W9-BJC-321

STREETWISE

# MARKETING
# PLAN

STREETWISE®

# MARKETING PLAN

## Winning Strategies for Every Small Business

### by Don Debelak

Adams Media Corporation
Avon, Massachusetts

Published by Adams Media Corporation
57 Littlefield Street, Avon, MA 02322. U.S.A.
*www.adamsmedia.com*

ISBN: 1-58062-268-2

Printed in the United States of America.

J I H G F E D C

**Library of Congress Cataloging-in-Publication Data**
Debelak, Don.
Streetwise marketing plan / Don Debelak.
p.    cm.
ISBN 1-58062-268-2
1. Marketing—Management.  I. Title.
HF5415.13.D3767 2000
658.8'02—dc21        00-028870

Cover illustration by Eric Mueller.
*This book is available at quantity discounts for bulk purchases.*
*For information, call 1-800-872-5627.*

**Visit our exciting small business Web site at businesstown.com**

# CONTENTS

Preface.....................................xi

## CHAPTER 1—MARKETING PLANS
## KEEP SALES GROWING .....................1

Change Happens Everywhere .................3

Your Marketing Goals .......................5

The Marketing Planning Process–
   It's More than the Final Document .........6

Writing the Plan............................8

A Successful Marketer ........................9

The Planning Process .......................10

Final Comments.............................10

Ask Five Customers to Take This Test ..........12

## SECTION ONE—CUSTOMER FOCUS

### CHAPTER 2—A CUSTOMER PROFILE .........15

Customer Profile ...........................16

Target Customer Group......................17

Functional Goals ...........................19

Major Interests.............................20

Type of Buyer..............................20

Self-Image.................................21

Importance to the Customer..................22

Brand Preferences ..........................22

Important Features .........................23

Customer Mood ............................24

Final Comments............................24

You Don't Pass Go Unless You Can
   Answer these Questions..................25

### CHAPTER 3—HOW THE CUSTOMER BUYS .....27

Customer Buying Patterns Form ..............28

How Customers Decide to Buy ...............32

Your Impact During the Buying Process ........33

The Customer's Information . . .
   Gathering Process.......................34

Competitor Advantages .....................35

Your Advantages ...........................35

Tactics That Work Best......................36

Evaluate Your Tactics .......................37

Keep Up the Momentum .....................37

Final Comments............................38

How Smart Have You Been? .................39

## SECTION TWO—THE SITUATION ANALYSIS

**CHAPTER 4—THE INTERNAL AUDIT** . . . . . . . . . . **43**

Internal Audit Form . . . . . . . . . . . . . . . . . . . . . . . 44

A Description of the Business . . . . . . . . . . . . . . . . 48

The History and Background of the
Business . . . . . . . . . . . . . . . . . . . . . . . . . . . . . 48

Target Markets . . . . . . . . . . . . . . . . . . . . . . . . . . . 49

Your Company's Specialty . . . . . . . . . . . . . . . . . . . 50

Sales Growth . . . . . . . . . . . . . . . . . . . . . . . . . . . . 51

Your Strengths and Weaknesses . . . . . . . . . . . . . . 51

Your Financial Capability . . . . . . . . . . . . . . . . . . . 53

Your Management and Marketing Expertise . . . . . . . 54

Final Comments . . . . . . . . . . . . . . . . . . . . . . . . . . 54

Don't Be Too Safe . . . . . . . . . . . . . . . . . . . . . . . . 55

**CHAPTER 5—THE EXTERNAL EVALUATION** . . . . . **57**

External Audit Form . . . . . . . . . . . . . . . . . . . . . . . 58

Target Markets . . . . . . . . . . . . . . . . . . . . . . . . . . . 63

Market Segments . . . . . . . . . . . . . . . . . . . . . . . . . 63

Competitor Advantages . . . . . . . . . . . . . . . . . . . . . 64

Competitive Positioning Strategies . . . . . . . . . . . . . 64

Competitive Rankings . . . . . . . . . . . . . . . . . . . . . . 66

Market Trends . . . . . . . . . . . . . . . . . . . . . . . . . . . 69

Opportunities . . . . . . . . . . . . . . . . . . . . . . . . . . . . 70

Threats . . . . . . . . . . . . . . . . . . . . . . . . . . . . . . . . 71

Final Comments . . . . . . . . . . . . . . . . . . . . . . . . . . 72

Don't Zig When the Market Zags . . . . . . . . . . . . . . 74

## SECTION THREE—MARKETING STRATEGY

**CHAPTER 6—MARKETING OBJECTIVES** . . . . . . . **77**

Positioning Strategy Form . . . . . . . . . . . . . . . . . . . 78

Marketing Sales and Objectives Form . . . . . . . . . . . 80

Target Customer Group . . . . . . . . . . . . . . . . . . . . . 82

Major Goals and Desires . . . . . . . . . . . . . . . . . . . . 82

Unmet Goals and Desires . . . . . . . . . . . . . . . . . . . 84

Strategies to Meet Unmet Goals and Desires . . . . . 84

Competitive Advantage . . . . . . . . . . . . . . . . . . . . . 86

Target Distribution Network . . . . . . . . . . . . . . . . . . 86

Unmet Desires of the Distribution Network . . . . . . . 87

Positioning Strategy for Distribution . . . . . . . . . . . 89

Positioning Statements . . . . . . . . . . . . . . . . . . . . . 91

Marketing Sales and Objectives . . . . . . . . . . . . . . . 91

Final Comments . . . . . . . . . . . . . . . . . . . . . . . . . . 91

Your Customers Have the Answers . . . . . . . . . . . . . 93

# CONTENTS

## CHAPTER 7—PRODUCT-BASED MARKETING TACTICS . . . . . . . . . . . . . . . . . . . . . 95
Product-Based Marketing Tactics Form . . . . . . . . . 96

Marketing Goals . . . . . . . . . . . . . . . . . . . . . . . . . . . 98

Product/Store/Service . . . . . . . . . . . . . . . . . . . . . . 98

Pricing . . . . . . . . . . . . . . . . . . . . . . . . . . . . . . . . . . 100

Packing/Store Display . . . . . . . . . . . . . . . . . . . . . . 101

Customer Service . . . . . . . . . . . . . . . . . . . . . . . . . . 103

Final Comments . . . . . . . . . . . . . . . . . . . . . . . . . . . 105

What Have You Done for Me Lately? . . . . . . . . . 107

## CHAPTER 8—COMMUNICATIONS-BASED MARKETING TACTICS . . . . . . . . . . . . . . . . . . . . . 109
Communications-Based Marketing Tactics Form . . . 110

Advertising . . . . . . . . . . . . . . . . . . . . . . . . . . . . . . . 112

Marketing Messages . . . . . . . . . . . . . . . . . . . . . . . 115

Brochures/Flyers . . . . . . . . . . . . . . . . . . . . . . . . . . 116

Trade Shows . . . . . . . . . . . . . . . . . . . . . . . . . . . . . . 117

Publicity . . . . . . . . . . . . . . . . . . . . . . . . . . . . . . . . . 118

Direct Mail . . . . . . . . . . . . . . . . . . . . . . . . . . . . . . . 120

Final Comments . . . . . . . . . . . . . . . . . . . . . . . . . . . 122

Communications Tactics Serve Three Masters . . . 123

## CHAPTER 9—MARKETING TACTICS FOR SALES, PROMOTIONS, AND DISTRIBUTION . . . . . . . . . . 125
Marketing Tactics for Sales, Promotions,
    and Distribution Form . . . . . . . . . . . . . . . . . . 126

Sales . . . . . . . . . . . . . . . . . . . . . . . . . . . . . . . . . . . . 129

Credibility Building . . . . . . . . . . . . . . . . . . . . . . . . 132

Distribution . . . . . . . . . . . . . . . . . . . . . . . . . . . . . . 133

Promotions . . . . . . . . . . . . . . . . . . . . . . . . . . . . . . . 136

Internet . . . . . . . . . . . . . . . . . . . . . . . . . . . . . . . . . . 138

Final Comments . . . . . . . . . . . . . . . . . . . . . . . . . . . 140

Are You Sleeping? I Hope Not. . . . . . . . . . . . . . . . 142

## SECTION FOUR—SAMPLE MARKETING PLANS

## CHAPTER 10—RETAIL/COFFEE SHOP MARKETING PLANS . . . . . . . . . . . . . . . . . . . . . 145
H&R Trains Marketing Plan . . . . . . . . . . . . . . . . . 146

Executive Summary . . . . . . . . . . . . . . . . . . . . . . . . 146

Marketing Objectives . . . . . . . . . . . . . . . . . . . . . . . 146

Current Situation . . . . . . . . . . . . . . . . . . . . . . . . . . 147

Positioning Strategies . . . . . . . . . . . . . . . . . . . . . . 149

Marketing Tactics . . . . . . . . . . . . . . . . . . . . . . . . . . 149

Implementation Plan . . . . . . . . . . . . . . . . . . . . . . . 152

Mighty Grounds Coffee Shop Marketing Plan . . . 154

Executive Summary . . . . . . . . . . . . . . . . . . . . . . . . 154

Internal Audit . . . . . . . . . . . . . . . . . . . . . . . . . . . . . 155

External Audit . . . . . . . . . . . . . . . . . . . . . . . . . . . . 159

Positioning Strategies . . . . . . . . . . . . . . . . . . . . . . 160

Marketing Tactics . . . . . . . . . . . . . . . . . . . . . . . . . . 161

Implementation Plan 2000 . . . . . . . . . . . . . . . . . . 164

Marketing Budget . . . . . . . . . . . . . . . . . . . . . . . . . 166

Final Comments . . . . . . . . . . . . . . . . . . . . . . . . . . . 167

Key Starting Points . . . . . . . . . . . . . . . . . . . . . . . . 168

**CHAPTER 11—SERVICE COMPANY MARKETING PLANS............ 169**
Resnick Associates Marketing Plan............ 170
Background ............................... 170
Strengths and Weaknesses ................. 172
Market Analysis .......................... 172
Positioning Tactics........................ 174
Tactics ................................. 175
Implementation Plan ...................... 177
Southwest Painting Marketing Plan/2000...... 179
1. Executive Summary...................... 179
2. Situation Analysis ...................... 179
3. Positioning............................ 182
4. Marketing Tactics ...................... 183
5. Implementation Plan.................... 186
6. Budget Summary....................... 187
Final Comments.......................... 188
Marketing on a Tiny Budget ................ 189

**CHAPTER 12—MARKETING PLANS FOR MANUFACTURING COMPANIES............. 191**
Safeplay Systems Inc. Marketing Plan 2000..... 192
Executive Summary........................ 192
Market Conditions ........................ 193
Situation Analysis ........................ 195
Strategy for 2000......................... 199
Marketing Tactics......................... 200
Implementation Plan 2000 ................. 203
Schulco Marketing Plan 2000............... 204
Executive Summary........................ 204
Marketing Objectives...................... 205
Situation Analysis ........................ 205
External Audit ........................... 207

Positioning Strategy ...................... 211
Marketing Tactics......................... 212
Implementation Plan ...................... 215
Budget Summary......................... 215
Final Comments.......................... 216
Are You Fast?............................ 218

**CHAPTER 13—MARKETING PLANS OF INTERNET COMPANIES ............... 219**
BHD Corp. Marketing Plan 2000 ........... 220
I. Executive Summary ..................... 220
II. Marketing Goals ...................... 221
III. Situation Analysis .................... 222
IV. Positioning .......................... 230
V. Marketing Strategy .................... 231
VI. Marketing Tactics..................... 231
VII. Implementation Plan/2000 ............ 233
Oil-N-Gas, Inc. Marketing Plan............. 234
I. Executive Summary ..................... 234
II. Situation Analysis ..................... 235
III. Marketing Strategy and Positioning ....... 239
IV. Marketing Tactics..................... 240
V. Implementation Plan Fall 1999/2000 ...... 244
VI. Expense Summary ..................... 246
C-Ya Greeting Cards Marketing Plan 2000 ..... 247
1. Executive Summary..................... 247
2. Situation Analysis ..................... 248
3. Positioning........................... 254
4. Marketing Tactics ..................... 255
5. Implementation Plan/2000............... 257
Final Comments.......................... 258
Traffic Stop ............................ 260

# Contents

## Section Five—Marketing Plan Workbook

**CHAPTER 14—THE OPENING** .............. **263**
Executive Summary Section ................. 264
Marketing Plan Table of Contents ........... 265
Marketing Objectives and Goals .............. 268
Final Comments............................ 269
Simplicity is Power......................... 270

**CHAPTER 15—SITUATION ANALYSIS......... 271**
Internal Audit............................. 272
Company Operations....................... 272
Sales Trends.............................. 276
Last Year's Commentary ................... 277
Strengths and Weaknesses ................. 278
The External Evaluation ................... 278
Customer Information...................... 279

Market Profile ............................ 285
Final Comments........................... 291
Do You Really Have the Answers?............ 292

**CHAPTER 16—STRATEGY, TACTICS, AND
IMPLEMENTATION** ...................... **293**
Positioning and Marketing Strategies.......... 294
Positioning Strategies ..................... 295
Additional Marketing Strategies .............. 296
Rationale for Strategy ..................... 297
Competitive Positioning ................... 298
Marketing Tactics.......................... 298
Implementation Plan and Budget............. 303
Final Comments........................... 308
Do You Have the Right Game Plan? .......... 309

## Appendices

**APPENDIX A—MARKETING PLAN
TABLE OF CONTENTS** ................... **311**

**APPENDIX B—IMPLEMENTATION PLANS FOR
PRODUCT BASED MARKETING TACTICS** ...... **313**
Sample Implementation Plan ............... 315

**APPENDIX C—IMPLEMENTATION PLANS
FOR COMMUNICATIONS-BASED
MARKETING TACTICS** ................... **325**
Sample Implementation Plan ............... 327

**APPENDIX D—IMPLEMENTATION PLANS FOR
MARKETING TACTICS FOR SALES, PROMOTIONS,
AND DISTRIBUTION ... .................. 337**
Sample Implementation Plan ................ 339

**INDEX.............................. 349**

I've been writing marketing plans for over 20 years working with all types of businesses from retail stores to high-technology medical, Internet, and electronics companies. As an independent consultant, marketing director, and part-time consultant for a Small Business Development Center, I've had the opportunity to talk to hundreds of marketers and business owners working on their marketing plans.

There has been a dramatic shift in the importance of a marketing plan over the past 10 years. For many companies, marketing plans were primarily a budgeting tool that offered a snapshot of their market position, but they were also put together to catalog the tactics a company would use during the next year. Today, marketers live in a fast changing world, where they need to constantly revamp their marketing strategies to adjust for new products, technologies, competitors, and their customers' rapidly changing environments. As an example, Hewlett-Packard, one of the first significant Silicon Valley start-ups, has announced that it is reinventing itself, with massive changes in its marketing program. Hewlett-Packard will be modifying its outlook on who its customers are, which distribution channels it should use, and how it will be delivering its marketing messages.

Marketing plans are now a survival tool. Marketers need to do much more than just dust off last year's plans when preparing their strategy. They need to re-evaluate every one of their core marketing principles and make sure they still have a viable strategy for the next year. Another reason companies need to start almost from scratch each year is that marketing tactics are changing rapidly. Ten years ago companies might have settled for a marketing plan that included using advertising, direct mail, sales materials, and trade show attendance to boost sales. Today those companies may offer seminars, enter into alliances with key associations in the market, develop three or four cross promotions, and sponsor several key events that target customers can attend. Marketing's focus is rapidly changing from delivering a message using advertising and promotion to delivering that same message by interacting with customers through promotions, distribution, and alliances

> Marketing plans work when they are based on unique, meaningful marketing strategies that focus on the current needs and desires of a target customer.

> A plan must identify a target customer group, explain what those customers want, and develop a positioning strategy that is important to the group.

Most books I've seen on marketing plans deal primarily with the format for writing the plan. My goal in writing this book is not only to offer readers a format but also to help them create innovative strategies that will help accelerate their business on a low-to-moderate budget. Effective marketing tactics don't have to be expensive. I want to help readers with a small budget prepare an effective marketing plan. I have geared this book toward readers who are writing their first plan, those who have written only a few marketing plans, and those who are re-evaluating their marketing program for the first time. I've also tried to include many new forms, tactics, and methods of evaluating a current marketing program; so readers with more marketing experience will still benefit from keeping the book handy as a resource tool.

In addition, I've included actual marketing plans from a variety of companies. One of the changes in marketing over the past five years is that companies are constructing their plans around the details of their customers' needs, desires, and buying behavior, rather than around marketing tactics such as advertising and distribution channels. As a result, the marketing plans prepared by companies selling to different customer groups can be quite varied. So I've included a sampling of plans to give readers more insight into the thought processes successful marketers use in creating an effective plan.

Since I've collaborated with the marketers or business owners who have prepared each of these plans, you'll notice that they are written in a similar style. Marketing plans may have different formats; that isn't what is important. What is important is that a plan identifies the target customer, explains what the customer wants, and then creates tactics that will allow the company to meet its sales and marketing objectives.

This book is divided into six main sections:

1. Section One—Customer Focus—concentrates on understanding your customer group, including what they want, how they buy, and what features are important to them.
2. Section Two—Situation Analysis—evaluates a company's current position, including an internal and external assessment of major threats and opportunities.

3. Section Three–Marketing Strategy–focuses on creating a marketing strategy and tactics. This deals with setting marketing objectives and goals, and creating a strategy to meet those goals. This section also discusses the various tactics that can be used to implement the marketing strategy.
4. Section Four–Sample Marketing Plans–contains actual plans from a variety of companies.
5. Section Five–The Marketing Plan Workbook–lays out a blank marketing plan format so readers can create their plan as they read.
6. Section Six–Tactics Implementation Plans–helps you create an implementation timetable for each marketing tactic.

My goal is for you to end up with a creative marketing plan. I want you to create a specific implementation plan that will be a working document for you to follow in the next year. This plan will help position your company for future growth, contain cost-effective marketing tactics, and be easy to follow. I hope that this book will occupy a prominent place on your bookshelf for years to come.

In this book you'll notice that I don't concentrate on the four Ps–product, price, placement, and promotion–that have been the cornerstone of past definitions of marketing activity. Instead I concentrate on knowing your customer, creating a positive impact (which includes creating high perceived value), and interacting with customers in a meaningful way. In today's marketing world, prospects and customers are just too busy to notice traditional marketing methods. Creating personal interaction is the most effective way to market products and services. This book is geared toward helping you create those interactions while still delivering a message that the customer wants to hear.

One last point: I have a tendency to refer to anything a customer buys–whether it is a service, an item, or an actual store–as a product. I believe that one aspect of marketing is establishing a strong link between you and the customer. Whatever you have to sell is your product. I have seen very little difference in the process of developing a marketing plan for any type of product, whether it is a product, service, restaurant, or store. Please don't be put off by the

> Implementing tactics is only part of the marketing challenge. Creating an effective strategy is the key to marketing success.

> Creating personal interaction is the most effective way to market products and services today.

word product if you are not marketing a manufactured *product*. I use the word to describe whatever it is that you are selling.

Staying on top of your competition isn't something that will just happen. You need to start with a strong marketing plan that (1) delivers the right product to the right customer at the right price, and (2) creates an impact on prospective customers with meaningful messages that are communicated in an interactive way. Your business won't succeed, no matter how hard you work, without an effective marketing strategy. I hope this book helps you create a plan that will keep customers knocking on your door while producing a steady stream of profits. In a way, business is a race against your competitors. A great marketing plan helps you run fast, run smart, and run strong, so you can consistently beat your competitors to the finish line. When reading this book, your goal should be to become a leader in your marketplace. Good luck and I hope to be able to hear about your success stories in the near future.

# Marketing Plans Keep Sales Growing

**1: MARKETING PLANS KEEP SALES GROWING**

2: A CUSTOMER PROFILE

3: HOW THE CUSTOMER BUYS

4: THE INTERNAL AUDIT

5: THE EXTERNAL EVALUATION

6: MARKETING OBJECTIVES

7: PRODUCT-BASED MARKETING TACTICS

8: COMMUNICATIONS-BASED MARKETING TACTICS

9: MARKETING TACTICS FOR SALES,
PROMOTIONS, AND DISTRIBUTION

Recently I worked on a marketing plan for a manufacturer of designer children's clothes. The company was concerned that its marketing strategy needed an overhaul because the market had changed considerably in just two years. Some of those changes included:

1. Two primary competitors had gone bankrupt.
2. Major new chains such as GapKids and Talbot Kids were having a serious impact in the market.
3. Other competitors were opening outlet stores in large outlet malls.
4. The company's primary customer group, children's boutiques, was being hurt by the new specialty store chains.
5. High-end department stores were shrinking their children's departments.
6. JCPenney became the third largest supplier of children's clothes (behind Wal-Mart and Kmart) and featured midpriced rather than high-end clothing.
7. Wal-Mart, Kmart, and Target all had gone to designer-type brands, which often simply mimic designer brands.
8. The company's 1998 brands hadn't sold as well as previous years' designs.

The company needed a new marketing direction to survive in this changed world. It had to look at every aspect of its marketing program and then create a new strategy. The company had run into what every marketer is faced with today. A fast-changing market that requires companies either to constantly revamp their marketing strategies or to face declining sales and possible bankruptcy. Most companies tend to be reactive, making one small change or another—such as adding a major discount program to department stores, for creating new product lines—without stopping to re-evaluate their basic strategy. That is a big mistake. Reactive moves are short-term Band-Aids at best, and in many cases fail to produce a significant benefit to the company. If companies want to be the clear market leader, marketers must take time every year to look at their marketing programs and to create a marketing plan.

> Marketers need to re-evaluate their strategy every year to respond to changes in the customers and the markets.

## Change Happens Everywhere

In the case of the children's clothing manufacturer, major changes occurred in its distribution channel and in its competition. But changes can occur in many other areas as well.

**Technology**. Manufacturers of computer network equipment are faced with computer upgrades, new software, new types of digital telephone lines, and new requirements due to the introduction of the Internet. Technology can change in other markets as well. For example, road bikes have given way to mountain bikes with more efficient crankcases, and changes in chip design have created a demand for different types of semiconductor equipment. Service business and retail stores can also be affected, as we have seen with the introduction of new types of camcorders, CDs, and technologically advanced equipment that customers don't know how to install. The telephone industry has had to constantly revise its products with cellular phones, high-speed modems, and a host of ancillary services such as voice mail, caller ID, and last call redial.

**Buying patterns**. In the past, people relied heavily on advertising messages and information from salespeople when making their buying decisions. Today they read product evaluations in specialty magazines, attend trade shows, go on the Internet, and discover a large amount of product information on their own. Industrial companies used to assign staff personnel to coordinate and monitor the products they purchased. Today they expect their vendors to take care of much of the paperwork and coordination involved in purchasing equipment and supplies. Restauranteurs, who once had wholesalers deliver food, now venture out to farmer's markets and fish markets to buy the freshest products possible in order to create the best meals.

**Public perceptions.** The public's antigun stance has strengthened after numerous gun-related tragedies occurred

> Marketers are adding value-added service to help customers cope with a changing world.

> In today's world, marketing strategies need to be re-evaluated at least once a year. Unfortunately I've found that most companies evaluate their strategies only when sales start dropping.

at schools throughout the nation. Yet Larami, manufacturer of the SUPER SOAKER has great sales. The company, which always used bright colors, has switched to neon plastics to ensure that the toy offers as little resemblance to a real gun as possible. Ten to 20 years ago most professionals believed they needed to "dress for success" and wear a suit to work; today many of those same professionals feel casual clothing is acceptable work attire. The foods we eat, the way we exercise, the games we buy for our children are all other areas where public perception constantly changes.

**Target customer groups**. There was a time when sports utility vehicles (SUVs), such as the Jeep Cherokee and GM's Suburban, were actually sold to people who needed four-wheel drive, either because they lived in the country or they went places where they could get stuck. When Jeep found out that their largest-selling dealership was in New York City, it became obvious that they were marketing to the wrong customer group. Once Jeep refocused their campaign to a new customer group, urban and suburban professionals, the SUV market took off. Dozens of competitors have since sprung up.

**Basic customer desires**. Today as you walk through my neighborhood, you'll see many elaborate wildflower and perennial gardens. Even five years ago people were content with a few shrubs and a small annual flower garden. Pasta Salads (a product that delivers a salad in five minutes), microwave cooking, and take-home supermarket meals are products that respond to a higher percentage of working couples. Housekeeping and lawn services, computer modems, Internet service providers, and new styles of comfortable bicycles are all innovations based on the changing needs and desires of a customer group.

These are just a few of the aspects of a marketer's world that can change in any given year. It's not unusual for a marketer to face three, four, or five major changes in one year. And of course your competitors are not sitting still, they are also making moves to better serve your target customer group. The result is that you need to do an effective marketing plan every year if you expect to survive in the market.

## Your Marketing Goals

Every year marketers strive to have a strategy that meets five important goals:

1. To give customers exactly what they want
2. To be highly differentiated, so the company stands out from competitors
3. To deliver marketing messages with high impact so targeted prospects will notice
4. To place the product in distribution where the customer can easily buy it
5. To provide the support required so prospects are comfortable buying and using the product

A marketing plan that delivers all five goals cost-effectively will generate the revenues you need to be successful. Unfortunately for marketers, a strategy that works well today may be the wrong strategy two years from now. Companies are forced to constantly create new strategies to meet their marketing goals. The good news is that rapidly changing markets create huge opportunities for increased market share for those who know how to adjust to changing market conditions. Companies can increase their market share 10 to 20 points in just a year or two by being attuned to the market. Otherwise, they'll have to slug it out with competitors for years to make even modest gains.

Ask five customers how they remember you. For example, a hardware store might have the best service, widest selection, best paint department, or some other distinguishing characteristic. If they can't tell you, you aren't doing an effective job positioning your company.

## The Marketing Planning Process—
## It's More than the Final Document

You won't have a sustainable marketing position if your marketing strategy doesn't change as your customers and competitors change.

The final marketing plan has two elements: an explanation of what your strategy is and a detailed implementation plan. The first part of the plan explains to everyone in the company, and is a reminder to you, exactly what your marketing strategy is trying to accomplish. The second part is an implementation plan that you use as a budget and as a calendar to be sure everything gets done. In effect, it is your yearly planner. A well written plan that meets these objectives may be only 12 to 20 pages long, but it still has all the information you need to properly implement your marketing strategy.

Before you start writing this plan, however, you need to decide what your strategy should be. The first part of the book shows you how to do that, and provides many forms and checklists to help you create a winning marketing strategy. As I've gone through the marketing plan process over the past twenty years, I've learned that every business has unique characteristics, and every marketing plan needs to deal with different key issues. In many cases the marketing elements that affect one customer group are much different than the elements that affect another group. Parents, for instance, have less disposable income than a childless couple and totally different concerns. The minivan was sold as a way of hauling around all the gear of a family, an important concern to parents, while childless couples were told that BMWs were a symbol of their professional success. You have to be flexible to adjust a marketing plan to your specific business. The wide variety of marketing strategies being used today convinced me to include nine marketing plans in this book. They show you some of the different thought processes and strategies people have employed to meet their marketing goals.

The second part of the marketing plan is to determine the tactics you will use. Many marketers figure out how much money they can afford to spend on marketing, and then base their plan on the money they have available. As a result, the marketing plan doesn't produce enough impact for the company to meet its marketing goals, so the company has low sales and never makes enough money. Companies in this position typically end up on a slow spiral to oblivion. You need to decide what sales levels you need, and then set up a marketing plan to meet those goals. For example, I consulted with a company that sold home soda-fountain systems that were smaller versions of the setup you see at fast-food restaurants. The sodas tasted better than can soda and the costs were much less than buying canned soda. The company had the following costs for each lead it generated with different marketing activities:

| | LEAD COSTS ($)* | NUMBER OF LEADS | CLOSING RATE ( PERCENT) | UNIT SALES |
|---|---|---|---|---|
| ADVERTISING | 16 | 180 | 7 | 13 |
| TRADE SHOWS | 7 | 330 | 12 | 40 |
| SEMINARS | 9 | 70 | 25 | 17 |
| PUBLICITY | 4 | 42 | 3 | 1 |
| DIRECT MAIL | 13 | 400 | 5 | 20 |

\* Lead costs were derived by dividing the total amount spent in the category by the number of viable leads generated from that activity.

The problem was that the company needed 180 sales to generate profits, but only had 81 sales. The company was planning on running the same plan as the year before, and hoping to raise its closing rate. The company had to dramatically change its marketing focus to succeed. I believed the company wasn't making enough impact on its prospects and needed to change focus and concentrate on fewer neighborhoods in order to benefit from referrals from customers and community groups.

One of the most critical steps in any marketing strategy is checking to make sure that the plan will deliver the sales the company needs and expects. In most cases, I've found that small business owners underestimate the investment they need to make in marketing programs, especially when they are changing strategic focus. If you are radically changing your market strategy, you should be prepared to spend anywhere from 4 to 10 percent of your sales volume.

The final plan is not the most important reason for doing a marketing plan. What's most important is actually going through the process of creating a marketing strategy.

## Writing the Plan

The actual task of writing a marketing plan is probably only 25 to 30 percent of the process of developing a winning plan. The rest of the process is determining just what your strategy should be. So don't just turn to Section Five, the Marketing Plan Workbook, without first completing the marketing strategy evaluation. Otherwise you will end up with a plan you can implement, but it won't meet your marketing goals. The rewards of a great plan are enormous. I introduced a dental product through seminars at major dental trade shows around the country. On one particular product I hit the right marketing combination of having the right product to solve a critical need of a high percentage of dentists. Over 250 dentists came to our introductory seminar while other seminars at the same trade shows were only attracting 25 to 30 dentists. A plan that's perfect can produce five to 10 times the business of a plan that is just acceptable, so take the up-front time required to produce a marketing strategy with high impact.

Emhart Fastening Technologies manufactures nuts, bolts, and a wide variety of other products that it sells to the automotive industry. Since Emhart is only one of the dozens of companies selling fasteners to automotive companies, its marketing messages were easily lost in the crowd. To start the marketing plan process, Emhart decided to determine what their customers' primary objective was. Emhart found that customers simply wanted to solve fastening problems quickly and easily. So the company put its marketing dollars to use by creating a technology center that showed exactly how its products worked and offered solutions to common automotive problems. Emhart also added two Mobile Innovation Centers, which took ideas directly to the plants in a converted truck trailer. The company decided to use the mobile center because the idea was totally different, and because the appearance of the vehicle in a customer's parking lot would generate awareness of the new program. The first mobile center visited five hundred customers and traveled over fifty thousand miles in its first year, successfully launching a change in strategic direction.

> A plan that's perfect can produce five to ten times the business of a plan that is just acceptable.

Emhart met the five major requirements of a successful program:

1. It developed a program that met the goals of its customers.
2. It had a strategy that wasn't commonly employed by its competitors.
3. It created tactics that had an impact on its prospects.
4. It offered an easy way to interact with its customers and take orders.
5. It gave customers the support they needed to realize Emhart's products would work in their applications.

> Your strategy has to have enough impact that people will stop and take notice of what you have to offer.

Emhart's key job was to figure out how to meet its marketing goals. Once it did that, the marketing plan was a straightforward process.

The first sections of this book are devoted to helping you develop a strategy that is going to help your business succeed. You will be filling out charts that you can use when you write the marketing plan. You should keep the charts handy, especially the ones that describe what your customers want, and refer to them every time you put together marketing materials.

## A Successful Marketer

Kitchen Koncepts, a gourmet gift shop, opened with a marketing plan that called for television, radio, and newspaper advertising that targeted the entire Beaumont, Texas community. That shotgun strategy didn't produce much in the way of results, and the company decided to go through the marketing plan process. Kitchen Koncepts started with the first point in any marketing plan, discovering their customers' goals. The customers wanted to cook gourmet dinners that had unique, delicious entrées, so that was what Kitchen Koncepts focused on while developing its marketing strategy. The owners started to appear on newscasts in their own cooking show segment, and they sponsored a local cooking show. To provide more help to customers, the store began giving cooking demonstrations at conventions their target customer group—women or men who liked to prepare special meals—were likely to attend. These events included the Golden Triangle Home Show, restaurant and food industry charity events, the Women's Junior League Style Show, and a Southern Living Cooking school. Kitchen Koncepts stopped concentrating on selling its products, and started helping customers meet their goal of cooking special entrées. Today Kitchen Koncepts is very successful because it delivers all the key elements of a marketing strategy.

> Do your marketing plan every year, before you get into trouble.

## The Planning Process

Kitchen Koncepts wasn't willing to go through a full-fledged planning process until it had some initial marketing failures. This failure to plan is typical of many of the small businesses I've encountered. New business owners are often too confident that they know how to sell their product. Unfortunately, they are frequently wrong. With luck the company can survive a rocky start and go on to be a successful company.

I shared the examples of Emhart Fastening Technologies and Kitchen Koncepts because they show that your final plan doesn't have to be a long, complicated affair. In fact, it should be focused on only a few main activities that deliver your message to your target customer. In the first sections of this book, I will be covering many marketing concepts that may not apply to your company. If a topic isn't a key point in your business, just move on to the next topic. You may only end up with three or four marketing aspects that will benefit your company over the next few years. That's an ideal situation because it limits the scope of your marketing plan and allows you to concentrate on tactics that will greatly improve your business success.

## Final Comments

"I'm just not very good at marketing" or "I just don't have marketing sense" are comments I've heard from dozens of small business owners. Well, marketing is no different from any other job. You just need to learn the process, follow the rules, and get some experience. I believe everyone can be effective at marketing. After all, the answers to a good marketing program don't lie with the marketing experts. They lie with the customers. If you listen to what your customers and prospects tell you about their needs, desires, and lifestyles, you'll be able to figure out pretty easily which strategies will work.

Anyone who follows the steps I've laid out in this book can become an effective marketer. All you need to do is get started. My last admonition is to start today. After all, your world is changing and your competitors are going to respond to those changes. You can either stay ahead of the pack, or fall behind. A good marketing strategy will set your company apart as the clear market winner. That strategy may have one bold component or several different tactics. The beauty of the marketing plan format is that it is flexible and allows you to create a winning plan for your business. Don't stop the process until you are confident you have all the elements in place for a successful plan. Before you know it, people will see you as a great marketer.

> Your world is changing and your competitors are going to respond to those changes.

You haven't done an
effective job of marketing if
people can't tell just whom
you are marketing to.

## Ask Five Customers to Take This Test

1. What customers are we (or your business name) trying to
   appeal to?

   _____

   _____

2. What do you feel makes us different from our
   competitors?

   _____

   _____

3. I completely understand what you want from our product
   or service.

   ____Strongly Agree   ____Somewhat Agree   ____Disagree

4. Your business is one that I would check out before
   buying.

   ____Strongly Agree   ____Somewhat Agree   ____Disagree

5. Do you remember any of our marketing messages?

   ____Yes              ____No

   If yes, what is our most meaningful message for you.

   _____

   _____

6. Do we offer you some feature or benefit that you feel is important?

   ____Yes              ____No

   If yes, which one is most important?

   _____

# Customer Focus

Chapters 2 through 9 concentrate on the preliminary analysis of your business and the selection of the marketing tactics you will use. Each chapter comes with a form to fill out, which you will use later when writing your marketing plan. The forms are designed to help you focus on creating an innovative marketing strategy. Each chapter will explain how to fill out the form.

In the first five chapters, there are two rankings at the end of each category. The first is Priority, which is the customer's priority. Rank the items 1 to 5, with 1 being the highest priority to the customer. If the items in a category are not a high priority to the customer, rank them 3, 4, or 5. Don't give an item a 1 unless it is a vital concern to the customer. The second category is Importance, how important is it that your marketing strategy deal with this issue. A 1 rating means it is vital you address this issue. Since you can only deal with three to five issues in your strategy, don't give a 1 rating too frequently. You should only give a 1 rating if (1) you can gain a differential advantage because customers are not being well served; (2) your product or service has definite advantages over competition; or (3) changes in the marketplace, or in customer goals, give you the first chance to respond to an opportunity.

**CHAPTER 2** A CUSTOMER PROFILE  **CHAPTER 3** HOW THE CUSTOMER BUYS

# A Customer Profile

1: MARKETING PLANS KEEP SALES GROWING

**2: A CUSTOMER PROFILE**

3: HOW THE CUSTOMER BUYS

4: THE INTERNAL AUDIT

5. THE EXTERNAL EVALUATION

6: MARKETING OBJECTIVES

7: PRODUCT-BASED MARKETING TACTICS

8: COMMUNICATIONS-BASED MARKETING TACTICS

9: MARKETING TACTICS FOR SALES,
   PROMOTIONS, AND DISTRIBUTION

## CUSTOMER PROFILE

Target Customer Profile:

. . . . . . . . . . . . . . . . . . . . . . . . . . . . . . . . . . . . . . . . . . . .

. . . . . . . . . . . . . . . . . . . . . . . . . . . . . . . . . . . . . . . . . . . .

* Rank Priority by the priority of the item to customers, and rank Importance by how important it is for your company to address the item. Rank each item 1 to 5, with 1 being a high value, and 5 a low value

|  | PRIORITY* (1-5) | IMPORTANCE* (1-5) |
|---|---|---|
| Customer's Functional Goals: | | |
| | | |
| | | |
| | | |
| Customer's Major Interests: | | |
| | | |
| | | |
| | | |

Type of Customer Buying Behavior:

| | |
|---|---|
| Maximizer | . . . . . . . . . . . . . . . . . . . . |
| Judicial | . . . . . . . . . . . . . . . . . . . . |
| Low Cost Buyer | . . . . . . . . . . . . . . . . . . . . |
| Minimizer | . . . . . . . . . . . . . . . . . . . . |

Customer's Self-Image:

. . . . . . . . . . . . . . . . . . . . . . . . . . . . . . . . . . .

. . . . . . . . . . . . . . . . . . . . . . . . . . . . . . . . . . .

. . . . . . . . . . . . . . . . . . . . . . . . . . . . . . . . . . .

## CUSTOMER PROFILE FORM

Why is your type of
product important to
the customer?:
. . . . . . . . . . . . . . . . . . . . . . . . . . . . . . . . . . . . . . . . . . .
. . . . . . . . . . . . . . . . . . . . . . . . . . . . . . . . . . . . . . . . . . .
. . . . . . . . . . . . . . . . . . . . . . . . . . . . . . . . . . . . . . . . . . .
. . . . . . . . . . . . . . . . . . . . . . . . . . . . . . . . . . . . . . . . . . .

|  | PRIORITY* (1-5) | IMPORTANCE* (1-5) |
|---|---|---|
| Why does the customer buy your brand? | | |
| Why doesn't the customer buy your brand? | | |
| What features are most important to the customer? | | |

As it relates to your product, what mood is your
customer typically in when buying your product?

| | |
|---|---|
| Fun loving | . . . . . . . . . . . . . . . . . . . . . . . . |
| Practical | . . . . . . . . . . . . . . . . . . . . . . . . |
| Serious | . . . . . . . . . . . . . . . . . . . . . . . . |

W ithout a doubt, all marketing activities start with knowing just what motivates your customer. After all, if the customer doesn't buy, you won't be in business. Starting with the customer will help you evaluate the effectiveness of your current programs and lead you to tactics that will produce significant sales and profit gains. This chapter deals with your customer's motivation and helps you decide which strategies you can use to have the biggest impact.

*The Blair Witch Project* had one of the strongest marketing campaigns of all time, even with a limited budget, because the movie's marketers understood their target customers' motivation—to be scared silly. During the movie's initial screening at the Sundance Film Festival in Park City, Utah, the marketers hung missing person's bulletins on telephone poles around town. The poster initiated the story line about the grim fate that befell the stars of the movie. A Web site chronicled the Blair Witch over a hundred-year period with grisly details of numerous deaths and disappearances. Then the movie was released to a small number of theaters, which quickly sold out to horror film fans. The limited distribution led to the buzz that the film was too scary for normal distribution. In its first weeks, the film sold out at virtually every theater it played in. Theaters averaged $56,000 a screen (versus a typical blockbuster's average take of $10,000 to $12,000 per screen). The buildup of a wicked story line and the limited distribution made the film the talk of the nation in the summer of 1999. Not surprisingly, the movie is projected to be the most profitable film ever made.

> All great marketing programs start with a thorough knowledge of the customer.

## Target Customer Group

The target customer group is the group of people you have chosen to sell to. Typically, marketers segment markets into various customer groups that have similar buying behavior. If marketers sell to more than one target group, they usually have marketing plans for each group or incorporate different elements of their marketing plans to account for each group. For example, teenage girls are not a target customer group for a clothing manufacturer because they do not all have similar buying behaviors. Teenage girls who prefer a "preppy" upscale look, take care of their appearance, and tend to buy at mid- to upper-priced stores are one customer group. This group might prefer mainstream music acts such as the Dave Matthews Band and read teen magazines like *Seventeen*. This is a distinctly different group from teenage girls in the "outsider" group who tend to wear older eclectic clothes and follow hard-core youth bands like Korn.

Industrial markets have the same type of differentiation. Value-added computer retailers may concentrate on customers who want to buy the latest technology or on those who want suppliers to do everything, including installation, to ensure that their product works right.

> A target customer group is one in which buyers behave in a similar manner. Defining exactly who in your target customer group is a marketer's first key step.

## Functional Goals

When a person buys a boat, what is his or her functional goal? It might be to go fishing, to have day trips on a local lake with the family, to cruise up and down a river, to fish in inlet bays of the ocean, or to go deep-sea fishing. Features, benefits, and marketing messages need to tie in directly to a customer's functional goal. Marketing a boat for family outings, for example, would focus on having extra seating capacity so kids can bring their friends along, extra storage capacity for food, and special rear-of-the-boat storage for skiing equipment. That message will connect to the target customer.

Although any given customer may have only one reason for buying your product, you may sell to a variety of customers for a variety of goals. For example, you may sell a lightweight lawn mower to people who have a small yard, a hilly yard, or a great number of bushes to maneuver around. You should list all three functional goals in the Customer Profile form.

Business-to-business products also frequently have multiple functional goals. A printer, for example, may be connected to seven to 10 users in an office. The customer's functional goals could include producing artwork for brochures and other marketing mailings, printing out letters and other correspondence, or printing engineering documentation for plant use.

## Major Interests

> People's major interests play a major role in their purchasing decisions. People buy when you help them achieve their major interests.

People have a variety of interests that, to a large extent, shape what's important to them. A businessperson's interests include being a leader in technology, providing high-quality products, and being the first to introduce the latest market trend. A consumer's interests can range from involvement in many sports activities to involvement in church activities.

I've listed some potential consumer interests to help you decide which fit your customer group. You should look for two or three interests that many, if not most, of the people in your target customer group share.

| | | | |
|---|---|---|---|
| Family | Home | Social events | Vacations |
| Hobbies | Sporting activities | Entertainment | Fitness |
| Community activity | Achievements | Recreation | Technology |
| Job advancement | Knowledge | High income | Security |

Business and industrial customers have different interests, but they are just as important to their buying decisions. Some of the interests businesses might pursue are listed here. Business customers are also interested in their desired self-image (see page 21).

| | | |
|---|---|---|
| Market leader | Cost savings | Quality conscious |
| Increase productivity | Employee satisfaction | Cut overhead |
| Maximize cash flow | Community oriented | Innovative |

## Type of Buyer

There are four general types of buyers that your customer group could fall into. An individual might exhibit more than one type of behavior, depending on the product he or she is purchasing. For example, a person might be a maximizer when purchasing products for a hobby, while being judicial when buying a VCR or a new TV. On the Customer Profile form, check the box for the type of buying behavior your customer exhibits when buying your product.

1. The **maximizer** buys the best affordable products that suit his or her needs—the biggest boat, the newest golf clubs, the latest electronics gear.
2. The **judicial** buyer weighs the features and benefits of a product versus its cost. Business buyers often operate in this mode, as do most people when buying a product they need, but one that doesn't play an important role in their life. People purchasing a washing machine, for example, often are in a judicial buying mode.
3. The **low-cost** buyer shops around to get the lowest price on a low-priced product.
4. The **minimizer** buys as few things as possible. Companies that use 50-year-old equipment even though old equipment has low productivity are often minimizers. This is a customer group marketers avoid because they are difficult, if not impossible, to sell to.

> With the rising wealth in America, I believe self-image has replaced value as the number one motivator in today's market.

## Self-Image

I believe that one of the biggest motivators for both consumer and business purchases is the buyer's self-image. A young professional whose self-image is that of a successful businessperson will have an elaborate wardrobe, often live in an upscale part of town, drive an expensive car, and be a member of a country club. These activities support the person's self-image. It's very rare that a person will buy a product that is counter to his or her self-image.

Not all people have a self-image of success; in fact there are a variety of types of self-images that may drive purchasing behavior. Just a few of those images are listed here.

| | | |
|---|---|---|
| Family oriented | Unconventional | High achiever |
| Progressive | Outdoors person | Fast climber |
| Financially savvy | Dedicated volunteer | Intelligent |
| Hard working | Party animal | Romantic |
| Adventurous | Cutting edge | Technologically savvy |
| Low profile | Conservative | Frugal |

## Importance to the Customer

Marketers are often far too quick to seize on the obvious importance of their product. For example, a marketer of tires may say people buy tires so their car has good traction and good braking power. But in reality, people buy for differing reasons. Buyers of high-end Michelin tires may purchase them because (1) they are concerned about car safety; (2) they want to support an image of a high achiever; (3) they want long tire life for convenience; or (4) they only buy dependable brands. Your marketing messages would vary depending on which reason you were trying to appeal to. Marketing opportunities would exist for Michelin if none of its competitors appeal to one of the reasons high-end tires are important to customers.

Taking this example one step further, what could be important reasons for midrange tire customer? They might be concerned about (1) car handling safety, (2) getting a good value, (3) buying from a reliable manufacturer, and (4) supporting their self-image as a smart buyer. The marketing campaign and product for a midrange tire should be different than for a high-end tire because the customers are value oriented.

## Brand Preferences

Some businesses like to use small consulting firms because they are less expensive, more customer oriented, and generally provide better service. Other businesses like to use larger companies because they can count on a certain standard of performance, and because many business executives value a report from a consultant who is known in the industry. For example, people may buy a bike because (1) it is available in bike specialty shops where they can get good service; (2) it has many features for its price; (3) it is used by well-known racers; or (4) they like its shifting mechanism.

One key strategy that marketers pursue is to strengthen their hold on their core customer group. You can't do that unless you know why your current customers are actually buying from you. This is the reason most warranty cards have a short questionnaire that helps marketers determine why you bought the product.

Ask your customers, either with a warranty card or by phone, why they bought your product. That answer is another key piece of the puzzle in determining how to influence your customers.

Most marketers get feedback from salespeople or customers about why they didn't buy the product or service. Generally, the product or service either didn't have one or two features they wanted or the price was too high. You will have very helpful information if you understand why the feature you are missing is so important to the customer. That information can help you design a product with features that are more innovative than your competitors. When customers say they didn't buy your product because of one or two missing features, be sure to find out why the missing feature was important.

A second major objective of marketers is to expand their customer base. People who investigate your product but don't buy it often find certain features attractive; otherwise they would have rejected it outright. These are often the easiest customers to acquire. All you need to do is understand why people aren't buying and then resolve the problem.

> Discovering why a feature is important to a customer will help you understand what the customer's real need or desire is.

## Important Features

I like to know what five features are most important to customers, and why they are important. The question is, How do you get this information? I've found that the best way is simply to call customers about six months after they buy a product or service or visit the store, and ask them:

1. How is the product or service working out for you?
2. What do you like best about the product, service, or store?
3. Which features were most important when you decided to buy the product or service or to visit the store?
4. Have any features of the product, service, or store worked out better than you thought they would?
5. Are there any additional features you wish the product, service, or store had?

I've always gotten insightful responses from about a third of the respondents when I ask these simple questions. You'll find that two or three features will be mentioned by 80 percent of the people you talk to. Those are the features that customers want.

## Customer Mood

In one of its commercials, Nike features Tiger Woods bouncing a golf ball off his club about a hundred times before tossing the ball up in the air and hitting it down the fairway. This fun commercial is great because Nike sells sports-related products and people use them to have fun. Another series of funny commercials focuses on cheese with the tag line "Behold the power of cheese." In one commercial an ice fisherman suddenly notices a plate of cheese. He grabs a piece and is instantly snagged by a fish that had his bait out for a human. I don't think these commercials are as effective as Nike's because people are in a practical mood when buying cheese. You want to match your buying mood to your customer's and to deliver an effective message. Humor is a tremendous marketing asset, but only when it incorporates the elements of a practical message. Eveready's Energizer Bunny, for instance, uses humor, but also promotes a practical point—the batteries last a long time.

## Final Comments

The Customer Profile form is designed to provide a snapshot of your target customers. It's crucial for your marketing plan because it gives you insight into how to impact your customers. There is only one way to get customers to notice you. You must have your product appear to be exactly what they want, and you can't do that without understanding them. You will be a much better marketer if you use the Customer Profile Form as a starting point for your marketing plans, strategies, and tactics. Every great marketing program starts with a direct connection to the customer. That's exactly what *The Blair Witch Project* marketers did. They understood the power of creating a buzz in the market by appealing to people's interest in real life (versus purely movie) horror. Appealing to that interest led to sold-out shows. You might not be able to produce the same impact as *The Blair Witch Project*, but I'm confident that you can generate a significant impact with an effective marketing program—an impact that will produce both profits and sales.

> Calling and talking to your customers is easy, and it's an inexpensive way to generate insights into their buying decisions.

## You Don't Pass Go Unless
## You Can Answer These Questions

Assume that you and your customer have no restraints such as man-power, technology, or making a profit:

1. What is the one thing that you could do that would have a dramatic impact on every one of your potential customers?

   _____

   _____

2. What would your customers buy if they could afford anything they wanted?

   _____

   _____

3. Who do your customers want to become?

   _____

   _____

You can't make everyone's dream come true, but you will have a more effective marketing plan if you know what your customer's dreams are.

People only worry about value or price when they can't get or can't afford what they really want. Worry about adding features that your customers value before you worry about cutting your price.

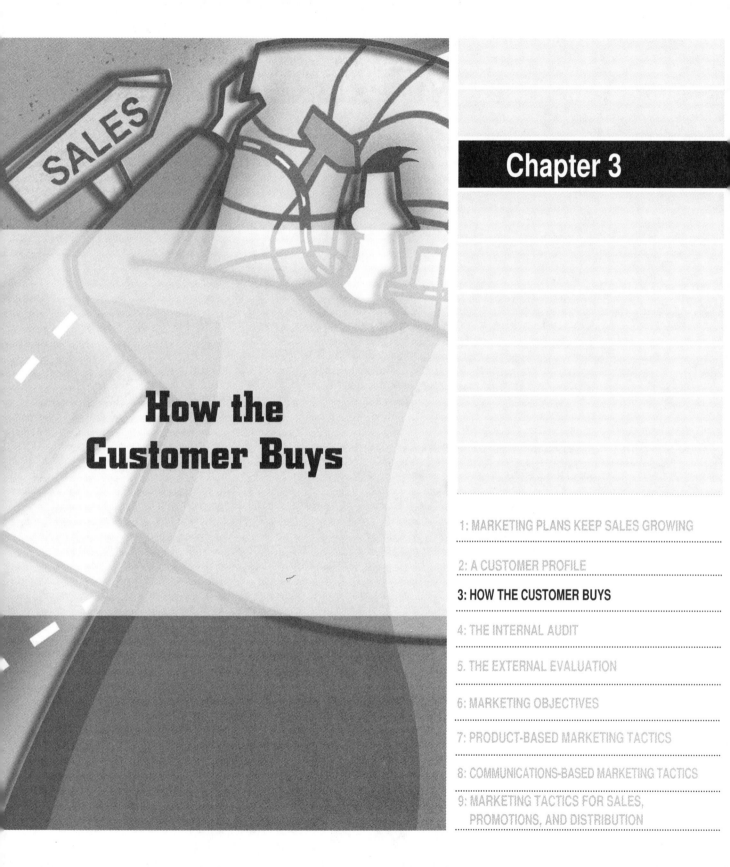

# Chapter 3

## How the Customer Buys

1: MARKETING PLANS KEEP SALES GROWING

2: A CUSTOMER PROFILE

**3: HOW THE CUSTOMER BUYS**

4: THE INTERNAL AUDIT

5. THE EXTERNAL EVALUATION

6: MARKETING OBJECTIVES

7: PRODUCT-BASED MARKETING TACTICS

8: COMMUNICATIONS-BASED MARKETING TACTICS

9: MARKETING TACTICS FOR SALES,
   PROMOTIONS, AND DISTRIBUTION

## CUSTOMER BUYING PATTERNS

How does the customer decide to buy?

........................................................................

........................................................................

........................................................................

........................................................................

\* Rank Priority by the priority of the item to customers, and rank Importance by how important it is for your company to address the item. Rank each item 1 to 5, with 1 being a high value, and 5 a low value

| | PRIORITY* (1-5) | IMPORTANCE* (1-5) |
|---|---|---|

What are the steps the buyer takes in his or her

buying decision?

Step 1. ................................... ............ ............

Step 2. ................................... ............ ............

Step 3. ................................... ............ ............

Step 4. ................................... ............ ............

Step 5. ................................... ............ ............

Step 6. ................................... ............ ............

How does your company impact a customer during

each stage of the buying cycle?

Step 1. ................................... ............ ............

Step 2. ................................... ............ ............

Step 3. ................................... ............ ............

## *CUSTOMER BUYING PATTERNS*

|  | PRIORITY* (1–5) | IMPORTANCE* (1–5) |
|---|---|---|
| Step 4. . . . . . . . . . . . . . . . . . . . . . . . . . . . . . . . . . . . . . . | . . . . . . . . . . | . . . . . . . . . . |
| Step 5. . . . . . . . . . . . . . . . . . . . . . . . . . . . . . . . . . . . . . . . | . . . . . . . . . . | . . . . . . . . . . |
| Step 6. . . . . . . . . . . . . . . . . . . . . . . . . . . . . . . . . . . . . . . . | . . . . . . . . . . | . . . . . . . . . . |

Where do customers gather information about
your product?

| 1. . . . . . . . . . . . . . . . . . . . . . . . . . . . . . . . . . . . . . . . . . . | . . . . . . . . . . | . . . . . . . . . . |
|---|---|---|
| 2. . . . . . . . . . . . . . . . . . . . . . . . . . . . . . . . . . . . . . . . . . . | . . . . . . . . . . | . . . . . . . . . . |
| 3. . . . . . . . . . . . . . . . . . . . . . . . . . . . . . . . . . . . . . . . . . . | . . . . . . . . . . | . . . . . . . . . . |

Where do competitors have an advantage over your
company in the buying decision?
Explain how.

| 1. . . . . . . . . . . . . . . . . . . . . . . . . . . . . . . . . . . . . . . . . . . | . . . . . . . . . . | . . . . . . . . . . |
|---|---|---|
| 2. . . . . . . . . . . . . . . . . . . . . . . . . . . . . . . . . . . . . . . . . . . | . . . . . . . . . . | . . . . . . . . . . |
| 3. . . . . . . . . . . . . . . . . . . . . . . . . . . . . . . . . . . . . . . . . . . | . . . . . . . . . . | . . . . . . . . . . |

Where does your company have an advantage
in the buying decision?

| 1. . . . . . . . . . . . . . . . . . . . . . . . . . . . . . . . . . . . . . . . . . . | . . . . . . . . . . | . . . . . . . . . . |
|---|---|---|
| 2. . . . . . . . . . . . . . . . . . . . . . . . . . . . . . . . . . . . . . . . . . . | . . . . . . . . . . | . . . . . . . . . . |
| 3. . . . . . . . . . . . . . . . . . . . . . . . . . . . . . . . . . . . . . . . . . . | . . . . . . . . . . | . . . . . . . . . . |

## *CUSTOMER BUYING PATTERNS*

Which tactics have worked best for your competitors?

1. . . . . . . . . . . . . . . . . . . . . . . . . . . . . . . . . . . . . . . . .    . . . . . . . . . . .    . . . . . . . . . . .
2. . . . . . . . . . . . . . . . . . . . . . . . . . . . . . . . . . . . . . . . .    . . . . . . . . . . .    . . . . . . . . . . .
3. . . . . . . . . . . . . . . . . . . . . . . . . . . . . . . . . . . . . . . . .    . . . . . . . . . . .    . . . . . . . . . . .

Which tactics have worked best for your company?

1. . . . . . . . . . . . . . . . . . . . . . . . . . . . . . . . . . . . . . . . .    . . . . . . . . . . .    . . . . . . . . . . .
2. . . . . . . . . . . . . . . . . . . . . . . . . . . . . . . . . . . . . . . . .    . . . . . . . . . . .    . . . . . . . . . . .
3. . . . . . . . . . . . . . . . . . . . . . . . . . . . . . . . . . . . . . . . .    . . . . . . . . . . .    . . . . . . . . . . .

List your major tactics, and indicate if they are
gaining, losing, or maintaining effectiveness.

|   | GAINING | LOSING | MAINTAINING |
|---|---------|--------|-------------|
| 1. | | | |
| 2. | | | |
| 3. | | | |
| 4. | | | |

ustomer groups gather information in certain ways leading up to the point at which they buy a product. An effective marketing campaign concentrates on how potential customers search for information, so the marketing information is available when and where customers are looking for it. For example, golfers can be divided into three groups of buyers: pioneers, early followers, and late followers. Pioneers like to be the first to buy and experiment with a new product. They enjoy the intrigue of being on the cutting edge of golf innovation. They look for information on new products in golf magazines, watch what various pros are using, and even search the Internet for tips on new equipment. A manufacturer of golf equipment usually starts out by giving their clubs to a few pros try to and by running publicity stories using the pros for endorsements. Increasingly those manufactures are also taking their clubs to driving ranges for customers to try and using the Internet as a way of finding their pioneering buyers. There is not much point in advertising a brand-new golf product to the general public. Most golfers won't use the product until the pioneers at their favorite course have endorsed it. The most effective marketing tactics coordinate marketing communication and promotions with the actual process the target customer goes through when deciding to buy a product.

Guinness, the Irish beer, has successfully penetrated the U.S. market, tripling its sales between 1990 and 1998. Guinness identified as its target customers people who experiment with new beers in taverns. These target customers are heavily influenced by what they learn about beer in their favorite bar. To reach these customers, Guinness concentrated on providing in-tavern and event marketing programs. Guinness hired 40 brew specialists who traveled from tavern to tavern, convincing owners to give Guinness a try. Then they worked with the tavern to develop customer interest and to show bartenders how to pour a Guinness correctly. Guinness also launched one contest to give away a free pub in Ireland, and another contest that encouraged customers to submit the "Great Guinness Toast." This is a great marketing program not necessarily because of its message, but because Guinness put its money on tactics that delivered its message in taverns, where its target customers decided which brand of beer was their favorite.

> You want to be sure to place your marketing messages in the places where customers look for information on your type of product or service.

This chapter is designed to help you make sure that your marketing dollars are spent where they will have the biggest payoff. I've found that this is an area of marketing that new entrepreneurs often overlook. Every business is different, so there are no general rules about which tactics you should use. What is important is to follow the examples of Guinness and the golf manufacturers and put your marketing messages in places where your customers are looking for information or where they make their buying decision.

> Your marketing dollars will have the highest return when you are selective in where and how you put out your marketing message.

## How Customers Decide to Buy

There are three important factors to consider when you try to understand how customers decide to purchase products and services or to patronize a store. First, is the purchase impulsive—buying a clock because of the way it looks—or deliberate—deciding which stereo system to buy and spending two months checking out purchasing options? Second, how willing are people to shop around for their purchase? When people buy a new kitchen, they often check out many potential suppliers. But when they decide to install a new deck, they may just decide to buy from the contractor who built their neighbor's deck. Third, how is the purchase made? For example, customers buy paint at a hardware store, businesses purchase office supplies from large suppliers who will deliver, and ice arenas buy their maintenance products from a catalog.

A wallpaper store might describe its customers' buying process in this way: Customers buy wallpaper at a wallpaper store that is convenient to their home, or that has been recommended by a friend. People consider redecorating for six to 12 months before actually moving ahead. During this period, they typically visit wallpaper stores two or three times to see what is available and to get a general idea of how they want to decorate their home. When they decide to buy, they know exactly what they want. What is the key moment for a wallpaper store's marketing program? It is those visits prospects make to the stores before they are ready to buy. The store should be set up to help those people who won't buy for another six months learn how to create a home interior that's right for them.

Some buying decisions are made quickly. People walk by a store in the mall and stop in. The appeal of the storefront catches their eye, and then the appeal of a new blouse or shirt encourages an immediate purchase. A prospect may simply decide to visit a restaurant because a friend recommended it. Other purchases have a long gestation period of several months to a year. People start thinking about buying a new boat when they start making more money. Then for six months to a year, they go to boat shows and look at friends' boats. Eventually they narrow their choices to two or three models, and finally they buy a boat.

Understanding what steps are involved in buying a product or service is especially important in industrial marketing, where many marketers and salespeople chase sales that can never happen. For example, one company I consulted with was trying to sell a new production-control software system. The marketing plan was to contact the head of the computer department and convince that person just how great their software system was. The sales rarely developed. We went back and analyzed the steps the customer took in making a purchase. First, management—either the plant manager or higher management—decided for any number of reasons that the plant needed improvement. Only rarely did a decision for change start with a lower-level employee.

The company's software was designed to reduce the amount of in-process inventory. Once the software company realized how companies actually decided to buy, it immediately changed tactics. The salesperson made contact with the person that ran the computer system, and then immediately tried to arrange for a presentation to top management. If he or she couldn't sell the benefits to top management, it was on to the next customer.

> You want to concentrate your marketing efforts on people when they start their buying process, which could be three months to a year before they actually buy.

## Your Impact During the Buying Process

Marketers want to have an influence on prospects the moment they start thinking about buying the product. Going back to our boat buyers, who has a better chance of getting the business: the boat dealer who attends trade shows to get prospects' names, invites them to

> Customers are more receptive to a marketing message when there is no sales pressure to buy immediately.

seminars and classes and sends out periodic mailings and newsletters, *or* the boat dealer who just waits until someone is ready to put down hard cash before starting any marketing efforts? Obviously, it's the boat dealer who has been with the prospect from the start.

Getting a prospect's attention early gives marketers another major advantage. You can approach the customer with information and helpful hints without any sales pressure. When you wait until the customers want to buy a product, you have no choice but to try to sell them. This raises their resistance and they become skeptical of any point you try to make. If you get customers earlier in the decision process, you can offer seminars or other non-sales-oriented programs and build customer trust *before* they are ready to buy.

You can influence customers with trade show attendance, seminars, presentations at association meetings, or a host of activities other than advertising. Try to place the emphasis of your marketing program as early as possible in the customer's buying process. Once you get prospects on your side, they are likely to stay there.

## The Customer's Information-Gathering Process

All types of customers, whether they are consumers or business-to-business accounts, typically gather information for a period of time before buying. Sometimes they attend classes, sometimes they look on the Internet, sometimes they go to stores, and sometimes they rely on their friends for input. Being present when people are looking for information is one way to get a leg up on competition. Burley Rink Supplies formed an alliance with an arena rink managers' association to put on seminars at association meetings on how to manage a rink, and how to maintain it for top performance. Burley doesn't try to sell its products; it only provides information. But the rink managers remember Burley in a favorable way, and that is all Burley needs to have a leg up on the competition.

Not surprisingly, most companies spend their marketing and sales dollars on prospects who are ready to buy. But the fact is you may only see 5 to 10 percent of the people who do buy if you wait that long to implement your marketing tactics. Your competitors will already have skimmed off the other prospects. Your goal should be to contact prospects as soon as possible, even if it is a year or two before they buy. That way you'll have a chance at over 70 percent of the prospects, which should improve your sales exponentially.

Retailers often feel that this buying process doesn't affect them, but they are wrong. Visibility is key for retailers, because people might go by a store 15 to 20 times before they decide to stop in. What a retailer does to impress a passerby has an incredible impact on their sales. People will go back to a store that they've seen before if they feel it delivers what they want.

> You are at an enormous competitive disadvantage when a competitor controls the prospect's information process.

## Competitor Advantages

You need to be concerned if one competitor does a much better job than you do in the early stages of the buying decision. For example, a restaurant may be concerned if another restaurant is recognized as the one that most people recommend. A boutique may have a competitor that is more visible or has easier access. A gardening store may have a competitor that offers established classes and seminars, or has some other tactic that appeals to prospective customers. An industrial supplier may have a competitor whose product is considered the industry standard. Marketing programs have to take into account the actions of their competitors. When a competitor has a big edge in a certain marketing area, you need to figure out how to establish your firm in an equal way. For instance, restaurants with lower name recognition can promote special days when they conduct taste tests of various dishes or have a family night when meals are served family style rather than in individual portions.

## Your Advantages

Marketers spend years building up market recognition of one or two aspects of their business. You always want to protect an advantage you've built up in the market. If you work hard to keep that advantage, rarely will you lose it. But if you are complacent, your advantage can be lost in as little as one year. Every market plan should incorporate tactics to keep your advantages in the market apparent to your customers.

A dental company I worked with provides a good example of what happens when you forget to preserve your market advantage. One of the key influences in the dentist's buying decision was input from the technicians who kept the dental equipment operating. Our products had a long history of reliability, and for over 10 years most technicians recommended our product line. Then one year our major competitor started a program that invited these service providers to their factory. They received three days of training, went fishing, were invited to baseball or basketball games, and were treated royally. We did nothing to counter the competitor's moves. In one year, we lost 7 market share points to them. We had to introduce two new products with advanced features just to reclaim our market share. That was a heavy penalty, but we deserved it for neglecting some of the people who mattered most to our customers.

## Tactics That Work Best

Marketing is a game of constant adjustments as marketers learn more about their customers, and about which tactics work in the marketplace. You are not interested in duplicating your competitors' programs. That is usually not a cost-effective tactic. But you do want to understand why a program worked, or didn't work, because that will tell you something about the customer. Your goal is to learn as much as you can about customers by judging the effectiveness of competitors' programs and understanding why they worked.

Going back to the competitor's program for dental service providers, we learned that the technicians really appreciated the perk of being sent out to our competitor's scenic location on the West Coast for three days of training. Our company was located in Des Moines, Iowa, which didn't (and still doesn't) have nearly as much appeal as the West Coast. But we learned that the technicians felt they were often overlooked, and that they appreciated some extra

> Building marketing momentum is like climbing a mountain. The way up is slow and arduous; but if you slip, the way down is fast and dangerous.

attention. We countered by holding afternoon training sessions at the dental equipment dealers' offices. Our salespeople brought food and beverages to the sessions. This program worked just as well as our competitor's because we treated every service person at the dealer, while our competitors invited only the top three technicians at each dealer.

## Evaluate Your Tactics

You should judge your tactics and their success as a way of evaluating your customers' behavior. You also want to keep consistency in your programs so you don't confuse your customers. If a program has worked well, keep its basic elements and just tweak it to make it more effective. Marketers often make too many changes to a successful program because they get bored with it. The fact is that marketers spend all their time thinking about their programs. Customers spend little time thinking about what a company is doing, and rarely get tired of a marketing program. Take Coppertone's ad, "Tan don't burn, get a Coppertone tan." That's run for at least 20 years, but the market isn't tired of the ad, or the message, and it still works great. I'm sure the marketers are sick and tired of the ad, but they have the discipline to realize that the person who counts is their customer.

Tactics work well when they address a desire or need of the customer. You are in a position to create innovative tactics when you understand what need or desire a successful tactic fulfills.

## Keep Up the Momentum

Momentum feeds on itself. The better your programs worked in the past, the faster start you will have with your programs the following year. If your programs aren't gaining momentum, you need to start worrying that the effectiveness of your marketing program and your sales level is going to decrease. The ideal plan is to keep the basic program that worked well for you in the past, and add new features to make the program more effective the following year. Keep up the excitement, keep up the momentum, and you'll keep increasing sales.

Starbucks is a good example of a company that just keeps adding to its basic program to create rapid growth. Starbucks started off selling gourmet coffee and bagels, muffins, and other treats in its

> Small companies can outperform consumer giants when they learn how to spend their money more effectively.

coffeehouses. The emphasis was that Starbucks cared about the consumer's cup of coffee. Then Starbucks started selling its coffee in supermarkets to enhance its reputation as a premium coffee supplier. To keep its momentum high in its storefront restaurants, Starbucks added Frappuccino, a milk-based coffee drink to its café menus. When that product was a success, Starbucks formed an alliance with Pepsi-Cola to sell Frappuccino in supermarkets. Consumers see Starbucks as a company that is constantly adding new and improved products. That is the type of public perception that every company would like to have. The real beauty of this momentum-based program is that it has allowed Starbucks to increase sales rapidly with a virtually nonexistent TV ad budget.

## Final Comments

As you go through this chapter, remember that you are only looking for two to three points where you can get a sustainable market advantage. By looking at every point in your customer interaction, you are doing everything you can to establish a marketing strategy that will be a runaway success. For example, the product Clean Shower went from the garage to over $100 million in sales per year because the inventor learned that people trusted the information they received from certain radio personalities. He gave leading personalities in various markets free samples of his product and paid for ad time when the personalities could say whatever they wanted about it. A simple fact about how people get information about a mundane job like cleaning their shower helped the underfinanced inventor of Clean Shower outsmart Procter & Gamble and other leading consumer product companies. You should be able to do the same in your market when you learn to understand your customer's buying process.

## How Smart Have You Been?

List your percentages of your marketing and expenses per category and then compare them to the recommend percentages. You might want to reconsider your spending patterns if they are substantially different from the recommended ranges.

| MARKETING FOCUS | YOUR PERCENTAGE | RECOMMENDED PERCENTAGE |
|---|---|---|
| Information during early stages of the buying decision | | 15–20 |
| Information where customers look for it | | 25–30 |
| Marketing contact with prospects who aren't ready to buy | | 10-15 |
| People who are ready to buy | | 40–50 |

People access information much differently than they did even two years ago. Be sure to adjust for those changes.

# The Situation Analysis

**CHAPTER 4** THE INTERNAL AUDIT **CHAPTER 5** THE EXTERNAL AUDIT

# Chapter 4

# The Internal Audit

1: MARKETING PLANS KEEP SALES GROWING

2: A CUSTOMER PROFILE

3: HOW THE CUSTOMER BUYS

**4: THE INTERNAL AUDIT**

5. THE EXTERNAL EVALUATION

6: MARKETING OBJECTIVES

7: PRODUCT-BASED MARKETING TACTICS

8: COMMUNICATIONS-BASED MARKETING TACTICS

9: MARKETING TACTICS FOR SALES,
   PROMOTIONS, AND DISTRIBUTION

## *INTERNAL AUDIT*

Describe your business or product.

. . . . . . . . . . . . . . . . . . . . . . . . . . . . . . . . . . . . . . . . . . . . . . . . . . . . . . . . . . . . . . . . . . . . . . . . . .

. . . . . . . . . . . . . . . . . . . . . . . . . . . . . . . . . . . . . . . . . . . . . . . . . . . . . . . . . . . . . . . . . . . . . . . . . .

Give its history and background.

. . . . . . . . . . . . . . . . . . . . . . . . . . . . . . . . . . . . . . . . . . . . . . . . . . . . . . . . . . . . . . . . . . . . . . . . . .

. . . . . . . . . . . . . . . . . . . . . . . . . . . . . . . . . . . . . . . . . . . . . . . . . . . . . . . . . . . . . . . . . . . . . . . . . .

Which markets do you target?

. . . . . . . . . . . . . . . . . . . . . . . . . . . . . . . . . . . . . . . . . . . . . . . . . . . . . . . . . . . . . . . . . . . . . . . . . .

. . . . . . . . . . . . . . . . . . . . . . . . . . . . . . . . . . . . . . . . . . . . . . . . . . . . . . . . . . . . . . . . . . . . . . . . . .

Which markets do you sell into but don't target?

. . . . . . . . . . . . . . . . . . . . . . . . . . . . . . . . . . . . . . . . . . . . . . . . . . . . . . . . . . . . . . . . . . . . . . . . . .

. . . . . . . . . . . . . . . . . . . . . . . . . . . . . . . . . . . . . . . . . . . . . . . . . . . . . . . . . . . . . . . . . . . . . . . . . .

Which markets do you choose not to compete in?

. . . . . . . . . . . . . . . . . . . . . . . . . . . . . . . . . . . . . . . . . . . . . . . . . . . . . . . . . . . . . . . . . . . . . . . . . .

. . . . . . . . . . . . . . . . . . . . . . . . . . . . . . . . . . . . . . . . . . . . . . . . . . . . . . . . . . . . . . . . . . . . . . . . . .

What is the company specialty?

. . . . . . . . . . . . . . . . . . . . . . . . . . . . . . . . . . . . . . . . . . . . . . . . . . . . . . . . . . . . . . . . . . . . . . . . . .

. . . . . . . . . . . . . . . . . . . . . . . . . . . . . . . . . . . . . . . . . . . . . . . . . . . . . . . . . . . . . . . . . . . . . . . . . .

. . . . . . . . . . . . . . . . . . . . . . . . . . . . . . . . . . . . . . . . . . . . . . . . . . . . . . . . . . . . . . . . . . . . . . . . . .

## INTERNAL AUDIT

What has the sales growth rate been over the past three years? ·····························

Give a brief summary of what occurred last year to increase, decrease, or maintain sales levels.

· · · · · · · · · · · · · · · · · · · · · · · · · · · · · · · · · · · · · · · · · · · · · · · · · · · ·

· · · · · · · · · · · · · · · · · · · · · · · · · · · · · · · · · · · · · · · · · · · · · · · · · · · ·

\*Rank Priority by the priority of the item to customers, and rank Importance by how important it is for your company to address the item. Rank each item 1 to 5, with 1 being a high value, and 5 a low value

| | PRIORITY* | IMPORTANCE* |
| --- | --- | --- |
| | (1–5) | (1–5) |

Company/Product/Service Strengths:

1. · · · · · · · · · · · · · · · · · · · · · · · · · · · · · · · · · · · · · · · · · · · · · · ·
2. · · · · · · · · · · · · · · · · · · · · · · · · · · · · · · · · · · · · · · · · · · · · · · ·
3. · · · · · · · · · · · · · · · · · · · · · · · · · · · · · · · · · · · · · · · · · · · · · · ·
4. · · · · · · · · · · · · · · · · · · · · · · · · · · · · · · · · · · · · · · · · · · · · · · ·
5. · · · · · · · · · · · · · · · · · · · · · · · · · · · · · · · · · · · · · · · · · · · · · · ·
6. · · · · · · · · · · · · · · · · · · · · · · · · · · · · · · · · · · · · · · · · · · · · · · ·

Company/Product/Service Weaknesses:

1. · · · · · · · · · · · · · · · · · · · · · · · · · · · · · · · · · · · · · · · · · · · · · · ·
2. · · · · · · · · · · · · · · · · · · · · · · · · · · · · · · · · · · · · · · · · · · · · · · ·
3. · · · · · · · · · · · · · · · · · · · · · · · · · · · · · · · · · · · · · · · · · · · · · · ·
4. · · · · · · · · · · · · · · · · · · · · · · · · · · · · · · · · · · · · · · · · · · · · · · ·

## *INTERNAL AUDIT*

|  | PRIORITY* (1-5) | IMPORTANCE* (1-5) |
|---|---|---|
| 5. ................................................. | ............... | ............... |
| 6. ................................................. | ............... | ............... |

Describe your financial capability.

...................................................................................................

...................................................................................................

...................................................................................................

...................................................................................................

...................................................................................................

What is your management and marketing expertise?

...................................................................................................

...................................................................................................

...................................................................................................

...................................................................................................

...................................................................................................

The internal audit is a snapshot of your company at this point in time, where it has been in the past, and what your strengths and weaknesses are. A company can't just pick one strategy that will work for its entire growth cycle. As growth occurs, the company's market position changes, and what once were assets may become liabilities. For example, a company may grow because it has the newest, most innovative inventory-management software on the market. That reputation as a leader in inventory-management software will be an asset as the company grows. But it becomes a liability if the company tries to branch out into a totally new market area, such as contact-management software. Customers will want to buy that product from a supplier that specializes in contact-management software and therefore will know the market best.

> An asset in today's strategy can become a liability in tomorrow's market. An effective marketing plan addresses these changes so the company's current positioning strategy matches its goals.

G-Vox Interactive Music, a $5 million business with 50 employees, is doubling in size every year. In 1993 the company started out with a hardware/software package that used a computer to transcribe music being played on a guitar into a sheet of music that could be observed on a computer monitor. Company founder Nathaniel Weiss believed that the product would be popular with guitarists, since they wouldn't have to stop playing to write down the notes as they composed a song. Instead, as they played, the G-Vox program would convert the song into sheet music.

When G-Vox started, its first major weakness was that Weiss was an unknown in the music business. He wasn't an established manufacturer, nor was he a well known musician. To overcome this weakness Weiss signed a distribution arrangement with Fender, a leading guitar manufacturer. Weiss's agreement with Fender had two components. Fender agreed to offer the guitar pickup as an option on its guitar, and to distribute the software and auxiliary hardware to major guitar stores under the G-Vox name. This agreement gave G-Vox the credibility it needed to penetrate the market.

In 1995 G-Vox's biggest weakness was that too much of its sales were tied up with one customer. To generate the next growth phase of his company, Weiss brought in a sales and marketing executive who had extensive experience in the guitar store market and who was able to add a whole new network of retailers to G-Vox's distribution outlets.

By 1997 G-Vox's market size, industry image, and expertise were limited by its role as a supplier to only the guitar industry. The strategy evolved to include alliances with major corporations like McGraw-Hill to sell products to schools. The products would help band and orchestra students practice correctly by allowing them to see the notes they were playing and compare them to the music they were supposed to be playing. G-Vox's evolution is typical of a growing company. Its situation kept changing, depending on its marketing objectives over time. As a result, G-Vox had to develop a new marketing plan and strategy every one or two years. This story illustrates just one of the reasons for developing an annual marketing plan.

An interesting experiment is to ask your employees to write their descriptions of your business. Your company won't be as effective as it could be if everyone doesn't write down similar descriptions.

## A Description of the Business

This should be a two- or three- sentence description of your business. G-Vox's company description could read: "G-Vox supplies hardware and software that allow musicians to see and save the notes they are playing. The product is aimed at musicians who write their own songs, and at schoolchildren who are learning to play an instrument. G-Vox sells its products to guitar stores through a network of distributors and through a private label arrangement with Fender Guitar Company. Products are sold and distributed to schools through an alliance with McGraw-Hill.

## The History and Background of the Business

G-Vox started out as a song-writing aid for guitar players. Before G-Vox, musicians had to stop playing to write their notes down on paper. This was time-consuming, and sometimes the musicians lost the concept of the song they were playing. With G-Vox, they simply plays the notes, and the program transcribe them onto a musical staff. G-Vox concentrated on this market for the first three to four years, establishing a strong reputation with guitar players. Then it decided to enter the school market and formed an alliance with McGraw-Hill. G-Vox is just starting to penetrate this market.

A company's background plays a big role in its strategy. G-Vox is well established in one market, and a new entrant into another. Its strategies in the marketing plan can only be understood if you have a modest amount of company background. Again, you should be able to give the pertinent historical details in three to four sentences. If your company has been in business for a long time, just concentrate on the past five years.

## Target Markets

A market is either a geographic area, or a group of customers who buy products for similar needs and in similar ways. For example, guitar players buy the equipment and supplies they need at guitar stores. Claire's Boutiques sell jewelry in mall stores to preteen and teenage girls. Preteen girls don't buy quite the same items as teenage girls, so Claire's Boutiques used different strategies for these two markets. Each of Claire's Boutiques also sold to different geographic markets. A Claire's Boutique in one town would have as its target market the preteen and teen girls in that town.

This sounds like a simple enough step, but surprisingly it is a tough assignment for many companies. One of the marketing plans presented in Chapter 12 deals with Safeplay Systems, a company that sells playground equipment. But the market isn't just playground equipment. Parks, schools, independent day care centers, day care chains, churches, and parents all buy playground equipment. Do they all purchase for similar reasons and make buying decisions in the same way? Probably not. Each group probably has a different set of purchase criteria, which makes each group a separate market. You want to choose a specific target market in order to understand the purchasing requirements for that market.

### Secondary Markets

I recently worked with a company that sold equipment for hockey rinks, including the board systems, ice resurfacers, and supplies. It targeted community skating rinks that catered to youth hockey programs and public skating. The company also received

> Small companies are almost always better off concentrating on a small market where they can give customers exactly what they want. This is their main advantage over large companies that have to compromise certain features so they can serve several markets.

inquiries and orders from roller hockey rinks. The company didn't target that market, didn't understand its needs, and didn't make much money on whatever orders it did get. Many companies get caught in a situation like this. Their resources are diverted into side markets that they don't target, and aren't prepared to compete in.

You should be very deliberate in choosing the markets you compete in. Either stop selling to side markets and spend all your efforts on your chosen market, or target the secondary market in a more intentional manner. This could be a growth market for you, or it could be a market you want to avoid. In the case of the ice rink supplier, there were several entrenched suppliers in the roller hockey market, and the market desire for lower-price, lower-quality products did not fit with the company's manufacturing expertise.

A marketing plan is a communication tool for people in your company. Salespeople want to get every order that they can. Unfortunately, they often chase after business in markets in which the company has chosen not to compete. Marketers will do best in their chosen market if they do everything they can to make sure their salespeople don't try to generate sales in markets that the company isn't prepared to serve.

## Your Company's Specialty

Why do your customers think your business is special? When people think of Bloomingdale's, they think of high fashion and unusual clothes. When people think of Wal-Mart, they think of low prices and wide selection. It is not uncommon for potential customers to associate a different trait with each company in the market. For example, Safeplay Systems, a manufacturer of playground equipment, is special because its equipment is made from recycled material. Other playground equipment manufacturers could be known for low prices, elaborate mazes, innovative swing sets, or jungle gym–type equipment.

In many cases the market may not have an established perception for a company or business. I have an OfficeMax close to my home, and I know it has low prices. There is also a Nelson Office Supply in the area, but I don't have any idea at all of what that

> One of the purposes of a marketing plan is to help employees understand exactly what the company is trying to accomplish.

store's specialty is. The market's perception of your company is a critical step. If the market doesn't perceive your company as having a specialty, you will have to develop a strategy to build an image the market will recognize. If you already have a specialty established, use it in your market strategy, either to reinforce the image, if it's positive, or to change the image, if it's negative or is no longer the perception you want. G-Vox, as an example, was known as a guitar player's song-writing aid. When it went into the school market, it had to overcome that established position, which was the main reason it formed an alliance with McGraw-Hill.

> Customers have a hard time remembering a company if it doesn't have a clear-cut lead product, service, or specialty.

## Sales Growth

Today's market is a rapidly changing place, and consumers are always looking for the business with the next red-hot idea. Once momentum swings to a new company, it can become a gargantuan force knocking off competitors. That means you can't afford to sit on a certain level of sales. If your sales aren't growing, they will soon start declining. The sales growth rate is a measuring point for how well your past strategies worked. Unless you have growth rates of 20 percent or more, or are limiting your growth rate due to financial constraints, you need to be modifying or drastically changing your strategy.

There are always events in the market that can have a drastic effect on your company performance. A major competitor could have gone out of business and held a huge inventory clearance sale that lowered your sales. Or the competitor could have just closed down and your sales went up. New competitors, new market trends, new products, new applications, or a changing economy could all impact your sales. You want to look at these explanations because they will give you additional insights into whether your strategies affected your sales or whether lucky, or unlucky, market events had more of an impact.

## Your Strengths and Weaknesses

All companies have both strengths and weaknesses in the market. I've listed a series of areas in which a company could be either strong or weak, but there could also be a number of other strengths and weaknesses that apply to your business. Remember to look at your company from the customer's point of view. If buyers think a competitor has a broader product line than you do, that's a weakness—even if you believe your product line is just as broad as the competitor's. Over the last 20 years of helping small businesses with marketing, I've come to the conclusion that one of the biggest problems these marketers have is that they look at their own efforts through rose-colored glasses. That doesn't help anyone. It just stops small businesses from taking the steps they need to compete effectively in the market. Another problem I've seen is that small businesses will often do all they can with the resources they have to overcome a weakness. Then they'll stop considering the situation a weakness because there is nothing else they can do. Unfortunately, the market will still see the weakness, and the market's perception is all that matters.

> If you don't think you have any weaknesses, just ask your customers if there are areas you need to improve. They will be happy to tell you.

### Potential Strengths and Weaknesses*

| | |
|---|---|
| Brand name recognition | Innovation |
| Features | Product or service design |
| Market focus | Application expertise |
| Alliance partners | Sales force |
| Distribution network | Experience |
| Established customer base | Meets customers needs |
| Customer service | Ease of use |
| Management | Financial strength |
| Penetration of key customers | Source of customer information |
| Reliance on one customer | Preferred customer brand |
| Geographic location | Market buzz |
| Perceived status of customers | Price/value |
| Perceived to be the safe choice | Quality |
| Referrals | Purchasing requirements |
| Happy users | Installation and technical support |
| Trade show attendance | Market understanding |
| Promotional programs | Strength of a lead product |
| Product line breadth | Offers a complete solution |
| Entertainment value | Endorsements |
| Field repair network | Product differentiation |
| Packaging | Displays |

Training/education
Company size
Industry standards
Manufacturing plant location

Events
Association memberships
Trustworthy reputation

\* Each category can either be a strength or a weakness. For example, in the product innovation area, a company's products could be considered either innovative or unnecessary.

Try to be objective when considering your company's strengths and weaknesses, and be sure to evaluate each aspect of your company from your customer's point of view. In the long run, objectivity is a key trait that will help your company grow profitably. An excellent example of perception versus reality is 7UP and Slice soft drinks. Before Slice was introduced, marketers discovered that people liked the taste of 7UP because they thought it contained natural fruit juices. The fact that there isn't any fruit juice in 7UP doesn't matter, because the public thinks there is. When Slice was introduced, it actually contained 10 percent fruit juice in order to meet the public's perception that soft drinks with fruit juice taste better. The only problem was that the public didn't perceive 10 percent to be a significant amount of fruit juice. As a result, Slice never really took off. Then Snapple came out with its fruit juices and succeeded. Of course, Snapple isn't 100 percent fruit juice either, but the public doesn't perceive that. When it comes to marketing, perception becomes the true reality, so marketers have to treat customer's perceptions as the truth, even though they may be a mirage.

> Before you implement a new program, check with at least five to 10 customers to make sure it has the impact you desire. You need customers to believe your program counters a weakness, or reinforces a strength, in a significant way.

## Your Financial Capability

The extent of the marketing programs you can implement depends on your ability to finance your marketing changes. Obviously, you have to focus on what you can afford to do. Fortunately, many marketing programs, especially for small companies, do not have to be expensive. What is important is to have a clear goal in mind. Once you have that, you can generate an effective program no matter what your finances are.

## Your Management and Marketing Expertise

An inexperienced marketer will have a tough time putting together an effective direct-mail campaign. Many marketing tactics are easily implemented by marketers and small business owners with any level of experience. Others take more expertise. Stay with the marketing tactics that you can execute, and bring in outside help if you decide to run a program that is more complex than you have run before.

The internal audit is a key point to any marketing program for two reasons. First, how you are perceived by your customers is a major factor in your success. Marketers need to control that perception; and they can't do it, if they don't check periodically to see how the market sees them. A major part of any marketing program is projecting to customers the image the company wants to be known for. Second, you need to be sure you are creating a marketing program that you can execute. For example, you can't implement a key account marketing program if you don't have enough salespeople or the financial resources to serve the needs of large customers. You want to pick a program that fits your capabilities.

> Marketers can expand sales by entering markets or by introducing new products. Knowing what resistance the market will offer a new company allows the company to create a strategy to overcome that market resistance.

## Final Comments

I've done many plans over the years, and I've found that the internal audit is the one area where companies constantly see themselves in a much more positive light than their customers do. It may be human nature. Perhaps people's self-image won't let them see too many of their weaknesses. Marketers need to look at their business world in a different light than their personal world. A marketer's weaknesses are not necessarily deficiencies; they are the facts of the market. G-Vox didn't have credibility in the school market because it was a new player. If you operate only in those markets where you don't have weaknesses, you will never expand sales. However, you have a limited number of resources to contend with a market full of hundreds of opportunities. You simply can't be strong everywhere, so go into those markets where you have the resources to overcome your weaknesses. Ignoring problems in your current situation will only lead you to make bad decisions.

## Don't Be Too Safe

One of the dangers of doing an internal audit is that marketers get too cautious and stay with their tried-and-true markets and strategies. This is a recipe for disaster. You must try new things to see what will work in the future. Fill out this chart for long-term growth to see if you are making enough changes every year to maintain market momentum.

| TYPE OF STRATEGY | ACTUAL PERCENTAGE | RECOMMENDED PERCENTAGE |
|---|---|---|
| Effective strategies from the past | | 25 |
| Variations and improvements over past strategies | | 25 |
| New tactics with an established positioning strategy | | 15 |
| Tactics that promote positioning strategies for new market trends | | 20 |
| Strategies that address new markets or opportunities | | 15 |

Marketers won't succeed unless they introduce bold new strategies every year.

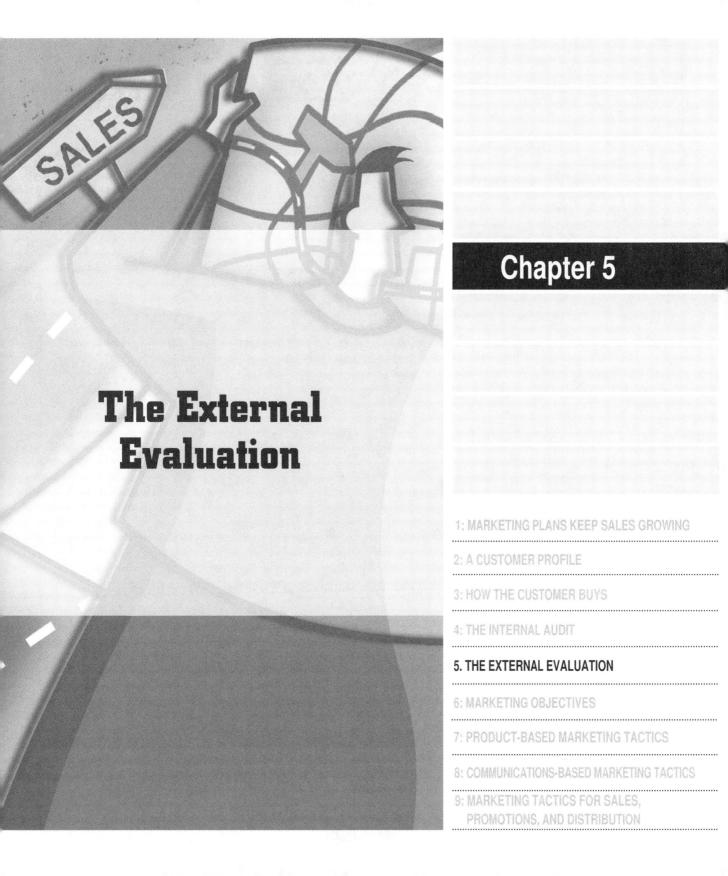

# The External Evaluation

## Chapter 5

1: MARKETING PLANS KEEP SALES GROWING

2: A CUSTOMER PROFILE

3: HOW THE CUSTOMER BUYS

4: THE INTERNAL AUDIT

**5. THE EXTERNAL EVALUATION**

6: MARKETING OBJECTIVES

7: PRODUCT-BASED MARKETING TACTICS

8: COMMUNICATIONS-BASED MARKETING TACTICS

9: MARKETING TACTICS FOR SALES,
   PROMOTIONS, AND DISTRIBUTION

## EXTERNAL AUDIT

List the markets you compete in.

. . . . . . . . . . . . . . . . . . . . . . . . . . . . . . . . . . . . . . . . . . . . . . . . . . . . . . . . . . . . . . . . . .

. . . . . . . . . . . . . . . . . . . . . . . . . . . . . . . . . . . . . . . . . . . . . . . . . . . . . . . . . . . . . . . . . .

\* Rank Priority by the priority of the item to customers, and rank Importance by how important it is for your company to address the item. Rank each item 1 to 5, with 1 being a high value, and 5 a low value

List the different segments of the market.

|  | PERCENTAGE OF MARKET | PRIORITY* (1–5) | IMPORTANCE* (1–5) |
|---|---|---|---|
| 1. | | | |
| 2. | | | |
| 3. | | | |
| 4. | | | |

Which segments do you target?  1. . . . . . . . . 2. . . . . . . . . . . 3. . . . . . . . . . . . 4. . . . . . . . . . . .

List your major competitors and their major advantage in the market. List your competitors by their importance, with your top competitor first.

|  | PRIORITY* (1–5) | IMPORTANCE* (1–5) |
|---|---|---|
| 1. . . . . . . . . . . . . . . . . . . . . . . . . . . . . . . . . . . . . . . . . | | |
| Major Advantage: . . . . . . . . . . . . . . . . . . . . . . . . . . . . . | | |
| Positioning Strategy . . . . . . . . . . . . . . . . . . . . . . . . . . . | | |
| . . . . . . . . . . . . . . . . . . . . . . . . . . . . . . . . . . | | |

## *EXTERNAL AUDIT*

|  | PRIORITY* (1-5) | IMPORTANCE* (1-5) |
|---|---|---|
| 2. | | |
| Major Advantage: | | |
| Positioning Strategy: | | |
| 3. | | |
| Major Advantage: | | |
| Positioning Strategy: | | |
| 4. | | |
| Major Advantage: | | |
| Positioning Strategy: | | |

** Important signifies when a competitor's position gives them a significant advantage in the market.

List in order your top competitors along with your company by category.

| 1. Price (top price first): | IMPORTANT** | 2. Features (most features first): | IMPORTANT** |
|---|---|---|---|
| a. | | a. | |
| b. | | b. | |
| c. | | c. | |
| d. | | d. | |
| e. | | e. | |

## EXTERNAL AUDIT

|                        | IMPORTANT** |                        | IMPORTANT** |

3. Service (best service first):

a. . . . . . . . . . . . . . . . . . . . . . . . . . . . . . . . . . . . . . .

b. . . . . . . . . . . . . . . . . . . . . . . . . . . . . . . . . . . . . . .

c. . . . . . . . . . . . . . . . . . . . . . . . . . . . . . . . . . . . . . .

d. . . . . . . . . . . . . . . . . . . . . . . . . . . . . . . . . . . . . . .

e. . . . . . . . . . . . . . . . . . . . . . . . . . . . . . . . . . . . . . .

4. Distribution (widest distribution first):

a. . . . . . . . . . . . . . . . . . . . . . . . . . . . . . . . . . . . . . .

b. . . . . . . . . . . . . . . . . . . . . . . . . . . . . . . . . . . . . . .

c. . . . . . . . . . . . . . . . . . . . . . . . . . . . . . . . . . . . . . .

d. . . . . . . . . . . . . . . . . . . . . . . . . . . . . . . . . . . . . . .

e. . . . . . . . . . . . . . . . . . . . . . . . . . . . . . . . . . . . . . .

5. Price/Value Relationship (list best first):

a. . . . . . . . . . . . . . . . . . . . . . . . . . . . . . . . . . . . . . .

b. . . . . . . . . . . . . . . . . . . . . . . . . . . . . . . . . . . . . . .

c. . . . . . . . . . . . . . . . . . . . . . . . . . . . . . . . . . . . . . .

d. . . . . . . . . . . . . . . . . . . . . . . . . . . . . . . . . . . . . . .

e. . . . . . . . . . . . . . . . . . . . . . . . . . . . . . . . . . . . . . .

6. Quality (who customers rank first):

a. . . . . . . . . . . . . . . . . . . . . . . . . . . . . . . . . . . . . . .

b. . . . . . . . . . . . . . . . . . . . . . . . . . . . . . . . . . . . . . .

c. . . . . . . . . . . . . . . . . . . . . . . . . . . . . . . . . . . . . . .

d. . . . . . . . . . . . . . . . . . . . . . . . . . . . . . . . . . . . . . .

e. . . . . . . . . . . . . . . . . . . . . . . . . . . . . . . . . . . . . . .

What new trends in the market could significantly impact your business?

|   | | FAVORABLE (YES OR NO) | IMPORTANT** |

1. . . . . . . . . . . . . . . . . . . . . . . . . . . . . . . . . . . . . . . . . . . . . . . . . . . . . . . . . . . . . . . . . . . . . . . . .

2. . . . . . . . . . . . . . . . . . . . . . . . . . . . . . . . . . . . . . . . . . . . . . . . . . . . . . . . . . . . . . . . . . . . . . . . .

3. . . . . . . . . . . . . . . . . . . . . . . . . . . . . . . . . . . . . . . . . . . . . . . . . . . . . . . . . . . . . . . . . . . . . . . . .

4. . . . . . . . . . . . . . . . . . . . . . . . . . . . . . . . . . . . . . . . . . . . . . . . . . . . . . . . . . . . . . . . . . . . . . . . .

# THE EXTERNAL EVALUATION

## EXTERNAL AUDIT

Opportunities:

|  | PRIORITY* (1–5) | IMPORTANCE* (1–5) |
|---|---|---|
| 1. | | |
| 2. | | |
| 3. | | |
| 4. | | |

Threats:

|  | PRIORITY* (1–5) | IMPORTANCE* (1–5) |
|---|---|---|
| 1. | | |
| 2. | | |
| 3. | | |
| 4. | | |

Distribution channels, customer needs, and technology are just a few of the many parts of a marketer's external world that are changing almost on a yearly basis. Marketers need to make the right adjustments or they will soon be out of business.

In every industry I know, the marketer's world is changing rapidly. One of the companies presented in the Sample Marketing Plans section (Chapter 10) is H&R Trains, a store that sells model railroad equipment. Model railroading may not have changed much in the 23 years since the store opened, but the world around H&R Trains is nothing like it was. Electronic games from Nintendo and Sega have enjoyed tremendous popularity, computers have become a mainstay in most homes, and the free time people have to enjoy a hobby has shrunk dramatically. H&R Trains has to adjust to this changing environment or it will go out of business. The store can't rely on existing model railroading enthusiasts. It has to encourage new people to take up the hobby, and it has to help fledgling model railroaders increase their interest in and satisfaction with the hobby. Most important, H&R Trains needs to keep attracting young people to support the long-term staying power of model railroading in its market.

Market trends are just one of the marketer's concerns. They also have to adjust to moves by competitors, changes in customer needs, and the opening of major new markets. Another primary concern is how their products or services interact with other products in the market. For example, modems have changed rapidly, as have the downloading capacities of most computers. US WEST, the telephone company, has been slow to react to these changes and has delayed providing high-speed connection lines. This deficit has left the company at a serious competitive disadvantage. Rarely in today's world do products exist in a vacuum, and marketers need to be on their toes. This isn't just a concern of major corporations. Sporting goods retailers have to adjust to the presence of category killer stores such as Golf Galaxy that specialize in just one area, and high-quality restaurants are now forced to compete with restaurants such as the Rainforest that make dining out an entertainment event. Consumers can only choose to do so many things. Consequently, in order to succeed, marketers have to understand the customer's total world and how it interacts with their products.

## Target Markets

This should be the same market you listed in Chapter 4, in the Internal Audit form. If you serve more than one market, list each one separately. For example, a piece of test equipment could be sold to the medical, machining, and semiconductor production markets. Or a retail store might concentrate on the teenage fashion market, the outdoor apparel market, or the high-fashion market.

> Small companies often thrive by attacking market segments that are too small to interest larger companies.

## Market Segments

A segment of a market behaves in some way that is similar to the primary market, but it has some differences that set it apart. For example, the test equipment manufacturer may be able to sell to hospitals, medical clinics, or sports therapy clinics. Each of these different customer groups would define a market segment. A clothing retailer for a women's high-fashion market may concentrate on high fashion for professional working women or on high fashion for a night on the town.

Of particular interest to marketers are segments that are not specifically targeted with a designated product by any one supplier. Often marketers can increase market share by simply targeting a segment that is being overlooked by the market's suppliers. In the case of our medical test equipment, other companies may compete vigorously for the hospital and clinic market segment, but totally overlook the physical therapy market segment.

### Target Segments

Many small business owners tell me that their marketing plan is in their head and that they don't need one written down. One function of a marketing plan is to provide a clear vision to every person in the company. True, people can have a marketing plan in their head, but the problem is that everyone in a company has a different plan. I've found the number one difference in employees' minds is what market segments the company targets. Everyone seems to think that a different segment is the best one for the company's products. You should clearly state which market segments you target, both to ensure that programs are aimed at your target markets, and that all your employees understand the company's focus.

## Competitor Advantages

Customers don't view your company, store, service, or product in a vacuum. It is one of many choices. So what competitors do has a direct bearing on how the market perceives your product. Typical marketers try to counteract a major competitor's advantage in two ways. They may try to figure out another advantage that would be at least as important to the consumer. Paper Warehouse is a big party supplies retailer. Its competitors—supermarkets, drugstores, and discount stores—typically have more convenient locations for most customers. Although these stores may be convenient, they don't have enough supplies to satisfy the market segment that works hard to throw a great party. Paper Warehouse has introduced a new strategy called "Party Smart." The company offers brochures on how to hold special parties and gives expert advice on every phase of holding a party. This marketing strategy is designed to get customers to drive a little farther to a Paper Warehouse store.

Marketers also may try to outdo the competitor at its own advantage. When MARS (Music and Recording Superstores) entered the guitar store market, its major competitors allowed musicians to come in and plug in any guitar and try them out. MARS went the competitors one better by putting in performing stages where guitar players could jam with other musicians. MARS even brought in well known guitar players on Saturdays to jam with its customers.

Most important, you must have a compelling advantage associated with your company that customers will notice. Every marketing plan revolves around creating an advantage and then developing tactics that ensure that customers will realize that you have that advantage.

## Competitive Positioning Strategies

A positioning statement is how a company tries to present itself so customers will remember them. Paper Warehouse wants to position

> You can respond to a competitor's advantage by creating another equally important advantage for your company. Don't try to duplicate your competitor's advantage unless you can do it better.

itself as the one stop people must make before throwing a party. Companies might position themselves as the biggest store, the highest value restaurant, or the paint store with the widest selection in town.

Competitors are not always obvious about their positioning statements (which is good for you). Perkins Restaurant, for example, in the Twin Cities of St. Paul and Minneapolis, where I live, advertises family food and a wide variety of choices. But in reality most of Perkins' customers appear to be businesspeople who have breakfast and lunch meetings at the restaurant. Perkins is a little more expensive so it doesn't have lots of kids making noise, which of course businesspeople like. But Perkins doesn't promote its true positioning strategy aimed at businesspeople, because it has a loyal customer base. Instead, Perkins tries to promote family dining to generate evening business.

You can figure out a company's positioning statement by first listing its target market segment, and then listing why the competitor believes the target segment should buy its product. For instance, one company's positioning statement may be: "Supplier of market's most innovative, brightly designed, upscale clothing for young children." This company's advantage in the market is that its clothing has won awards for the creativity of their designs.

There are times when a company's advantage doesn't tie in with its position statement. For example, a competitor's major advantage may be an extensive distribution network, while its positioning statement may be as a full-line supplier for metallurgical laboratories. Another example may be that a restaurant happens to have the best location in a mall because it is next to the mall's top attraction. But its positioning statement may be its spicy barbecue and great bands for young adults. A supermarket may have an advantage of being in a market for 20 years, but its positioning statement may be that it has the broadest selection of premium meats in the area.

In Chapter 2 you looked at your target customer groups and their needs and desires. You don't want to have the same positioning statement as the major competitors in the market. You won't be able to get customers to notice you if you don't have anything new to offer. Instead you want your eventual strategy to let customers know

> Every marketing plan revolves around creating a compelling competitive advantage and then developing tactics that ensure that customers will realize that you have that advantage.

that you sell something different, and that the difference you have is meaningful for them. Wendy's, a fast-food supplier, does a great job at their positioning strategy. Wendy's competitors, McDonald's and Burger King, seem to talk about low-cost meals, things for kids, and special promotions. I believe they have indistinguishable positioning strategies. Wendy's concentrates its marketing communications on its food, and the fact that its food tastes good. Every ad focuses on food, and Wendy's founder is always in the ads, proud of the quality of the meals it serves. Wendy's attracts a higher percentage of adult customers than Burger King or McDonald's because they buy into Wendy's positioning statement that its food tastes better.

> People will remember a positioning statement when they observe with firsthand experiences that it is true.

## Competitive Rankings

In most markets, competitors are not perceived as being quite the same and marketers need to understand those differences. I recently conducted a little survey of how people perceived Target, Wal-Mart, and Kmart. I found out that people perceived a difference between the three. They felt Target had the most upscale clothing, was slightly more expensive, and that people who went to Target wouldn't go to Kmart or Wal-Mart. They felt Wal-Mart had good values on many common items and had good-quality clothes. They felt Kmart had the best values on items like automotive supplies, paint, and sporting goods but had poor-quality clothing. Target was perceived to have the best customer service, but Wal-Mart was felt to have the best hours, primarily because they are open 24 hours a day in the Twin Cities. The point is, your customers do perceive differences between you and your competitors, and you need to know what they are.

**Price**. Having the highest price in a market is not a detriment, as long as the public views that the highest price goes with the best product. In many markets, a high price implies a better product and people will gladly pay the price. For years Michelob claimed it had a premium beer and charged a higher price. I'm not sure if the beer was better, but there advertising strategy and pricing sold the consumers on its better taste.

**Features**. Having the most features appeals to some people, but not to everyone. For example, a standard drip coffeemaker sells for $30 to $40 and has a certain number of features. Fancy coffeemakers may sell for $80 with extra features that some people like but that really don't make the coffee taste better. Most people buy the $30 to $40 coffeemaker because all they want is a decent coffeemaker. Lawn mowers with mulching capability, or extra bagging capacity, offer extra convenience, but all lawn mowers still cut grass the same. Most home owners buy the lawn mowers that they perceive to have the best value. At other times, extra features provide better performance and do offer an advantage. Antilock brakes on cars offer better braking. Frozen dinners with gourmet food offer a better tasting dinner. Production equipment that offers quicker setup times, more through-put capacity, or tighter tolerances all provide better performance. In these cases people who want the best product will buy the product with the most features. Competitors with additional features that produce better performance typically have a major market advantage.

**Service**. Customer service, loaner equipment, technical support, field service networks, field service repairs, fast delivery, and training and installation help are all part of service. Overall the service levels in America appear to be dropping, led by voice mail and automated phone answering systems. Having significantly better service is a big advantage in today's market, and customers are more willing than ever before to pay for service.

**Distribution**. This term applies to all aspects of how you get a product, service, or store to a place where a customer can buy it. In the case of a store or restaurant, distribution is simply its location. The best distribution is where customers can

> Marketers have trouble succeeding when they don't know what their customers see as the differences between their company and their competitors.

> A competitive advantage in the distribution network is by far the most important advantage a marketer can have.

easily find the store, without the rent being prohibitive. For a manufacturer, the distribution network can include wholesalers, distributors, retailers, salespeople, brokers, manufacturers' representatives, or catalogs. As a general rule, the more times a company can get its product in front of customers, the more times the customer will buy.

Setting up an effective distribution network is the most difficult and time-consuming aspect of marketing. A company with the best distribution network is difficult to dislodge in the market: usually that can only be done with a great deal of effort. Apple Computer, as an example, locked up school sales early in the 1980s. Apple maintained an enormous lead in this market until the late 1990s. Usually, marketers get around a broad distribution network by targeting a narrower market segment. For instance, a restaurant that has a poor location might add a jazz pianist to attract jazz lovers, bring in a well known chef with a gourmet reputation, or put in an outdoor eating area. Those features will appeal to a limited segment of the market, but that segment will be willing to go to a little extra effort to visit a restaurant that caters to its desires.

**Price/value relationship**. Some customers only buy the best products. Others buy the lowest priced products. But some customers buy when they feel the price is a good value for the features and performance of the product or service. The percentage of the market that is concerned about value depends on the market. Most people buying soup at a supermarket are concerned about the price/value relationship. A man buying flowers for his girlfriend on Valentine's Day isn't going to be overly concerned about the price/value relationship. People buying an economy car will look at price/value. Buyers of luxury cars are much less worried about price/value relationships.

**Quality**. People expect quality products, and often will not even consider buying from a company that they feel has less than outstanding quality. As a result, quality is no longer an effective positioning statement because consumers expect it.

They no longer consider quality to be an unusual feature for a company. One way to generate sales is to look at the segments that companies with poor quality compete in. There are times when those markets are just waiting for a new supplier to finally give them a quality product.

## Market Trends

The market has changed as never before. The high-fashion children's apparel market used to be concentrated in small children's boutiques and high-end department stores. Now chains such as Baby Gap, Baby Guess, and Talbot Kids make it hard for the individual boutiques to exist and siphon business away from major department stores. At the same time Wal-Mart and Target are adding lines with a designer look, midpriced stores like JCPenney are expanding their children's departments, and high-end retailers like Sweet Potatoes are opening outlet stores. All these changes have happened in the past five years. Amazon.com has had a major impact on the book-selling business, and the MP3 program that allows people to download music off the Internet is threatening to revolutionize the music industry.

Often marketers have watched new trends and waited to act until they were sure how they would turn out. That strategy was dangerous in the past, but it is incredibly hazardous today. Barnes & Noble and Borders ignored Amazon.com for several years and have paid the price. Amazon.com has grown into a major market competitor. The same situation exists today. Tommy Hilfiger clothing and Old Navy stores rose up primarily because Levi Strauss, the apparel giant of the 1980s and early 1990s, didn't respond to the market's desire for distinctive, brand-label clothing.

The first companies to jump onto a new trend often establish a long-term predominant market position. Yahoo, Excite, Infoseek, and Lycos were the first companies to see that the Internet was going to be moving into the homes of everyday consumers. They are still the leading search engines on the Internet, and the stock market has placed a high value on all four. Gopher, which was one of the leading search engines when the Internet belonged to computer savvy

> People spend a lot of money on products, and they are unwilling to settle for anything but top quality.

engineers and university researchers, stayed true to its original client base and is now used far less than its major competitors.

In today's market, if you miss the trend, you'll be either out of business or a significantly smaller company. Your goal is to start capitalizing on potential trends by adding new products or services to meet those trends, and then to continually modify your existing products and services so they serve the needs of the new trends. Unfortunately, many, if not most, new trends fizzle out before taking over the market. So sometimes fast-moving marketers chase markets that don't develop. That is just a risk businesses have to accept. Don't throw all your resources into a developing trend, but do get your foot in the market so you can move quickly if a trend takes hold.

## Opportunities

As a rule, you don't want to slug it out with a competitor in an established market. That's an expensive strategy that customers don't really care about and that rarely produces a successful campaign. Look at the battles between Coke and Pepsi, or between McDonald's and Burger King. The companies engage in a high-cost marketing war, without anybody gaining much ground.

Instead, concentrate on opportunities in the market. These are usually easier to exploit, primarily because it is much easier to gain customer attention. The minivan is a good example. Families with children did not have a vehicle that suited their needs. Chrysler saw that opportunity and introduced the minivan, which had phenomenal success on a fairly limited marketing budget. FUBU (For Us By Us) is a leader in the urban sportswear market with high-color fashions. In 1998 the company landed a major deal with Macy's. The reason Macy's decided to handle the line was that it was targeted at a market that no one had bothered with before, inner-city youth.

The forms in the earlier chapters have been focused first, on finding opportunities in the marketplace where you can find eager customers, and second, on creating a low-cost, effective marketing strategy. New trends, new developing markets, new distribution

> Companies that miss trends in today's market go out of business or are severely damaged. Trends can move in and take over a market in less than a year. Marketers can't afford to wait to make sure a trend will last before responding.

outlets, new customer needs, and new technology can create opportunities for you.

There are two critical steps in developing a marketing strategy. The first step is to decide which aspect of the market to focus on. The second step is to develop a positioning statement and strategy that make it obvious that your company is the perfect solution for that opportunity. The best way to create a marketing strategy is to find an opportunity and then create your positioning strategy. The Saturn car is a perfect example of using an opportunity to develop a positioning strategy. General Motors decided that young adults didn't have a car designed for them. That market wanted a sporty, economical car, instead of a boxy, cheap car. GM also discovered that young adults were intimidated when buying a car at a traditional dealer. As a response, General Motors introduced the Saturn as a sporty model for young people, and it set up a separate "no haggle" network of dealers to sell the car.

> Don't try to take on competitors head-on in the market. Instead, look for opportunities that you can meet first to gain market share.

## Threats

Most companies use a reactive marketing strategy. When a competitor adds a feature, drops a price, or opens a new distribution network, most companies follow with a similar action. A threat arises on the market, and they take a reactive step to try to counter it. For example, when Dell Computer came out with its direct sales and low-price strategy, most of its competitors followed by dropping their prices. When Old Navy started to succeed with low- to moderately-priced merchandise, discount store chains and mass merchandisers like JCPenney responded by offering their own line of designer-styled clothes.

Reactive marketing is a losing proposition. First, it is simply trying to market a feature or benefit that someone else has. Marketers will have a tough time catching the attention of customers with a "me-too" approach. As a result, companies that market reactively invest in programs that will generate only marginal sales. A much better approach is to look at the market threat and try to understand

> Respond to competitive threats by differentiating your product rather than by dropping your price or running new promotions.

why it exists. Then marketers can design their own innovative programs to address the issue that created the threat.

Why are computer users willing to buy from a mail-order house at a discount? Is it because computers have become an undifferentiated standard product? Or is it because technical support and service on computers is so dismal? Probably both are major reasons for Dell's success. Is the best reaction for a computer company to respond with lower prices? I don't think so. The companies should respond by differentiating their products. Instead of selling a standard computer that can be modified for different users, computer companies should realize that most consumers want a product that just does what they want. Computer companies should concentrate on selling different models that meet the needs of various users, including models with great sound cards and high-speed graphics for game users, models dedicated to easy Internet use, and models focused on office use with great networking capability.

Marketers need to know what their threats are. But instead of reacting to those threats, they need to learn how to turn them into opportunities. A threat typically occurs when customers aren't getting what they want. You'll be taking several major steps toward success when you learn to look at threats as a first step in uncovering market opportunities.

## Final Comments

Almost all successful investors will tell you that only strong marketing companies will sustain long-term success. What is a strong marketing company? It is one that understands its customers and their needs and desires, the trends in the market, and what new opportunities can be pursued profitably. With that knowledge, a strong marketing company goes out and develops the products and services that meet the customer's needs. That sounds pretty easy, doesn't it? Well, in fact, most companies are not marketing, or customer oriented. They are product oriented. In other words, a company develops a product, and then tries to figure out how to sell it.

As an example, the satellite TV market is struggling in urban areas where cable TV is available. It may be a great idea to be able to get three hundred channels, but just who can watch that much TV? The product is driven by the satellite company's love of the technology, not by what customers really want or need. Computer companies can fall into the same trap. They concentrate on making computers go faster and store more information. After a certain point, more speed isn't an asset. Computer companies are focused on the computer, and not on what customers want, which is an easy computer to use.

Your marketing success always starts with knowing your customers and your market. This was the focus of the first five chapters. Now you are ready to focus on creating strategies and tactics that will create long-term success for your company.

> Strong marketing companies know their customers, what they want, and how they'll buy.

Marketers can double or triple market share with innovative tactics.

## Don't Zig When the Market Zags

Go back five years in your market and list the five to 10 companies with significant market share. Then put a check mark by the ones that have fallen on hard times and list the reasons for it. Typically the reason is that they just didn't or couldn't adjust to changes in the market.

Next, list the market leaders today that were not market leaders five years ago, and write down the reason they have succeeded. Typically those companies have responded to market changes with the perfect product or service. Keep these charts handy for those times when things are going well. Your success could turn around if you don't stay on top of the current market.

**MARKET LEADERS FIVE YEARS AGO**
Check the ones that are no longer leaders.

_____ 1. _____
_____ 2. _____
_____ 3. _____
_____ 4. _____
_____ 5. _____

Explain what happened to the companies that have dropped off the list.

_____
_____

**MARKET LEADERS TODAY**
Check the ones that are new.

_____ 1. _____
_____ 2. _____
_____ 3. _____
_____ 4. _____
_____ 5. _____

Explain why these companies gained market share.

_____
_____

# Marketing Strategy

**CHAPTER 6** MARKETING OBJECTIVES **CHAPTER 7** PRODUCT-BASED MARKETING TACTICS
**CHAPTER 8** COMMUNICATIONS-BASED MARKETING TACTICS **CHAPTER 9** MARKETING TACTICS FOR SALES, PROMOTIONS AND DISTRIBUTION

# Chapter 6

# Marketing Objectives

1: MARKETING PLANS KEEP SALES GROWING

2: A CUSTOMER PROFILE

3: HOW THE CUSTOMER BUYS

4: THE INTERNAL AUDIT

5: THE EXTERNAL EVALUATION

**6: MARKETING OBJECTIVES**

7: PRODUCT-BASED MARKETING TACTICS

8: COMMUNICATIONS-BASED MARKETING TACTICS

9: MARKETING TACTICS FOR SALES,
   PROMOTIONS, AND DISTRIBUTION

## POSITIONING STRATEGY

Who is your major end-user target customer group? . . . . . . . . . . . . . . . . . . . . . . . . . . . . . . . . . . . .

What are the major wants and desires of your customers?

1. . . . . . . . . . . . . . . . . . . . . . . . . . . . . . . . . . . . . . . . . . . . . . . . . . . . . . . . . . . . . .

2. . . . . . . . . . . . . . . . . . . . . . . . . . . . . . . . . . . . . . . . . . . . . . . . . . . . . . . . . . . . . .

3. . . . . . . . . . . . . . . . . . . . . . . . . . . . . . . . . . . . . . . . . . . . . . . . . . . . . . . . . . . . . .

Which need or desire is not being met by competitors? Is there one that you are able to meet better than competitors? . . . . . . . . . . . . . . . . . . . . . . . . . . . . . . . . . . . . . . . . . . . . . . . . . . . . .

What positioning tactics or strategies can you employ to better meet this need or desire?

1. . . . . . . . . . . . . . . . . . . . . . . . . . . . . . . . . . . . . . . . . . . . . . . . . . . . . . . . . . . . . .

2. . . . . . . . . . . . . . . . . . . . . . . . . . . . . . . . . . . . . . . . . . . . . . . . . . . . . . . . . . . . . .

3. . . . . . . . . . . . . . . . . . . . . . . . . . . . . . . . . . . . . . . . . . . . . . . . . . . . . . . . . . . . . .

What is your competitive advantage? . . . . . . . . . . . . . . . . . . . . . . . . . . . . . . . . . . . . . . . . . . .

. . . . . . . . . . . . . . . . . . . . . . . . . . . . . . . . . . . . . . . . . . . . . . . . . . . . . . . . . . . . . . . . . . .

Who is the major target group in your distribution network? . . . . . . . . . . . . . . . . . . . . . . . . . . . .

What are the major wants and desires of this group?

1. . . . . . . . . . . . . . . . . . . . . . . . . . . . . . . . . . . . . . . . . . . . . . . . . . . . . . . . . . . . . .

2. . . . . . . . . . . . . . . . . . . . . . . . . . . . . . . . . . . . . . . . . . . . . . . . . . . . . . . . . . . . . .

3. . . . . . . . . . . . . . . . . . . . . . . . . . . . . . . . . . . . . . . . . . . . . . . . . . . . . . . . . . . . . .

## *POSITIONING STRATEGY*

Which need or desire is not being met by competitors? Is there one that you are able to meet better than competitors? . . . . . . . . . . . . . . . . . . . . . . . . . . . . . . . . . . . . . . . . . . . . . . . . . . . .

What positioning tactics or strategies can you employ to better meet this need or desire?

1. . . . . . . . . . . . . . . . . . . . . . . . . . . . . . . . . . . . . . . . . . . . . . . . . . . . . . . . . . . . .

2. . . . . . . . . . . . . . . . . . . . . . . . . . . . . . . . . . . . . . . . . . . . . . . . . . . . . . . . . . . . .

3. . . . . . . . . . . . . . . . . . . . . . . . . . . . . . . . . . . . . . . . . . . . . . . . . . . . . . . . . . . . .

What is your competitive advantage? . . . . . . . . . . . . . . . . . . . . . . . . . . . . . . . . . . . . . . . .
. . . . . . . . . . . . . . . . . . . . . . . . . . . . . . . . . . . . . . . . . . . . . . . . . . . . . . . . . . . . . .

**Your basic positioning statement for end users** should read as follows:

. . . . . . . . . . . . . . . (your company name) provides . . . . . . . . . . . . . . . . (your product or service) to . . . . . . . . . . . . . . . . (your target market). . . . . . . . . . . . . . . . . (your company name) offers . . . . . . . . . . . . . . . . (your competitive advantage) to the . . . . . . . . . . . . . . . . (target customer group) to meet or satisfy the . . . . . . . . . . . . . . . . (target customer group's major want or desire that your company meets).

**Your basic positioning statement for the distribution network** should read as follows:

. . . . . . . . . . . . . . . . (your company name) provides . . . . . . . . . . . . . . . . (your product or service) to . . . . . . . . . . . . . . . (your target part of the distribution network). . . . . . . . . . . . . . . . . . . . (your company name) offers . . . . . . . . . . . . . . . . (your competitive advantage) to the . . . . . . . . . . . . . . . . (target customer group) to meet or satisfy the . . . . . . . . . . . . . . . . (target customer group's major want or desire that your company meets).

## *MARKETING SALES AND OBJECTIVES*

Sales Dollar Objectives: . . . . . . . . . . . . . . . . . . . . . . . . . . . . . . . . . . . . . . . . . . . . . . . . . . .

Percentage Increase from Prior Year: . . . . . . . . . . . . . . . . . . . . . . . . . . . . . . . . . . . . . . . .

Market Share: . . . . . . . . . . . . . . . . . . . . . . . . . . . . . . . . . . . . . . . . . . . . . . . . . . . . . . . . . .

Percentage Increase from Prior Year: . . . . . . . . . . . . . . . . . . . . . . . . . . . . . . . . . . . . . . . .

Major Target Customer: . . . . . . . . . . . . . . . . . . . . . . . . . . . . . . . . . . . . . . . . . . . . . . . . . . .

Market Share: . . . . . . . . . . . . . . . . . . . . . . . . . . . . . . . . . . . . . . . . . . . . . . . . . . . . . . . . . .

Percentage Increase from Prior Year: . . . . . . . . . . . . . . . . . . . . . . . . . . . . . . . . . . . . . . . .

Other Measurable Marketing Objectives (e.g., number of new retailers opened, number of new accounts, products introduced, new markets penetrated, decrease in cost per sale, increase in the closing rate, number of salespeople hired, or percentage of customer complaints):

1. . . . . . . . . . . . . . . . . . . . . . . . . . . . . . . . . . . . . . . . . . . . . . . . . . . . . . . . . . . . . . . . .
2. . . . . . . . . . . . . . . . . . . . . . . . . . . . . . . . . . . . . . . . . . . . . . . . . . . . . . . . . . . . . . . . .
3. . . . . . . . . . . . . . . . . . . . . . . . . . . . . . . . . . . . . . . . . . . . . . . . . . . . . . . . . . . . . . . . .
4. . . . . . . . . . . . . . . . . . . . . . . . . . . . . . . . . . . . . . . . . . . . . . . . . . . . . . . . . . . . . . . . .
5. . . . . . . . . . . . . . . . . . . . . . . . . . . . . . . . . . . . . . . . . . . . . . . . . . . . . . . . . . . . . . . . .
6. . . . . . . . . . . . . . . . . . . . . . . . . . . . . . . . . . . . . . . . . . . . . . . . . . . . . . . . . . . . . . . . .

# MARKETING OBJECTIVES

There are two types of objectives in a good marketing plan. First, there are the objectives you achieve in your positioning in customers' minds, or in how the customer thinks about you. Second, there are the measurable objectives, such as sales numbers, number of new retailers opened, number of new accounts, percentage increase in business, products introduced, new markets penetrated, salespeople hired, and service levels increased. You need to set positioning objectives, so you can gear your marketing program toward those objectives. But specific objectives are also important. After all, your positioning strategy isn't doing the job if it's not generating higher sales and profits.

Boise Cascade sells a wide variety of office supplies. Its primary target customers are female office staff who order supplies—typically administrative assistants or office managers who are 18 to forty-nine years old. Boise's goal was to increase sales 20 percent. The question was what type of positioning strategy to use to attract the loyalty of this target group. Boise decided to try a promotion program that was fun and gave away lots of freebies that the office supply buyers could take home. All of the prizes tied in with the music of the 1970s, which Boise discovered was the favorite music of its target audience. Boise sent out a catalog that looked liked a double album, and had a '70s music theme. There was also a poster for "Peace, Love, and Harmony" to remind customers about the Boise brand. Then Boise put in monthly promotions including free posters, CDs, and other items tied into the '70s music. The program was fun, it created brand awareness for Boise, and most of all, it increased sales 22 percent.

Boise Cascade's campaign delivered all of the key elements of a marketing strategy. It had a measurable objective, a positioning strategy that clearly differentiated Boise's brand, and finally tactics that clearly communicated the positioning strategy to its customers. The best feature of the campaign was that it was clearly driven by a characteristic of its target customers: a desire to add some fun to offices that are boring. Marketing is an easy task when you clearly know who your target customers are, and what they want.

> The bottom line for marketers is always sales and profits. A great positioning strategy isn't effective unless it produces sales and profits.

## Target Customer Group

Chapter 2 discussed choosing your target customer group. Everything you do in marketing starts with your target customer group. I like to list it as many times and in as many places as possible, so there isn't any chance people will forget just who that all-important group is.

> Great marketing strategies are clearly driven by a key characteristic of its target customer group.

## Major Goals and Desires

To determine the major wants and desires of your target market in business-to-business marketing, start by asking this question: Which of the following describes your target customers' operating mode at work?

1. They excel at their job in a way that everyone will notice.
2. They do a good job and stay out of trouble.
3. They do whatever is necessary to make it through the day.

The answers will help you determine which one of the three basic groups your customers fall into.

1. People who want to look like heroes.
2. People who want to avoid any controversy.
3. People who want to have fun or reward themselves.

One of these motivations is always the first major want or desire of any business-to-business customer group, and it dictates to a large degree how those people will buy. Boise Cascade obviously felt a major portion of its target customer group fit into category 3, and used that group's desires as a starting point for formulating the promotion. Office managers who wanted to look like a hero or avoid controversy probably didn't buy into Boise's program. Boise doesn't need to worry about whether or not its program appeals to every office manager. Boise only needs to worry about whether 25 to 40 percent of the managers fall into category 3.

What made Boise's campaign shrewd is that it realized that everyone else was marketing to the first two categories of motivations, either looking like a hero or avoiding controversy. Boise chose to market to the third group because competitors weren't targeting them.

You can determine the primary reason consumers buy most products by asking:

1. Does the customer choose the product for status-related reasons?
2. Does the person choose the product for function-related reasons?
3. Does the person choose the product for price-related reasons?

> Features and benefits don't dominate business-to-business purchases. The key marketing factor is the overall personal goals of the employees who make the decision.

Again you may find that the customer group is split into different motivations. Food processors are a good example of this. Some people buy the fanciest processor because they like to entertain and enjoy showing off their latest gadget. Other people are more concerned about the functions that the food processor performs, while the final group may only buy a processor that is priced below $49.95.

The second major want or desire is typically goal oriented. What is your customer trying to do? For example, the office managers were trying to keep the office fully stocked with supplies. In the case of the food processors, some people may want to prepare interesting or complicated food items when they entertain. Another group may be trying to reduce meal preparation time during the week. A third group may want to be able to prepare a wider variety of meals. But they all have one goal or another that they are trying to meet.

The third category is either functional performance or price/value relationship. Most marketers worry about function first, when it is at best the third most important want or need. In Boise's case, the third category would be delivery times, emergency shipments, or pricing. For the food processors, the function might be either size, or the number of features such as the number of food items it can process, or the number of different power settings. For complicated or industrial products, you may have to address two or three functional wants or needs. I only list three items on the form because I want you to remember that people buy for a limited number of reasons, and you only obscure your understanding of the customer's real goals when you list too many desires.

## Unmet Goals and Desires

Buyers have a quick, positive response when they see a product that meets a need or desire that no other product or service meets. Being perceived as unique in the marketplace is one of the most beneficial marketing assets any company can have.

## Strategies to Meet Unmet Goals and Desires

The one comment I occasionally receive from small business marketers is, "Everything that can be done has already been done by someone else." I used the Boise Cascade example because it is in the office supply category, which is about as dull a product category as there is. The fact is you can always come up with an innovative marketing strategy when you focus on customers' desires and needs and find an area where those needs and desires are not being met.

Your job with strategies and positioning tactics is to reinforce in the customer's mind that your product, store, or service is the perfect solution for their situation. A positioning tactic reinforces the image you want to project. Chapter 7 will talk about the whole range of marketing tactics. To look at positioning tactics, let's go back to our example of a food processor for someone who enjoys entertaining. This person is concerned about looking good to his or her friends, preparing meals that people will talk about, and owning an easy-to-use product.

To increase status, the company could employ a wide variety of positioning tactics, such as:

- Getting an endorsement from a well known chef or restaurant
- Adding styling features to give the product a "designer look"
- Selling the product exclusively through high-end department stores and kitchen shops

- Branding the product with a well known celebrity. (For example, the manufacturer could strike a deal with Julia Child and the product could be called the "Julia Child" Food Processor.)
- Furnishing food processors, a chef, and recipes for high-end charity dinners and events

To help position the product so that it will help create meals that people will talk about, the company could:

- Include a cookbook with 25 easy-to-prepare gourmet meals.
- Add a special feature that allows it to knead dough
- Get a chef's endorsement or brand the product with a chef's name
- Package the product with some cooking molds to help present food in an exciting way (For example, add a series of molds for pâtés or include coupons for a variety of exotic-looking molds or serving dishes.)
- Highlight on the package some of the special foods that the processor can make (For example, the package might announce, "Prepares 28 Gourmet Party Dips.")

To help position the product to be easy to use, the company might:

- Enlarge the buttons (People associate large buttons with an easy-to-use product.)
- Add a timer that indicates how long the processor has been going
- Add a resistance meter to the blades that beeps when the processing is complete (For example, a bisque should have a certain consistency. The resistance to the blades can be correlated to that consistency and trigger a buzzer when it's reached.)

The positioning tactics used each year are one of the most important tasks of any marketer. Positioning tactics make all of your other marketing tactics work more effectively because you are

> Marketers want their product, service, or store to be perceived by the customer as the perfect solution for them.

delivering a message the customer wants to hear. The way to beat a path to the customer's door, through the maze of thousands of other marketing messages, is simply to be sure you are sending the message the customer wants to hear.

Many small business marketers worry about which tactics to use, such as direct mail, advertising, and special promotions. But they never worry about positioning tactics that clearly convey their company's image to the customer. Those companies rarely come anywhere near their sales potential. Always create innovative positioning tactics before you worry about your standard marketing tactics.

> Your competitive advantage should be significant to your customers, easy to understand, and have enough impact to get customers to take some action immediately.

## Competitive Advantage

Your competitive advantage is why your customers should want to buy from you instead of from your competitors. The Positioning Strategy form starts with the customer's needs and desires that aren't being met by competitors or that you meet better than competitors. It then lists positioning tactics or strategies that you can use to communicate clearly to the customer that you meet those needs. Your competitive advantage should be obvious to both you and your customer. If it is not obvious, you need to go back and take another look at your positioning tactics.

## Target Distribution Network

Selling the distribution network is almost always the most difficult sale that the manufacturers need to make. Retailers, wholesalers, distributors, and sales agents for other manufacturers are some of the organizations in distribution networks. You won't make many sales if you can't get your product placed where consumers can actually purchase it. So you should spend as much time gaining a competitive advantage in your distribution channel as you do trying to gain an advantage with consumers.

## Unmet Desires of the Distribution Network

The distribution network's goals, desires, and needs usually revolve around four issues:

1. The level of sales compared to the amount of work required
2. Profitability created by each sale
3. Access to new and important markets
4. The extent to which a supplying manufacturer's requirements are hassle free

> Companies need a competitive advantage with their distribution channel that is just as powerful as the advantage they create with their customers.

*Level of Sales.* A manufacturer's sales agent is an independent contractor who agrees to sell products for a variety of different manufacturers. A sales agent in the ski industry will always want a line of skis and ski boots to sell. These products are big-ticket items that generate plenty of revenue. The agent will be much less likely to carry a ski accessories line, which will not generate nearly as high a sales level.

The distribution channel is also likely to carry products that they don't have to expend much effort on. These are products their customers are familiar with—and request—because of the manufacturer's advertising and promotional activity. No company in the distribution channel wants to turn a customer away because it doesn't carry the product he or she requests. Many companies will use big events to drive their distribution system. For example, a ski accessory manufacturer may sponsor a race at a ski resort. The company will approach the distribution network in that area to carry the product while the event is occurring, and hope that the distribution network will keep the product if it sells well during the race.

*Profitability.* Manufacturers with products that are big sellers typically offer lower discounts to distributors and lower commissions to sales agents than accessory manufacturers. That's because accessory manufacturers need to increase the profitability of their sales to ensure that distributors will want to carry their products. Often companies with minor market shares will offer bigger discounts or promotional programs to try to gain market share.

A distribution network always responds positively to an opportunity to penetrate a major new market.

Distribution networks always care about profitability. It is one of the areas that companies can target when they need to increase sales quickly. Safeplay Systems, whose marketing plan appears in Chapter 12, lets its sales agents set their own prices on playground equipment. This allows agents to add their own value-added services to the bid, so they make more money on each sale. This strategy helps Safeplay land top-quality representatives even though it is much smaller and not as well known as some of its major competitors.

*Access to New Markets.* Like virtually every other company, distribution networks are always looking for new customers. If a new market opens up, the distribution networks will search out new products. I've found that meeting the desire for new markets and customers is one of the best ways to sell a distribution channel. For example, consider distributors of equipment for beauty salons. The distributor may have a 20 percent market share of typical salons, but it may not have any share of the salons in nursing homes, assisted-living facilities, or retirement apartments. A distributor may be able to crack that market if it adds a manufacturer of an adjustable sink that allows salon operators to shampoo their customers' hair while they stay in their wheelchairs. Once it cracks the elder-care market, the distributor would not just increase sales from the adjustable sinks, it would also increase sales of its entire product line.

*Hassle-Free Requirements.* Major manufacturers often take their distribution networks for granted. Sometimes they have rules about returning goods, or a warranty service, or large purchasing requirements that the distribution network doesn't like. The distributors have no choice but to acquiesce because the manufacturer's products represent a sizeable portion of their income. As a result, the distributors are sensitive to the requirements of all manufacturers. In many cases there are items you can address that will make you look like a hero to your distribution network. For example, one company sold compressors to industrial users through a distribution network. The pumps were warranted for one year from the day of shipment. But if the distributor didn't sell the compressor for three or four months, it had to support the one-year warranty to its customer. That meant the distributor had three or four months (from the time it purchased the compressor to the time of sale) when it was responsible for the warranty. One company picked up significant market share by simply starting its one-year warranty on the date the distributor sold the compressor.

You want to discover the unmet needs and desires of your target distribution channel in the same way you discovered your customers' unmet needs and desires.

> You will have loyal distributors once you convince them that your company has a competitive advantage that improves their profitability.

## Positioning Strategy for Distribution

Again this section is similar to the earlier section that focused on consumers. However, tactics will be much different for each of the four categories.

1. The level of sales compared to the amount of work required
2. Profitability created by each sale
3. Access to new and important markets
4. The extent to which a company's sales policies are hassle free

*Level of Sales.* There are a wide variety of tactics you can use to make distributors realize your product generates enough sales for the effort involved. Some of the tactics commonly used include:

- Providing additional sales support from your company on large accounts (Distributors appreciate your sending out technical experts to help their sales representatives land major accounts.)
- Staging major events in the distributor's areas
- Promoting the product through advertising and direct mail
- Offering promotional programs that distributors can pass on to their customers to spur more sales
- Partnering with other small suppliers to offer complete packages of products that distributors can offer to their customers

*Profitability.* You can increase the profitability of your product for distributors by offering some of the following incentives:

- Co-op advertising programs (Distributors often print up catalogs with special pricing at various times in the year. You can help fund that catalog to ensure your product is in it. (Chapter 9 includes additional details on co-op advertising programs.)
- Promotional pricing, if distributors purchase certain quantities of your product
- Consignment spare parts (The distributor only pays for the parts once they are sold.)
- Partial payment for a booth at regional trade shows where your product is displayed

*Access to New Markets.* Access to a new market is a tactic that works best when you supply much of the initial impetus to get the distributor in the market. Give some thought to the following strategies:

- Sharing market research information with distributors
- Turning over sales that you've made on a direct basis to distributors
- Offering training and support on selling to the new market, such as sending in a company salesperson to do on-on-one training
- If needed, telling the distributors about other suppliers that would give them a complete line for the new market
- Supplying mailing lists, key contacts, and other pertinent sales information

*Hassle-Free Service.* Here you need to address the networks' major concerns. These concerns can be involved in almost any aspect of their business.

When you decide to put together a program be sure to do it with a little pizzazz. Give it a name, like Performance Plus or All-Star, and be sure to announce it with a flyer. Your program won't get anywhere unless it has enough fanfare for the distributors to know it is important.

Companies in the distribution network often make just a 1 to 2 percent profit on sales. They respond favorably to any program that gives them a higher profit margin.

## Positioning Statements

A positioning statement indicates what your product is, who your target customer is, and why your target customer should buy from you. It is not a marketing slogan meant for customers. A positioning statement is meant for internal use as a guideline for every marketing campaign your company undertakes. Every aspect of your program should be designed to reinforce your competitive position in the minds of your customers.

> If you put together a great plan, you should be willing to project a significant increase in sales and market share.

## Marketing Sales and Objectives

Most companies use the marketing plan as a starting point for their next year's budget. You should list your marketing sales and objectives so that you know whether or not your program worked. If you failed to meet your goals, you want to know why. Sometimes the economy was too difficult, sometimes a competitor had a better program, and sometimes the program wasn't implemented effectively. You won't be able to evaluate your performance if you don't have objectives. Most of the marketing plans in this book don't list the companies' objectives, because they were considered confidential.

## Final Comments

I've seen many stories in newspapers and magazines about how we've entered the information age because so much information is now available to everyone. From a marketing point of view, what we've entered is an era of information clutter, in which it has been increasingly difficult for marketers to take their message to their prospective customers. Small to midsize company marketers have trouble finding ways to reach a high percentage of prospects and make an impact. This is one reason that marketing positioning and strategies become more and more important each year. Since marketers will make far fewer contacts, they have to do everything they can to make each contact count.

Marketers need to keep close tabs on their customers and markets, and be ready to readjust their positioning strategies if a significant shift occurs in market conditions or customer desires.

Positioning has also increased in importance because America has entered an era of unprecedented affluence. People no longer purchase according to value pricing based on their needs; instead, their buying is based on their desires. Functional performance is becoming less and less of a factor in purchasing decisions. Meeting personal goals, reinforcing a self-image, and satisfying a sense of fun and adventure are becoming key purchasing criteria. As a result, people are purchasing products for a wider variety of reasons, and marketers must position their products to meet their customers' new buying criteria.

The marketers' world is in a tremendous state of flux; virtually every aspect of it is changing. If you're going to succeed, you must have a positioning strategy that is right for current market conditions. That means you need to re-evaluate your positioning strategy at least once a year. The up side for small business marketers is that big companies can't respond quickly to market changes. The tremendous growth in small company start-ups and successes is really occurring because entrepreneurs are taking advantage of all the opportunities created by market changes. The marketing environment has never been better for a small business that is nimble and ready to move as opportunities present themselves. Marketers who successfully seize those opportunities will start by finding the right positioning strategy. That is the foundation for rapid market growth in a rapidly changing world.

## Your Customers Have the Answers

In a fast-moving world, marketers need to keep their fingers on the pulse of the market. Look at the following list and then check the items you routinely use to keep abreast of what's happening in the market. If you can't check off any of the items, then you are relying on your intuition of what the market wants. Intuition isn't valuable in a changing world. Direct contact with customers is the only way to uncover what customers want.

|  | YES | NO |
|---|---|---|
| 1. Do you have an advisory council of customers you meet with periodically? | ___ | ___ |
| 2. Are members of your target customer group in key management positions? | ___ | ___ |
| 3. Do you have staff who attend events of your target customer group, and key conferences, or participate in the life of the customer group? | ___ | ___ |
| 4. Do you talk to your customer group on a regular basis? | ___ | ___ |
| 5. Do you have a procedure for showing new programs, products, or services to customers to get their input? | ___ | ___ |
| 6. Do you have an open submission policy for new product ideas? | ___ | ___ |
| 7. Do you have alliance partners that you share market information with? | ___ | ___ |
| 8. Do you use survey results from warranty cards? | ___ | ___ |
| 9. Do you use questionnaires or surveys from customers? | ___ | ___ |
| 10. Do you use focus groups as a source of market research? | ___ | ___ |
| 11. Do you have customer advisors who provide periodic advice? | ___ | ___ |
| 12. Do you have a feedback form for salespeople who have new market insights? | ___ | ___ |

Marketers can't rely on past experience to understand today's customers, marketers need constant customer feedback.

# Product-Based Marketing Tactics

1: MARKETING PLANS KEEP SALES GROWING

2: A CUSTOMER PROFILE

3: HOW THE CUSTOMER BUYS

4: THE INTERNAL AUDIT

5. THE EXTERNAL EVALUATION

6: MARKETING OBJECTIVES

**7: PRODUCT-BASED MARKETING TACTICS**

8: COMMUNICATIONS-BASED MARKETING TACTICS

9: MARKETING TACTICS FOR SALES, PROMOTIONS, AND DISTRIBUTION

# PRODUCT-BASED MARKETING TACTICS

Marketing Goals

1. ..................................................................................................
2. ..................................................................................................
3. ..................................................................................................

*Note:* Use the following form to fill in the tactics you plan to use in the upcoming year.

Product/Store/Service

1. ..................................................................................................
2. ..................................................................................................
3. ..................................................................................................

Pricing

1. ..................................................................................................
2. ..................................................................................................
3. ..................................................................................................

Packaging/Store Display

1. ..................................................................................................
2. ..................................................................................................
3. ..................................................................................................

Customer Service

1. ..................................................................................................
2. ..................................................................................................
3. ..................................................................................................

# PRODUCT-BASED MARKETING TACTICS

You execute a marketing strategy with marketing tactics. Most people think of tactics as advertising, direct mail, pricing, sales, distribution, and promotion. But I recommend you think of marketing tactics with a much broader perspective—one in which marketing represents any tactic you employ to create a bond between you and your customer. This chapter and the next two chapters contain over 90 tactics that marketers use to implement their positioning strategies. I've listed a large number of tactics to help you realize the wide variety of tactics that are available and to help you create new tactics to better market your product.

Street Glow manufactures neon lights that go around auto license plates, underneath cars, on dashboards, and in glove compartments. The company sells fun for the young car owner who wants to show off. The target customers are young men, 18 to 32 years old, who are extremely proud of their cars. Their main buying motivation is to be noticed. Some of the company's marketing tactics include:

> Marketers today are employing a broad range of tactics that go far beyond advertising, direct mail, and public relations programs.

1. Sponsoring Light Offs, contests in which people compete for an award for the best lighted car at auto accessory shows throughout the country
2. Selling through auto stereo dealers that also market to Street Glow's target customer group
3. Promoting through car stereo and auto accessory magazine ads and publicity stories
4. Adding new products every year to help prevent competitors with a smaller product line
5. Introducing a line of neon lights for in-line skaters to broaden market exposure
6. Adding music to a few neon products and packaging them in a display that occasionally plays the music to attract attention in stores
7. Continuing to sell exclusively through auto accessory and auto stereo stores to keep the exclusive "show off" image for its core customers
8. Forming an alliance with the producers of Sound Offs, contests for the best car stereo system, to combine Sound Offs and Light Offs into one, more noticeable mega-event in each auto accessory show

This program addresses Street Glow's target customer group—young males who like to show off—and its target distribution channel—auto stereo and auto accessory retailers. All of the company's events promote the show of image its customers want, and the company's new products and innovative displays keep bringing customers into the retail stores, which is exactly what the stores want. Items 4, 5, and 6 are product-related tactics, which are covered in this chapter. Item 3 is a communications-related tactic, which is covered in Chapter 8. Items 1, 2, 7, and 8 are sales promotion, and distribution-related tactics, which are covered in Chapter 9.

> Marketers can reinforce their image by choosing tactics that, by themselves, send a message to customers. Street Glow uses Light Offs contests as a marketing tactic because they are fun and allow customers to show off.

## Marketing Goals

In the next three chapters you will list the tactics that you are planning on implementing over the next year. Each chapter's form starts out with the marketing objectives. These are the same positioning objectives that you put on the Marketing Sales and Objectives form in Chapter 6. I like to repeat the objectives on each form so you can be sure that your tactics reinforce them. In today's marketing world you must use every opportunity to project your positioning strategy to your customers. You simply can't afford to send out mixed or confusing messages.

## Product/Store/Service

*Adding performance features.* You may want to add features to position your product as the best one for a certain application or customer group. You could also add features so the product goes further toward meeting customers' goals. For example, microwave ovens now have a feature that automatically sets cooking times and power levels for foods from popcorn to hot dishes. That feature helps the product go further toward meeting the customer's goal of tasty food. You might also add a product feature to overcome a perceived product deficiency. A few years ago, customer complaints convinced car companies to start equipping minivans with sliding doors on both sides.

Stores and service organizations work the same way. Stores constantly add lines or product sections for new uses and applications. They also offer value-added services such as installation, free repairs, alterations, overnight delivery, and shopping consultants to help customers pick out gifts in order to separate themselves from competitors. Service businesses strive to adjust to changing market conditions with new services, more complete services, and even services that allow customers to save money by doing part of the work.

*Introducing new models for specific markets or applications.* You may decide to reinforce your dedication to a certain market by introducing a special model that serves that market. You may also introduce a model for a special application such as phone systems for telemarketing firms, or database management software geared to small home businesses. Stores add sections for different types of buyers, and service companies offer a variety of products for different people. For example, a septic tank cleaning service will have one type of service for car washes that need frequent cleaning, and another service for residential homes that need service every year or two. Some companies sell their service work on a monthly contract basis, repairing the product anytime in return for a monthly fee, while other service providers just charge for the service when it's rendered.

*Packaging products together.* Manufacturers will often package two products together to better meet consumers' goals. Laundry detergents may be packaged with a laundry presoak, bird feeders may come with bird feed, or an accountant may package manufacturing cost accounting, payroll, monthly statements, and tax service into one complete product offering for manufacturers.

Companies also put products together to be at a more attractive price point for stores or TV infomercials. For example, TV products should be priced at a minimum of $29.95. If a marketer of fishing lures finds its lures are too inexpensive, it might sell several lures together, throw in a rod and reel, or offer a video and instruction manual to bring up the product's price point. Companies also add in promotional items to create more value in the product. America's Best Glasses offers a pair of sunglasses and a pair of regular glasses for one low price. Service businesses, especially ones that have travel time to the customer, often give a package price for three

> Packaging products together can increase a product's perceived value, offer a more complete solution for the customer's goals, and differentiate a product from the competition.

or four services. A well drilling company, for instance, may offer to change-out the well to home piping for half price when it replaces a submersible pump.

*Packaging in accessory materials.* An example of this tactic is when a food processor manufacturer adds a cookbook to its package. This tactic can reinforce the company's positioning strategy for very little cost. Service providers that offer free booklets, resource lists, or checklists are all examples of using an accessory product to reinforce the company's image.

*Changing design features.* Products and stores can change the price image of their products with design features. Fancy displays, more space between clothes, more elaborate mannequins all give a store an upscale image. Products made of molded plastic look better, and have higher value, than plastic products that are vacuum formed. The look of operation controls on products or the look of a store entryway also reinforces the image. Service companies that have shiny trucks and drivers in clean uniforms project a higher-priced image. The pricing of professional service providers such as lawyers, doctors, or accountants is often dictated by the type of building they are in and the way their office looks.

*Adding new products or services.* Marketers often introduce a new product or service and stores remodel when they want to change their image. If a drastic adjustment in positioning is needed, introducing a new product is often the best way to change the way customers perceive your company.

## Pricing

*Trial pricing.* An introductory price is designed to encourage people to try a new product or service. Typically, the price is held for a few months, but it is an excellent way to familiarize people with a new product or service.

*Image pricing.* Price the product for the image your customer wants. Upscale restaurants charge $100 per person because it gives them an elite image that its target customers desire. Value products, low-priced products, and high-performance products are all priced to

> Don't be afraid of charging for the value you provide. Low prices demean your product and service and appeal to customers who buy on price alone. That is a very difficult path to follow for success.

establish an image. Minivans are priced about a third less than sport utility vehicles because they are targeted at families, while SUVs are targeted at upscale couples.

*Tier pricing.* This tactic gives customers lower prices once they pass certain quantity purchase points. This is a strategy commonly employed by industrial suppliers and distributors of frequently-used products like maintenance or office supplies.

*Bundling pricing.* Selling products together as a package is called bundling. Furniture stores do this when they package a suite of living room furniture at a special price that is often much lower than the price of the items purchased separately. Machinery suppliers also use bundling to encourage complete system purchases.

*Value-added pricing.* Including value-added services without lowering the price is one way to counter a competitor's lower price. Free installation, free service, free seminars or training, and free magazines or CDs are all value-added features that can be thrown in at no charge to create value-added pricing.

*Captive pricing.* The most common example of this tactic is to sell a razor at a low price in order to receive later razor blade sales at a profitable price. Marketers frequently set a low price for original equipment when it locks customers into purchasing their machinery supplies.

*Pay-one-price.* Amusement parks, Internet providers, and even some service businesses charge one fixed fee no matter how much service customers use in a year.

*Non-negotiating pricing.* Saturn auto dealers promise customers that they always put their lowest possible price on every car, and that they are, therefore, non-negotiable.

> Value-added pricing is the best tactic to employ when facing price competition. It sets your company apart as a premium supplier.

## Packaging/Store Display

*Image.* When a customer looks at a company, one image needs to stand out. Every customer's experience with your company makes an impression, whether it's a business card, a product package, a brochure, or the salesperson. In the 1970s IBM took a lot of heat for requiring all their salespeople to wear conservative suits and white shirts, but that tactic sold the concept that an IBM computer was reliable.

*Positioning visuals.* People remember visual images better than they remember anything else. A memorable visual image helps consumers remember your company. The ideal visual also promotes your positioning statement. For example, Prudential Insurance's Rock of Gibraltar is a great visual symbol because it sells the concept that Prudential is dependable, a key point for an insurance company. In today's market Old Navy has a great visual in the plain way its letters look. The visual conveys an image that is simple, but with high perceived value.

Packages of products should have a visual that ties immediately to the product's benefits to the customer. Bags of Scott's lawn fertilizers, for example, always picture a beautiful lawn. Software packages typically show the results the software produces. Food products show the final prepared product, often in a meal setting.

*Enticements.* When people walk by a store, what draws them? A store will almost always attract more visitors if it has a feature that draws people inside. H&R Trains, the model train store discussed in Chapter 10, has a railroad yard for children and an elaborate model train layout to attract people. Other stores may feature an exclusive high-end line in the window. It doesn't matter if people often buy the line due to its price; it only matters that they come in to see it. Perfume shops may have a collection of miniature perfumes in the back of the store that people want to look at, and record stores may have listening headphones as an enticement.

Packages might promise a special recipe, a pamphlet, or a promotional item, or even frequent flyer miles. Marketers need to get people to look at their package, so they often will make a bold statement on the package to attract interest. Statements such as "50 percent less fat," "twice as moist," or "50 percent better coverage" encourage people to pick up a package and check it out a little more closely.

*Demonstrations.* Every time I go to the state fair, I see people demonstrating knives, mops, cooking utensils, miracle painting devices, and green thumb gardening equipment. Every demonstration has a crowd of people around it. People love a demonstration and nothing convinces them to buy as effectively. Cooking stores are

> We live in a visual world, and your visual impression will create over 75 percent of the image customers have of your company. If you have a dull image, prospects will believe you are part of a dull company.

increasingly adding demonstration areas, as are hardware stores. Home Depot offers classes on most Saturdays on a variety of home improvement projects. Clothing stores have fashion shows, beauty supply stores do makeovers, and garden shops demonstrate proper plant care. Demonstrations attract people to a store, convince them to buy, and create a perception that this store is a place where things happen. That perception alone will draw people in.

Product packages often show a series of photos that detail how a product works. People like to see the pictures because they are curious about how a product works, and also because they will be more likely to believe a product's claim if they can see it work.

## Customer Service

*Technical service.* Technical service can incorporate having a service network in the field, placing in-depth technical service information on the Web, making technical service experts available on the phone 24 hours per day, and even offering to send in a repair representative within 24 hours to any customer location. People like good technical service, and what they appreciate most is someone who will come out and take care of their problems. For example, the biggest selling point Value Added Computer Resellers have is error-free installation, and that's a service people will gladly pay for. Technical service is typically expensive to provide, but it is also an extremely effective tactic if your product is even a little bit difficult.

*Hours of operation.* Banks, with traditional banking hours, aren't very customer friendly. On the other hand, bank branches located in supermarkets that stay open until 10:00 P.M. are customer friendly because they are open when people aren't working. Customer service departments for customer friendly business-to-business marketers are open twelve hours per day to provide eight to nine hours of service for their East Coast and West Coast customers.

*Return policies.* Retailers will often take back a product for six months to a year because they want to keep their customers happy. They can have these liberal policies because they simply send defective products back to the manufacturers. Most companies, however,

> You won't sell many products if you can't catch your customers' attention. Catching people's interest is done most effectively with bold visuals and bold statements. Timid messages are an indication of a ho-hum product.

The bidding process is an important, and often overlooked, marketing tactic. You have more contact with prospects during a bid than during a normal sales call. Your bid format and bid procedure should help convince customers of the value of your product or service.

don't have anyone to send returns back to, so the return is a loss if it can't be resold. You don't want a return policy that attracts customers who return everything, but neither do you want to chase away good customers. Return policies can increase sales, and help build customers' confidence in you.

*Bidding policies.* When you get a bid from an auto mechanic, do you ever worry that the final price will be much higher than the price quote? Of course you do—and so does everyone else. Customers like service companies that guarantee that the final price won't exceed 110 percent of the bid price. The distant second-best alternative is a company that promises to notify you immediately if additional work is needed.

Another part of the bid procedure that bothers customers is when the bid doesn't specify what work will be done. That makes it difficult for a customer to compare bids, plus it leaves the customer feeling he or she is being overcharged. Companies that submit bids or proposals should spell out clearly all the work that will be done. Customers will find that type of bid more reliable, and they will believe that the company that submits it is trustworthy.

*Installation assistance.* Customers like to follow the slogan "Don't worry—be happy," which means they want everything to work right the first time. People will pay for this assurance, and it will often be the one factor that makes a sale. For example, the manufacturers of industrial and office equipment usually install the equipment as well. They too have found that their customers are worried that products won't work as promised.

*Delivery times.* If you need a plumber, you need him or her right now. Amazon.com might have lower prices; but when people want a book, they often want it today. Twenty years ago most people were happy with ordinary mail. Then overnight delivery became popular, and now we have courier services everywhere. Delivery time is a big consideration in most purchases, and the company that can meet the customer's delivery criteria often gets the business. For example, Today's Man's biggest feature isn't low prices, it's the store's instant alteration policy.

*Flexibility in ordering.* Grocery stores order products in case lots to get the lowest prices. Of course, they sell a lot of product and don't mind bringing in large quantities of inventory. Most companies, on the other hand want, to buy smaller quantities to minimize inventory costs. Often manufacturers have an order minimum or other purchase requirement that customers find annoying and, in some cases, expensive. You may be able to increase sales by changing your ordering requirements to accommodate your customers' needs.

Service companies can be flexible in how they allow work to be done. For example, my friend wanted to use his well water to irrigate his plants, but minerals in the water caused the plants to turn brown. To get rid of the minerals, he had to pump water out of his well into a constant-level pond where the minerals could settle out. Then he could use the pond's water for his plants. The drilling company let him do about two-thirds of the work himself to minimize costs. In the same vein, consultants will often work with one or two employees from their client company to cut costs.

*Payment terms.* For example, when golf club manufacturers ship products to a pro shop in the spring, they don't require payment until the fall. The manufacturers know the pro shops can't afford to pay for products before they are sold. They also know they won't get an order without extended terms. Other companies will offer catalog retailers "5 percent 10 net 30" terms, which means companies that pay within 10 days get a 5 percent price discount. Catalog retailers like those terms because they can pay promptly, and the selling companies like the terms because they get their money right away.

*Credit policies.* Boutiques with high-end children's clothes are often small shops that are owned by a mother with young children. They tend to come and go quickly, and often don't have a credit history. A manufacturer can increase its market share by offering smaller delivery quantities and by being willing to extend a small amount of credit to these small businesses.

> Burger King's "Have it Your Way" campaign was great because it said people were in charge of what they ate. People like control and customers appreciate being given the flexibility of buying your product or service just the way they want it.

## Final Comments

I listed product-oriented features in the first chapter on tactics because in the long run, your product, service, or store has to be right or people just won't keep buying from you. Product-oriented

> It can take several years to rebuild your sales base if your company is perceived to be outdated.

tactics are also typically the most difficult and expensive tactics to implement, which is why many small business marketers don't pay as much attention to them as they should. That neglect is a big mistake. Computer technology has made customers very conscious of buying the latest technology. If your product or service isn't constantly upgraded, customers will start to think they are buying yesterday's products. Customers want to buy the most up-to-date products, and you can't risk being perceived as "old hat." Marketing can't compensate for a bad product, and it can take two or three years to rebuild market share if your product is perceived to be outdated. The product, service, or store itself is always the foundation of a business, and without a strong foundation, a business will fail.

## What Have You Done for Me Lately

Marketers live in a hard cruel word today, and they can't afford to rest on their laurels. People expect things to change and in many cases, they want to buy the best. That is why you need to make changes on a regular basis that set you apart from the competition. Otherwise you could end up like Barnes & Noble's Internet site, a nice site that produces sales but is absolutely no threat to Amazon.com, which is constantly adding innovative features to its site.

If you can't check yes on at least two or three of the following questions, you need to try harder to be innovative.

|  | YES | NO |
|---|---|---|
| 1. If you asked five to ten random customers, could they list two innovations in product, price, or customer service that you've made in the past two years? | _____ | _____ |
| 2. Can prospects recognize your product when they see it being used by someone else? | _____ | _____ |
| 3. Have you made at least two dramatic visual changes over the past three years? | _____ | _____ |
| 4. If you asked 10 prospects to rank your company from 1 to 5 as a market leader in product technology, would they rank you 4 or 5, if 5 is the top score? | _____ | _____ |
| 5. Would 10 prospects or companies in your distribution network rank your company in the top three in customer service? | _____ | _____ |
| 6. Do you use your pricing strategy as a marketing tool to enhance your image (this could include an image as a full-line supplier, the company most closely associated with customers' desires, or the premium product or service on the market)? | _____ | _____ |

Many market leaders would answer yes to each of these questions. Most companies are lucky to answer yes to even one. Companies that rise to the top set the bar for their own performance. You should do the same, even if you only have the resources to answer yes to one or two of these six points. Make your product, service, or store memorable and you'll find that success will follow.

In an overcrowded market, you have to use high-impact tactics and strategies. Otherwise, no one in the market is going to notice. It is better to have two or three tactics with high impact than ten tactics with moderate impact.

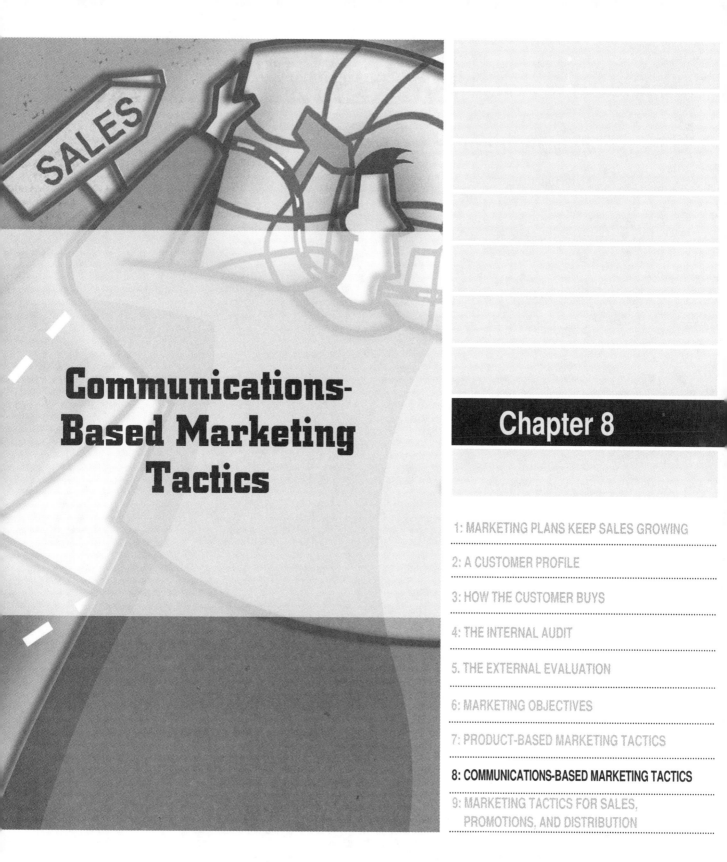

# Communications-Based Marketing Tactics

## Chapter 8

1: MARKETING PLANS KEEP SALES GROWING

2: A CUSTOMER PROFILE

3: HOW THE CUSTOMER BUYS

4: THE INTERNAL AUDIT

5. THE EXTERNAL EVALUATION

6: MARKETING OBJECTIVES

7: PRODUCT-BASED MARKETING TACTICS

8: COMMUNICATIONS-BASED MARKETING TACTICS

9: MARKETING TACTICS FOR SALES,
   PROMOTIONS, AND DISTRIBUTION

## COMMUNICATIONS-BASED MARKETING TACTICS

Marketing Goals

1. ........................................................................
2. ........................................................................
3. ........................................................................

*Note:* Use the following form to fill in the tactics you plan on using in the upcoming year.

Advertising

1. ........................................................................
2. ........................................................................
3. ........................................................................
4. ........................................................................

Marketing Messages

1. ........................................................................
2. ........................................................................
3. ........................................................................
4. ........................................................................

Brochures/Flyers

1. ........................................................................
2. ........................................................................
3. ........................................................................
4. ........................................................................

# COMMUNICATIONS-BASED MARKETING TACTICS

Trade Shows

1. .....................................................................................
2. .....................................................................................
3. .....................................................................................
4. .....................................................................................

Publicity

1. .....................................................................................
2. .....................................................................................
3. .....................................................................................
4. .....................................................................................

Direct Mail

1. .....................................................................................
2. .....................................................................................
3. .....................................................................................
4. .....................................................................................

**T**raditionally most small business marketers have relied on communications tactics—such as direct mail, advertising, trade shows, publicity, and brochures—to do a cost-effective job of creating consumer awareness for their companies. Today's world is a much different place for marketers. Consumers have so much information that they end up ignoring, or not hearing, or not remembering most marketing messages. As a result, marketers have started to rely more on distribution and promotional tactics to get their message in front of customers. Although the importance of communications tactics has shifted, they are still used by virtually every company. Communications tactics can still be cost effective if marketers are careful to use them only in the proper situations.

GoRu Toys is a small toy company that produces Conscience, a board game dealing with life and business ethics. GoRu decided to put most of its marketing emphasis on distribution tactics. The company started selling its game exclusively through Starbucks and eToys, a major Web retailer. Starbucks liked the game because it was a conversation piece for its target customers, who are business professionals. eToys liked the product because it was unique and it wasn't sold by the big toy retailers. One of eToys' strategies to differentiate its business from traditional toy retailers is to offer different games, especially games aimed at adults. GoRu didn't promote Conscience with the traditional big advertising budget. Instead, GoRu distributed its game in a way that enhanced its position as a great game for adults. But GoRu did support its distribution strategy with flyers, brochures, and a big publicity campaign.

Some communications tactics—such as brochures, flyers, and catalogs—produce materials customers expect marketers to have. Other tactics such as publicity, trade shows, direct mail, and advertising can still produce cost-effective exposure to customers for your product, service, or store.

> Successful small company marketers are cutting back on expensive advertising programs and switching to promotional and distribution programs to convey their messages.

## Advertising

*Yellow Pages.* This is an important marketing tool if people look in the Yellow Pages to find your type of business. People look for a dog-clipping business in the Yellow Pages, so dog-clipping salons better advertise in them. People typically go to an optical shop that they notice in their neighborhood rather than looking in the Yellow Pages. Optical stores are better off with a small Yellow Pages ad and a premium location or a big sign.

*Directories.* These are the Yellow Pages for industrial and business-to-business marketers. Suppliers to print shops in Minnesota are all listed in the *Printing Supplier Directory of Minnesota*. That's where printers look for items they only need occasionally. Almost all industrial markets have a directory, often published by a trade magazine, that suppliers can advertise in. Probably the best known directory is the *Thomas Register of Manufacturers*, which lists manufacturers that supply virtually any type of product used by a manufacturer.

*Classifieds.* I like to follow the rule, "Advertise where people look for information on your type of product." If people look in classified sections when they want to buy your type of product, be sure to advertise there. Don't overlook trade and consumer magazines. They often have classified ads sections, which customers peruse for certain types of items, especially services. For example, I was looking for a contract manufacturer for a small plastic part. I looked in the classified section of a magazine called *Job Shop Technology* to find the type of manufacturer I was looking for. *Popular Mechanics* has a large classified section that its readers scour for ads for innovative automotive or mechanical tools.

*Magazines.* Trade and specialty publications are great spots to place ads because people read them for information on specific topics. Whenever I do a project around the house, I look through *Today's Homeowner* for ads and articles related to the project. Many people read *Entrepreneur* or *Business Start Ups* because they have ads and articles about business franchises. If marketers have a product or service that nobody knows about, they will advertise in print magazines directed at their target customer to build customer awareness. The drawback to magazine advertising is that it can be expensive; your best results occur after you run the ad repeatedly.

*Newspapers.* Newspaper ads work best when they have a call to immediate action, which is why retailers like them. On Saturday

> Trade and specialty magazines aimed at a company's target market are often a cost-effective advertising vehicle.

> The rising cost of TV advertising dramatically reduces the chance of a small business getting enough exposure to impact customers.

morning, people who are planning to shop for furniture read the newspaper to see where the good deals are. Retailers that have sales, special promotions or events, or that want to announce the arrival of a new product line all use newspapers to get the message to people who are ready to buy. Restaurants and other entertainment businesses also benefit from newspaper ads. People deciding to go out on a weekend frequently look at a paper for either a restaurant with an interesting review, or for a coupon at a restaurant they like.

*Radio.* People listen to the radio to be entertained or to be informed, not because they are looking for information about a specific purchase they are going to make. Radio advertising works best for building awareness and for getting top-of-the-mind awareness for products that people think about buying for a long time. Jewelry stores may advertise on the radio because they want to build awareness that they have an exclusive line of diamonds. People getting married may hear the ad 15 to 20 times, maybe more, before they decide to buy their diamond ring. Radio advertising may help them decide to visit a specific jeweler before making the final selection. A pizza delivery business may also advertise on the radio because it is a purchase people make repeatedly. If people hear the ad often enough, they just might decide to try a pizza from a radio advertisement.

*Television.* This is the best place to advertise when you want to quickly build awareness in a market. It is also an expensive tactic. Small businesses can benefit from TV advertising when they sponsor specialty shows such as cooking or fishing, or sports shows that cover local high school athletes.

Larger businesses benefit when they want to build awareness for their business, or when they want to build awareness about a new direction they are taking. This could range from changing their image or merchandise to adding new departments or new customer service capabilities. For example, TV is an effective way for a series of car dealerships to create awareness that they have changed their service hours.

*Direct-Response TV.* These are the ads that ask you to call an 800 number to make an immediate purchase. They may be a one- to two-minute commercial such as K-Tel runs for its music collections, or they could be infomercials. These commercials can work for small businesses when they advertise on local TV shows that their target customers watch. The direct-response ads have also been effective for many companies that want to get local stores to carry a product. Fishing stores often add products that have been offered on direct-response ads, just in case their customers request the products. Most stores will carry products with a "Seen on TV" label in order to avoid losing an order.

## Marketing Messages

*Slogans.* Marketers want people to remember their products, stores, or services. One way to help people remember a message is a visual image. Another tactic is to develop short slogans. Customers hear "Where America Shops," and it reminds them that Sears has values for everyone. Ford trucks have a great slogan, "Built Ford Tough." It is easy to remember and it promotes an image of durability that Ford wants. The Quaker Oats slogan, "Warms your heart and soul," reinforces both the Quaker Oats tradition as a family breakfast food and the cholesterol-lowering properties of oat-based foods. Good slogans are short, to the point, and easily remembered. Coke's "The Real Thing" or 7UP's "the Uncola" are excellent slogans. A slogan is a tremendous aid in positioning your product. Try to create one because it will constantly reinforce your message to your customers.

*Tag lines.* Tag lines are a little longer than slogans and appear on the bottom of ads or near the end of commercials. They also help position your product, service, or store and help customers remember you. Aetna Life Insurance Company's tag line is "The Company You Need for the Life You Want." MasterCard's ad campaign features the tag line. "There are some things money can't buy. For everything else there's MasterCard." Effective tag lines are memorable, and they reinforce the message a company wants to project.

*Trademarked features.* One method marketers use to emphasize the unique aspects of their business is to trademark the names of certain features or services. For example, when I worked at a dental company, we trademarked the name "Compensating Traverse," which was a special feature that we couldn't get patented. The

> Marketers can help prospects and customers remember their company with slogans, tag lines, and a catchy or clever product or service name.

feature allowed the patient's head to stay in the same vertical plane when the back of the dental chair was raised or lowered, a benefit that was important to dentists. The trademark called attention to the fact that we were the only ones with this feature, and we prominently promoted it with all our ads and packaging. Service businesses may trademark the name of special services they offer, and stores may trademark a special section of their stores or a service they offer.

*Names.* A great name tells customers who you are, what you do, your competitive advantage—and it implies a certain price point. It is difficult to incorporate all four factors in your name selection and still keep it short enough for people to remember, but try to do everything you can with your name. Batteries Plus is a good name because it is clear what the company does, and it implies a service orientation that differentiates the company from its competitors. Yahoo is a good name because it differentiates the product from other search engines. Yahoo says that its search engine is more fun than other search engines. What do the Lycos or Alta Vista names imply? Not very much.

> Obtaining a trademark on the name of a special feature or program your company runs often encourages customers to consider that feature an important benefit.

## Brochures/Flyers

*Referral flyers.* Local companies often pass out black-and-white or two-color flyers to customers to hand out to their friends. These flyers are usually less expensive than a promotional flyer and have more detailed information, including a list of all the product's features and benefits. They are designed to help customers explain what a great choice they've made in buying a product or service. Referral flyers don't try to grab people's attention, because your customer is doing that for you.

*Promotional flyers.* These flyers are designed to be distributed to people who do not know about you. Typically they are designed to (1) grab people's attention with a stunning visual; (2) highlight your product, store, or service's major benefit; and (3) call the prospect to some action, either to request more information or to call for an appointment.

*Product catalogs.* If you have a broad product line, you may want to print a catalog for your distributors or customers so they know all the products you carry. Catalogs also help reinforce your image as a full-line, knowledgeable supplier.

*Product or company brochures.* You may want to print an extensive product brochure explaining the benefits of your product. Brochures are helpful when you don't have the sales staff to contact every prospect personally. To save money, many companies put extensive brochures on their company Web site so customers can download the information.

*Trade show pass-outs.* Hundreds of people may pick up a brochure at a trade show and then discard it when they decide the product is not what they're looking for. Since many brochures cost $2.00 to $5.00 apiece, companies will print a one-page pass-out for a trade show that highlights their competitive advantage and tells prospects how to request a full brochure.

*Seminar or event flyers.* If you are planning a big event, seminar, or special demonstration, you should promote it with a flyer that can also be posted as a sign. The biggest benefit you receive from a big event is that it reinforces your credibility with every person who hears about it, even if they don't attend. You want to be sure to send an event flyer to every prospect you know, even if you don't expect them to come.

> Trade shows typically produce the lowest cost leads of any communications strategy. They also are the best vehicle for a new company to attract its first customers.

## Trade Shows

*Major industry shows.* I've found these shows to be the most cost effective way for small manufacturers with specialized products to find prospects. Many times small companies don't have the resources to discover which target companies need their product. At a major industry show, hundreds if not thousands of people will walk by the manufacturer's booth, and those interested in the product or service will probably stop.

*Regional shows.* These smaller industry shows work better for small businesses that sell to a regional market. The trade magazine for most industries will contain information on both national and regional trade shows.

*Company-promoted shows.* In some cases companies band together and promote their own minishow. Bridal shows are often put on by local businesses. Manufacturers of production equipment also band together to demonstrate a full manufacturing setup at a hotel or conference center so prospects can actually see the equipment operating.

## Publicity

*Press releases.* Trade magazines frequently publish stories about a new product. The information is often taken from a press release. Companies use press releases to inform the media—newspapers, magazines, radio, and TV—of newsworthy events in their business. Trade magazines typically use an informational story, but other media prefer an intriguing angle. For example, GoRu Toys may send out a press release on how the Internet is changing the toy industry, mentioning their Conscience board game only as an example of Internet retailing.

Marketers also use press releases to announce big events, seminars, survey results, contest winners, and just about any other major company activity. The local newspaper's weekly calendar is one of the best press release formats for small retailers and service providers. You can send in an announcement about a class, demonstration, event, or any other informational activity, and the paper will typically publish it in the weekly calendar. Stores will often announce a contest for kids, celebrity appearances, or an unusual display or demonstration on Saturdays, during a big event to generate publicity.

Press releases to radio and TV shows should be sent to the show you'd like to appear on or be featured on. If a station has more than one show you're interested in, send your press release to each show. The *Radio-TV Interview Report,* published by Bradlee Media Publications in Lansdowne, Pennsylvania, will help you promote appearances on national TV and radio publicity programs.

*Surveys.* Newspapers and magazines constantly publish surveys or projections on just about every topic. For example, magazines and

> Marketers use press releases to announce big events, seminars, survey results, contest winners, and just about any other major company activity.

newspapers picked up the Direct Marketing Association's information about the level of catalog, Internet, and retail sales in the United States. InterMedia Advertising Solutions, an advertising supplier for the Internet, had magazines and newspapers publish its survey data about what industries are the top advertisers on the Web. Food companies publish survey details on how many times a family eats together. Sporting goods companies publish surveys on how much time kids spend watching TV. So many surveys are done because newspapers and magazines like to publish them. These publications also list the source of the survey data, which is great publicity for the company or association that initially conducted the survey.

*Informational stories.* Another way to generate publicity is to write informational stories for magazines or newspapers that only briefly list your company's name. Resnick Associates, an estate and business planning succession firm whose marketing plan is presented in Chapter 11, has had many informational articles published, including "Increasing your Cash Flow Through Charitable Giving." "Addressing Vanishing Premiums," and "Buy-Sell Agreements Can Be Crucial to Succession Plans." The firm's name isn't listed anywhere in the article, except in the credits. But that's all the company needs. Its name is still associated with an article that was informative and interesting to its target audience.

*Joint presentations.* Companies will often join with other companies, associations, and customers to hold presentations and round-table discussions on key issues involving their industry or on items of concern to consumers. People involved in the presentation build credibility and increase name awareness for their company. These presentations can be made at trade shows, association meetings, resorts, a community center, or at a customer's location. The information is frequently published after the meeting, so speakers have printed material to send out to prospects to reinforce their image.

*Newsletters.* Newsletters are considered direct mail when their content focuses on one company. But they become publicity when they are related to a topic and the company is just listed as a sponsor. These newsletters can be sent to customers, trade publications, and interested prospects. The Internet has made a topic-centered newsletter more viable since prospects can start receiving the

> Informational stories build an expert image for your company, attract prospects to your business, and are an effective tool to build company credibility in a direct-mail program.

newsletter after finding it on the Internet. Those prospects increase the newsletter's readership and help make it a cost-effective marketing tool.

*University studies.* Research funding at universities around the country has been cut back. As a result, professors are often scrambling to find research projects that graduate students and seniors can conduct for their required papers. A study published by a university about a product, process, or service offers tremendous benefits to a marketer because it is considered impartial and produces the type of results that magazines like to publish. Universities often have liaison offices to help connect them with interested companies. You have to pay the university for conducting the research, but it is usually a reasonable charge.

## Direct Mail

*Postcards.* Universities and colleges frequently buy the names of high school students who score well on ACT or SAT tests. Since the schools don't know which students will be interested, they typically send out a postcard that allows students to request additional information. Postcards are inexpensive to send out to a large group and can be read quickly. They are cost effective for approaching hard-to-find customers. For example, the best chance of locating prospects for a company that installs underground sprinklers is to send out postcards to a large number of home owners offering an incentive to request either more information or a price quote.

*Trading prospect names.* A better direct-mail option is to trade the names of prospects and customers with like-minded businesses. Charitable groups such as Boys Town and the Omaha School for Boys have been either buying each other's donor names or trading them for years. Trendy restaurants that target 20- to 30-year olds can trade lists with health clubs, art galleries, and comedy clubs. Wallpaper stores trade names with paint stores, and bakeries and florists exchange the names of future brides. Industrial companies trade names with other companies that serve the same target market. For example, companies that sell high-technology office equipment often trade names with a noncompetitive high-technology

> Prospects will view as important studies when they are done by universities or a consortium of companies in an industry.

company because they know that customers who buy the latest technology in one product are likely to use advanced technology as a criterion for purchasing other equipment.

*Lead follow-up programs.* Once marketers find an interested prospect, they don't want to lose him or her. A lead follow-up program, commonly called database marketing, sends periodic mailings to prospects. It is an essential marketing tool when a purchase decision takes a long time, or when a company doesn't have the sales staff to follow up personally with each prospect. The follow-up mailings should offer more information, free seminar tickets, or some other incentive for the prospect to call the company and request more information. Try to also include articles or studies that the customer will find interesting.

*Mailing lists.* A targeted direct-mail program is typically more effective than advertising, provided you can find a mailing list that only contains your target customers. You can buy mailing lists from hundreds of sources listed including brokers that can be found in the Yellow Pages. Your best lists will come from catalogs or magazines that are aimed exclusively at your target customers. Attendance lists from conventions can also work, provided the convention was tightly aimed at your target market. Don't use a list if fewer than 80 percent of the names have a high probability of becoming a customer.

*Direct-mail packages.* Whatever you send to customers has to contain many powerful elements to have any chance of working. The components of a direct-mail package include:

1. *The envelope.* It needs to have a strong enough message for people to open it.
2. *Proof statements.* Testimonials, test results, explanations of why your product or service works, newspaper and magazines quotes, and success stories can all be used as proof statements.
3. *A relatedness piece.* This is information about your company, who you are, and why you are trustworthy and reliable.
4. *The offer.* Explain what you have, what it costs, and how the prospect will benefit by buying your product.

> Every marketer needs an effective lead follow-up program because the cost of obtaining a lead has skyrocketed over the past ten years.
>
> A direct-mail campaign will rarely be cost effective unless at least 80 percent of the recipients have a high probability of becoming customers.

5. *Offer for an immediate response.* If people don't respond immediately, they probably won't respond at all.
6. *Guarantee.* People like to know they can return a product and get their money back if it doesn't work as promised.
7. *Reply card.* Be sure to make it as easy as possible for people to respond.

*Free promotional items.* You might also direct mail free promotional items or samples. Plumbers and other service people frequently send out refrigerator magnets, pens, or calendars so people will have something to remember them when they need the service they provide. Food companies send out samples directly to consumers, and manufacturers of consumable products frequently mail out samples for prospects to try out.

*Special product offerings.* Direct mail is especially effective if something special is happening with your business. Direct mail is an effective way for a store to communicate that it has a new line, that a special collector's edition is being released, or that a celebrity will be in the store to autograph pictures. Anytime your business has an event, use publicity and direct mail to get the message out to as many people as you possibly can.

## Final Comments

Communications tactics will always be important to marketers because they maximize the effectiveness of every other tactic. Marketers derive the most benefit from a big event when they support the event with advertising, publicity, and direct mail. Product changes, sales, promotion, and distribution tactics all are enhanced with communications tactics. Your communications tactics also create the message that helps customers remember you first when they need your product or service. Once you decide on your major tactics for the year, see how communications tactics can be used to support them. Combining the tactics reinforces your message and frequently can double the effectiveness of the original tactic.

> Direct mail is extremely effective when you can tie it in to a special event that is occurring in your company. People will frequently remember the event if they don't attend.

## Communications Tactics Serve Three Masters

The three key tasks are finding prospects, nurturing prospects, and creating a memorable message. You need to be able to do all three tasks effectively to create a successful marketing program. If you have a high-performance marketing program, you should be able to answer yes to most the following questions.

|  | YES | NO |
|---|---|---|

**GENERATING LEADS**

1. Do you generate enough leads that you can afford to discard marginal leads?  _____ _____

2. Is a minimum of 50 percent of your leads viable buying prospects?  _____ _____

3. Do you have new leads generated throughout the year?  _____ _____

**LEAD FOLLOW UP**

4. Do you have a follow-up program that contacts active prospects and customers at least every three to four months?  _____ _____

5. Do your lead follow-up programs include a method for prospects to indicate when they are ready to buy?  _____ _____

6. Does your lead follow-up program tie in with other events designed to provide prospects information about meeting their goals and desires?  _____ _____

**CREATING A MEMORABLE MESSAGE**

7. Can at least 50 percent of your customers and prospects state your marketing message?  _____ _____

8. Does your marketing message reinforce your major competitive advantage?  _____ _____

9. Does your marketing message convey a point that is significant to your customers?  _____ _____

> Generating leads and getting prospects to call is a key marketing task.

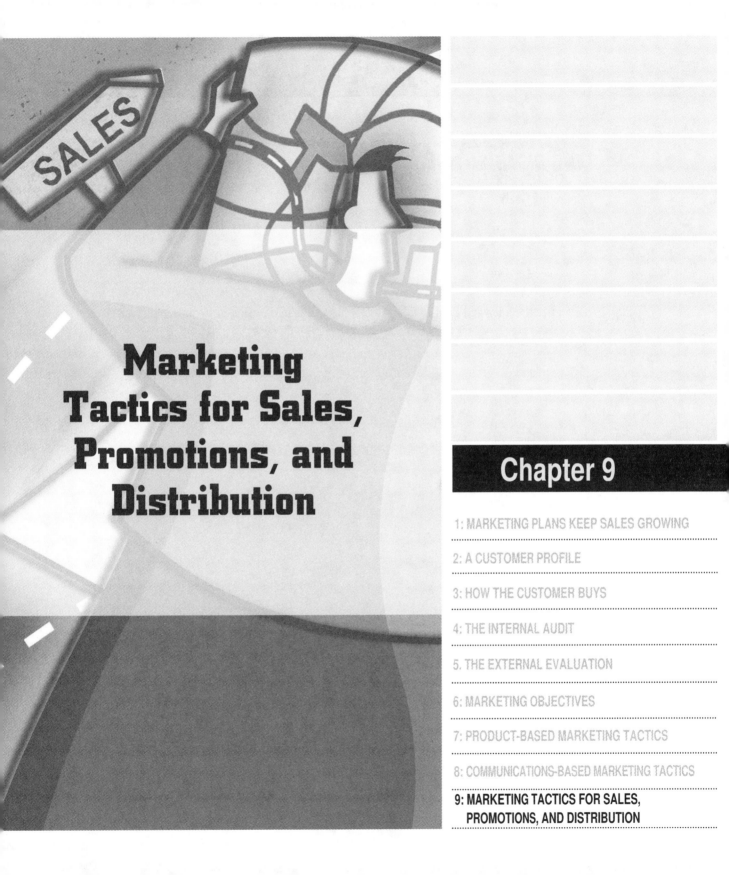

# Marketing Tactics for Sales, Promotions, and Distribution

## Chapter 9

1: MARKETING PLANS KEEP SALES GROWING

2: A CUSTOMER PROFILE

3: HOW THE CUSTOMER BUYS

4: THE INTERNAL AUDIT

5. THE EXTERNAL EVALUATION

6: MARKETING OBJECTIVES

7: PRODUCT-BASED MARKETING TACTICS

8: COMMUNICATIONS-BASED MARKETING TACTICS

9: MARKETING TACTICS FOR SALES, PROMOTIONS, AND DISTRIBUTION

## MARKETING TACTICS FOR SALES, PROMOTIONS, AND DISTRIBUTION

Marketing Goals

1. ......................................................................................................
2. ......................................................................................................
3. ......................................................................................................

*Note:* Use the following form to fill in the tactics you plan on using in the upcoming year.

Sales

1. ......................................................................................................
2. ......................................................................................................
3. ......................................................................................................
4. ......................................................................................................

Credibility Building

1. ......................................................................................................
2. ......................................................................................................
3. ......................................................................................................
4. ......................................................................................................

Distribution

1. ......................................................................................................
2. ......................................................................................................
3. ......................................................................................................
4. ......................................................................................................

## MARKETING TACTICS FOR SALES, PROMOTIONS, AND DISTRIBUTION

Promotions

1. ........................................................................................
2. ........................................................................................
3. ........................................................................................
4. ........................................................................................

Internet

1. ........................................................................................
2. ........................................................................................
3. ........................................................................................
4. ........................................................................................

Distribution has always been the most important method of getting a product in front of customers. Today marketers are starting to expand the use of promotions as a distribution tactic.

In my opinion, distribution has always been the most important part of any marketing strategy. *Distribution* is a marketing term that relates to the system or network marketers use to place their product in front of customers so they can actually enter a store, or buy a product or service. Distribution for a store could include its location, its alliances, its Web page, and its catalog. Distribution for a service business could include its alliances, its location, its Web page, direct salespeople, independent sales agents, and telemarketers. Distribution for a manufacturer could include distributors, wholesalers, retailers, direct salespeople, independent sales agents, , its catalogs, or its Web pages. As a rule, the company with the most effective distribution network will become the market leader.

In today's market, getting to the customer is still the most important marketing task. Marketers, however, are expanding the number of ways they are accomplishing it. Promotional strategies, which have traditionally been focused either on discount or loyalty programs, are now focused more on major and minor events that put companies in direct contact with their customers. Distribution strategies are incorporating more and more alliances so companies can expand their market presence without significantly increasing their expenses. Sales strategies have evolved from putting a salesperson in front of every customer to becoming a resource for the customer so they can achieve their goals. This change in marketing orientation has caused marketers to focus even more than ever before on sales, promotion, and distribution tactics. Their effectiveness is the key determining factor in how successful a company will be in the future.

Southwest Painting, a small painting company whose marketing plan is presented in Chapter 11, is an example of how distribution and sales strategies have changed. Southwest Painting's competitive advantage is that it specializes in Multispec Speckle Effects Coatings, an upscale substitute for wallpaper that produces a new look in the home. Southwest Painting does use traditional tactics of placing an ad in the Yellow Pages, putting up signs on the lawns of its customers, passing out referral cards, and promoting its service through direct mail and publicity. But it also has three loose alliances. One alliance is with a chain of 10 carpet stores. Southwest has painted part of the carpet stores with the Multispec coatings. The carpet store refers customers who like the way the paint system looks. In turn, Southwest Painting refers customers who are going to buy new carpet. The carpet store is a perfect partner because the customers of both businesses are redecorating their homes. Southwest also has an alliance with a catering firm, and with a multilevel marketing company that sells home décor products through parties in people's homes. Those extra alliances are a crucial part of Southwest Painting's distribution plan. They gain the company much broader exposure than it would otherwise have.

The sales force is typically a company's largest sales and marketing expense. Its performance should be constantly monitored to ensure high performance. Don't be afraid to shake things up anytime the sales force is not performing.

## Sales

*Database marketing.* Database marketing is when marketers use a contact management system to store information about each customer and then use that information to send out periodic flyers and mailings. This is an essential part of any marketing strategy if your customers take a long time to make a purchase. For instance, a person may think of remodeling the kitchen for six months before actually deciding to move ahead. Without database marketing, many companies that are approached by a prospect discard the person's name when he or she doesn't immediately buy. With database marketing, the company keeps sending prospect mailings, hoping to be remembered first when they finally decide to buy. The materials you send out in database marketing are discussed in Chapter 8 under lead follow-up programs.

*Networking.* Salespeople often network, which just means they talk and exchange the names of likely customers. Insurance salespeople network with stockbrokers, accountants, and financial planners to get the names of prospects who'd be interested in insurance. In return, the insurance salesperson offers the names of other people who may be interested in other services. In this example, networking is operating as a loose alliance.

Business-to-business salespeople also network by joining associations or other industry trade groups to meet prospective customers. Experienced people in the trade group are usually willing to offer suggestions to newcomers on where and how to sell their product.

*Changes in the sales force.* A company might add salespeople or independent sales agents, move salespeople closer to the customer, or consolidate salespeople in a regional office. There is almost no limit to the number of options a company has to maximize a sales force's effectiveness. Typically companies deploy their sales force to create the effort it needs to close a sale. If a salesperson is selling to major companies, he or she may need to sell 15 to 20 people on the merits of the company's products. In those cases, a company wants the salesperson near the customer's site. If a salesperson only needs to call on purchasing, the marketer will want salespeople located in a large city central where they can reach more accounts.

*Sales materials.* One of a marketer's key jobs is to give salespeople the tools they need to close sales. Sales books, testimonial sheets, diagrams on how a product works, success stories, and results from university studies are just a few of the items you may want a salesperson to show customers.

*Key account strategy.* A small service company may want to land one large account. In a key account strategy, the company develops a strategy for getting the business, and employs all of its assets to accomplish that task. Business-to-business marketers may have five key accounts. Scheduling visits from the company president and top management would ensure that those customers realize how important they are to the selling company.

*Specialist strategy.* Some companies that sell to many different types of industries employ specialists in each industry. For example, one salesperson may specialize in the automotive industry and another in the computer industry. A cleaning service may have a salesperson who specializes in selling to large companies in office buildings, while another salesperson specializes in shopping centers. A specialist strategy lets salespeople learn all they can about one small target customer group so they can sell to it more effectively.

*Management visits.* Customers like to feel important, and a visit from company management usually impresses them. Management visits are extremely effective when a customer isn't convinced your company can meet all of their requirements and needs to be sold on the company's capabilities. Management visits also help close deals and gain access to higher management at the customer's location. For

> Management visits impress the customer and keep management aware of the customer's changing needs.

example, a salesperson may not be able to get past the purchasing agent in a target company. The salesperson has a better chance of meeting with plant management if he or she brings in the company president for a sales call.

*Bidding process.* A company that is closing only 5 to 10 percent of its bids may have a problem with the bidding process. The bidding form may not contain enough details for the customer to realize all the work the bid includes. The customer may not be able to understand the value the company can offer them. Or the company may be wasting its time bidding on jobs it will never get. The company bid may include higher-cost materials than the customer needs. There are many reasons a bidding process isn't producing results it should. Marketers should check their closing rate every year to determine if changes in the bidding process are needed.

*Customer commitments.* Salespeople typically have "hot account" lists or "will buy" lists that indicate sales will be four to five times higher than they end up being. The problem is that the sales force isn't getting a formal commitment from the customer. Marketers counter this fall off from hot prospects to sales by having a process to generate customer commitment. They might offer a loyalty program in which a company can get discounts based on projected annual purchases. Golf suppliers offer discounts to pro shops that order by November 1 for shipment in the spring. Another tactic is to place the expected customer order in the production schedule, with the understanding that the order will be released on a certain date. Retailer's layaway plans are also a tactic for generating customer commitment.

*Leasing options and time payment plans.* Marketers who sell expensive merchandise often offer a leasing option, so a customer can make payments on the product(s) purchased. Many infomercials let you purchase a product in four monthly payments rather than in one large payment. Department stores have their own credit cards, which are another form of a time payment plan. Leasing is a great option for manufacturers. The leasing company pays them immediately for the purchase, and it allows companies on tight budgets to make an immediate purchase. The drawback is that you may have to sign an agreement to take the product back if the customer fails to make their payments.

> Most small business marketers need to include credibility tactics because prospects have so many choices they can get confused. Often they will buy from the first company they feel they can trust.

## Credibility Building

*Advisory councils.* A new company adds credibility when it has advisors who are well known in the industry. Advisors can be key customers, researchers, retired managers, or end users of the product. Members of an advisory council typically receive a small annual payment and/or stock options. A second benefit of advisory councils is that the advisors know more about the market than the small company and their advice is often valuable.

*Endorsements.* These can be from industry experts, well known end users, university professors, magazine editors, or virtually any other source your customers find credible. People generally only endorse products they like, but they may require payment if you use their endorsement to promote your product. The endorsement payment can be free products, stock options, or cash. Some small companies offer the endorser a percentage of the company. Ownership in the company by a well known industry person adds tremendously to a small company's credibility.

*Alliances.* Teaming up with another company or an association is another way to establish credibility. An alliance can take many forms. A small deck builder may subcontract to a larger contractor to establish its reputation. A lawyer may make a presentation on preserving intellectual rights for a local entrepreneur association. Two companies may partner to deliver a fully functioning production line at a manufacturing location. A small consultant may agree to put together a venture fair sponsored by lawyers, accountants, and the Small Business Administration Office. The consultant would be named as one of the sponsors of the event in return for doing all the legwork to organize it.

There is almost no limit to the type of alliances a company can establish. A group of small suppliers of maintenance services for shopping centers may team up to offer a complete maintenance service to shopping centers. A dry cleaner may take in shoes for a shoe repair shop across town. Four restaurants may band together to form dinner groups that rotate from one restaurant to another. A small dental supplier may post documents from the American Dental Association on its Web site so dentists could download them. All of

> Success stories work best when they are written by an outside freelance writer and focus on the customer rather than on your company. Freelance writers can also get more stories into trade publications than a company can.

these alliances benefit both parties, and most of that benefit can come on a modest marketing budget.

*Research projects.* I was helping a supplier of metal processing equipment try to penetrate a new market. Our big break came when we loaned some equipment to a university researcher who was doing a study on improving the performance of metal in high-stress applications. The results of the study were favorable to our equipment, and we were listed as a sponsor. Our credibility was established. I have furnished free supplies, free products, testing sites, and material for evaluation for a wide variety of research, most of which got the company listed as a sponsor. A low-cost method of becoming involved in research studies is to attend association meetings or trade shows and see who is presenting research information. Let them know that you are willing to furnish products or material for their future studies. They will often give your name to other researchers even if they don't have any current projects planned that could use your products.

*Success stories.* You can generate publicity for your company if one of your customers has a success story with your product or service. You can write the story yourself but you are better off hiring a freelance writer. That way the story will have less promotional information about your company and more information about the customer. When you do a success story, be sure to include a sidebar that clearly spells out the customer's situation. For example, I wrote a story about a manufacturing facility and how it increased its efficiency 20 percent with our product. That story didn't do much for our company because people thought the company in the story was operating inefficiently before they started using our product. People started to pay attention to the article when I included the material the company was machining, the actual machine operation being performed, the machinery the company was using, and the speed and feed rates that the machines were operating under.

## Distribution

*Alliances.* I mentioned alliances in the credibility section, but they can also be used as a distribution tactic. A fast-food restaurant chain

> Small marketers can often tap into a large distribution network by offering exclusive rights to a large retailer, distributor, or wholesaler.

> Salespeople in your distribution network are your primary customer contacts. Your sales will go up as you increase their effectiveness.

that puts a restaurant inside a convenience store is using an alliance to cut its operating costs. A manufacturer that sells goods on a private label basis is using an alliance to distribute its products. A printing company that offers graphic artists a 10 percent finder's fee is using an alliance to gain additional business. Companies that combine their products into a complete product line and use the same manufacturer's sales agents to sell their products are distributing their product under an alliance arrangement.

A company may have its products sold by another company with a larger market share. Or it may strike a deal in which the larger company will give away discount coupons for the smaller company's products to every one of its customers. For example, a small company that sharpens Zamboni blades for ice arenas offers a 20 percent discount to arenas that are members of a large ice rink supplier's loyalty buying program.

*Exclusive distribution.* A company trying to get established in a market might offer a distributor or retailer exclusive distribution rights to its products. In return for exclusive rights, which give the distribution network a competitive advantage, the distributor and retailer will be expected to promote the product with advertising, specials, and other strategies. Companies may offer exclusive distribution for just one market, either a geographic market or an end use market. For example, a company selling an insulated spray bottle may have an exclusive agreement for the sale of the bottle for wallpaper removal in home improvement stores, and an exclusive agreement with another company for distribution to the hair salon market.

*Adding new distribution.* A consumer products company may start selling to catalogs. A record store may open up a record section in a department store. A regional retailer may open stores in a new region of the country. A service company that seals abandoned wells may arrange with a real-estate company to promote its services to home owners who need their wells sealed before they can sell their home. A dentist may open a satellite office on the other side of town in order to attract more customers. A manufacturer may start selling products through a distributor that serves a new market, or sales representatives in a certain part of the country. These are all examples of companies increasing the access of their products to their customers, which is the goal marketers want to achieve when they decide to expand distribution.

*Distribution sales materials.* You want the best sales materials available in the hands of your distribution channel salespeople when they talk to your potential customers. Those salespeople won't know your products nearly as well as you do, and they need materials that guide them through the sales presentation. I recommend marketers visit their distributors at least a few times a year to see how they are selling your products, and to ask them what additional sales aids they need.

*Inventory support.* A store that sells maternity dresses may display just one dress of each style and size and then replace the sold inventory every night from an off-site warehouse. This offers more variety for the customer, and probably requires a smaller amount of floor space for the store.

Manufacturers may offer a certain number of products for overnight delivery to hold down their distributor's inventory, or they may guarantee 24-hour delivery of service parts. Another tactic is to send in extra inventory for a big sale with the understanding that the retailer or distributor can return anything that is unsold. Some companies even keep a truckload of inventory on a customer's premises that the customer doesn't pay for until they sell it.

*Support for distribution network salespeople.* Training and special sales incentives or contests are one way companies support distribution network salespeople. They can also send technical specialists into the field to help key customers or provide installation on big sales, have company salespeople available for joint sales calls, and offer the services of a customer service contact to handle any sales problems.

*In-store or showroom displays.* Marketers should do everything they can to put their best foot forward once they get a prospect in the door. Furnishing distributors with displays, demonstration units, and other materials will keep them happy and encourage more customers to buy.

> When done correctly, events generate a tremendous amount of impact for their cost. They build credibility, find prospects, and establish the sponsor as a leader in the market.

## Promotions

*Events.* Bicycle stores sponsor bike races for their best customers. Industrial suppliers may bring guest speakers to a big dinner. Service or professional businesses may sponsor forums or panel discussions at association meetings. These are all events that a business runs to gain exposure, build credibility, and find new prospects. Events are a cost-effective marketing program that companies are using more and more to place their name in front of their customers. For the past 10 years, H&R Trains, whose marketing plan is listed in Chapter 10, has run a major model train event that attracts over ten thousand visitors each year. Local media provide extensive coverage both before and after the show. That one event is probably the major reason the store is known throughout the market.

Marketers are also using events marketing when they run their own golf tournaments, take customers to sporting events, or sponsor a show or musical tour. Game manufacturers frequently introduce a game by sponsoring contests where people playing their games can win prizes. That type of contest generates free publicity and can draw big crowds. For years, Parker Brothers held an annual nationwide Monopoly contest that effectively generated interest in the game both before and after the contest was run.

*Special pricing.* Marketers also support events with special pricing. A bike manufacturer may bring in a large volume of products for a bike race, and the sponsoring dealer and manufacturer may offer the products at 40 percent off. That adds more value to the event and boosts the dealer's and the manufacturer's image. The manufacturer may also bring in a large amount of out-of-stock inventory that it will sell for the dealer at a 70 percent discount. This tactic adds value to the customers because it offers them an especially good deal, produces incremental sales for the bicycle dealer, and unloads unwanted inventory for the manufacturer. Special pricing is also used in tent sales, truckload sales, and other events retailers run when they bring in a large amount of inventory to sell at a reduced price.

*Seminars.* A well publicized educational seminar does several things for a company. It builds credibility, and it produces a large number of quality leads. You can hold seminars along with other

> Loyalty programs can be a tremendous help in creating loyal long-term customers. Offering free or discounted value-added services is a better approach than offering straight discounts because it enhances your company's image.

companies, with a local association, with a university professor, or on your own on any topic of importance to your customers. Seminars are an effective marketing tool if you have information your target customer group wants to know.

*Loyalty programs.* Airline frequent flyer miles are a loyalty program. They reward customers for repeatedly flying on the same airline. Loyalty programs can also be clubs that offer certain incentives when customers purchase designated quantities of products or services. Loyalty programs can offer discounts, free services, free merchandise, memberships into exclusive clubs, free golf tournaments, or just about any other benefit people can think of. Another type of loyalty program is the General Mills Box Tops for Education program that offers free computers to schools that collect enough box tops from students and their parents.

*Co-op advertising.* Manufacturers of consumer products that want retailers to advertise their products in local newspapers will often run co-op advertising programs. These programs offer the retailer a rebate of from 1 to 10 percent to pay for up to half of the cost of advertising the manufacturer's product in newspapers or catalogs. Manufacturers typically prefer to give co-op advertising rebates instead of offering straight price promotions because the co-op programs help stimulate demand for their products.

*Sampling.* You can give samples to people at grocery stores or on street corners or at events. Sampling is a tactic that marketers frequently use at events where target customers go. Samples of ski wax and lip balm are passed out at ski events. Sports drink companies have samples of their products at in-line skating events. Candy manufacturers pass out samples at children's concerts. The Trivial Pursuit board game was actually launched with a sampling program. The marketer simply gave away hundreds of games so people would start playing it. The Trivial Pursuit fad was on once people played and enjoyed the game.

*Contests.* A company I once worked with sold advertising to small retailers. One of the biggest selling points for their product was that every advertiser was allowed to display a poster promoting a free trip for two to Hawaii. People saw the poster and registered for the contest. The contest was a big success for every retailer. For the

> Contests are an effective marketing tactic when the contest is something unique. For example, Guinness offered a prize of a free bar in Ireland. This was a great contest because the prize was so much better than the traditional trip to Hawaii.

Putting a Web site up on
the Internet is not going to
attract many visitors
unless you learn the tricks
of getting your Web site
listed early by Internet
search engines.

company, which sold advertising nationwide, the cost of one trip for two to Hawaii was a small fraction of the benefit the contest provided, because it helped salespeople line up hundreds of new accounts. Contests are extremely effective, and usually don't cost very much compared to the benefit they produce. Contests can be trips, cash awards, or free merchandise.

The type of contest you run is limited only by your creativity. A manufacturer of industrial springs trying to attract design engineers ran a contest for a European vacation through a quarter-page ad in a trade magazine. To enter, all the engineers had to do was tell a story about the worst spring problem they ever encountered. Nine thousand engineers entered the contest. The spring manufacturer ended up with more leads than they ever dreamed possible, at a fraction of their normal cost per lead. People like to win prizes, and the best contests offer a significant prize that catches people's attention.

*Cross promotions.* A maid service is running a cross promotion when it gives free coupons to purchasers of a new carpet at a major department store. The maid service benefits when the carpet store advertises the promotion and picks up a prospect when they provide the service. The carpet store benefits because it offers customers a little extra incentive to make a purchase. The cross promotion helps both companies and produces significant benefits at a very modest cost. Other examples of cross promotion are the Marriott Hotel's offering of airline frequent flyer miles to hotel guests and Tommy Hilfiger's arranging for Nintendo to feature its clothes on skiers in Nintendo's 1080 Snowboarding game.

## Internet

*Web page.* The idea that a company can put up a Web site and have hundreds of visitors log on every month hasn't worked out well for most companies. But Web pages have succeeded as a method of disseminating information to visitors who already know about a product, service, or store. Stores post their specials, new products, and upcoming events on their Web pages. Manufacturers have their brochures, technical information, and past news releases on their Internet site. This tactic allows customers to download the information they want about the company when they want it, and helps companies cut printing, mailing, and customer service costs.

*Magnet Web page.* Web search engines have a certain protocol they use for assigning which sites come up first in a Web search. One of their protocol's rules is to list sites with free information first. Free or noncommercial sites also have an easier time establishing links to similar sites. Some companies will set up a free site to attract visitors, and then have prominent links from those sites to their commercial sites. The marketing plan for the Financial Ad Trader in Chapter 13 details how to use this strategy.

*Links.* Sites often have many links to similar sites in order to increase traffic to their sites. This is a tactic that requires a staff person to spend at least 10 hours per week establishing new links, checking to make sure links are still operating, updating information, and adding new reasons for people to click on your link.

*Alliances and partnerships.* Content is king on the Internet. Many companies can't put together a site with enough content to stand out. One option is to form an alliance with other companies to establish a magnet Web site, or band together with industry associations to present a content-rich information site.

*Banner page advertising.* When you do an Internet search, an ad is typically posted across the top of your monitor. That is known as a banner ad. Most search engines will sell you banner ad space that appears when their names are entered. For example, you could have your ad come up every time someone uses Lycos to search for inventors. You can also buy banner ad space on other sites that attract a great deal of traffic. Embark, for example, has a Web page that sponsors an $80,000 scholarship for high school seniors. You can buy a banner ad on Embark's Web site that high school students will see when they look into the scholarship offer. There are also banner ad trading services. A company targeting young males interested in heavy metal music might trade banner ads with a similar site, or they may join a banner ad network where they can place banner ads on other similar sites in return for allowing other companies to place free banner ads on their site.

> If you have an Internet site, be sure to join as many banner ad trading programs as you can. Don't expect a big return if you decide to pay for banner page advertising.

Some Internet companies are writing new business plans every six months to adjust to new market conditions. Marketers have to be on their toes in just the same way if they want to succeed.

*Search engine strategies*. People will typically only look at the first ten to twenty sites listed in an Internet search. The rules that dictate which sites come up first are getting more complicated. Most companies are hiring outside vendors to keep their sites search engine friendly. To find these vendors, start at the *www.virtualpromote.com* site, a tremendously helpful site on promoting a product or service through e-commerce.

*Free products or services*. With thousands (if not millions) of Web sites on the Internet, companies have to work hard to get attention. One of the best ways to get attention is to offer something free to site visitors. Most sites try to offer free items that can be downloaded, because it doesn't entail a significant cost to the site. Pamphlets, pictures, music, recipes, home project instructions, and pertinent articles are just some of the items offered at no charge. Giving something away allows the company to know who the interested visitors are so it can follow up with additional offers.

*E-mail updates*. Now that the Internet is so crowded, finding a site once doesn't mean you'll be able to locate it again. One way to counter this problem is to have visitors register on your site so you can keep in touch with e-mail updates. These updates may be newsletters, product specials, or just an interesting news item. Most effective Internet marketers employ some type of e-mail strategy to keep contact with people who visited their site.

*Web site changes*. People won't keep coming back to your site unless it changes significantly every three to six months. Most companies can't run an effective e-commerce strategy without at least one full-time employee to handle site updates and link exchanges. The cost of these employees needs to be incorporated into the marketing budget.

## Final Comments

Distribution, promotion, and Internet tactics are the three areas where the marketer's world is changing at unprecedented rates. Most marketers' worlds are already dramatically different than they were five years ago, and there is no telling how much their worlds will change in the next five years. Marketers need to be prepared to use the new tactics now being employed. But it is risky to throw all your efforts behind a new tactic, because it is still uncertain how it can be most effectively done. I believe each marketer should incorporate at least two or three new tactics into their program every year so they have the opportunity to gain experience with how these tactics can best be used by their business.

Rapid market changes convinced me to write this book from the view that marketing is a process in which marketers stay in touch with their markets, learn what their customers want, and then deliver it. Marketers can't depend on absolute marketing tactics anymore because every year they will face a different set of circumstances. That is why I'm convinced there will be renewed interest by every small business in the marketing plan process.

Most companies are only going to use five to 15 tactics in a given year. I listed a wide variety of tactics because I want you to take a fresh look at your strategy every year to see if there are new tactics you can use to energize your marketing efforts. After all, you want your customers to have a reason to keep checking your business out. Using new marketing tactics is one way to keep your business interesting to your customers and prospects. Remember that the phrase "tried and true" no longer exists in marketing. You have to either innovate or face a slow (or rapid) decline in your business.

> Markets should incorporate at least two or three new tactics into their program every year.

Read trade magazines, attend seminars and join associations to keep abreast of tactics developing.

## Are You Sleeping? I Hope Not.

There is no such thing as a marketing comfort zone today. You are either ready to join the innovations that are happening all around us, or you are going to fall down. On the following chart, check the appropriate column if you are going to investigate a new tactic on an information basis; if you are going to actively prepare to implement a tactic by attending events, classes, talking to other companies; or if you will actually implement the tactic. Be sure your chart looks as though you are at least leaning toward innovation. It is your best chance of success.

| | INFORMATION | PREPARE TO IMPLEMENT | IMPLEMENT |
|---|---|---|---|
| Database Marketing | | | |
| Customer Commitments | | | |
| Advisory Councils | | | |
| Alliance | | | |
| Success Story Publicity | | | |
| Event Promotion | | | |
| Seminars and Joint Presentations | | | |
| Cross Promotions | | | |
| Magnet Web Page | | | |
| Banner Page Advertising | | | |
| Search Engine Strategies | | | |
| E-mail Updates | | | |
| Other Innovations | | | |

# Sample Marketing Plans

**CHAPTER 10** RETAIL/COFFEE SHOP MARKETING PLANS **CHAPTER 11** SERVICE COMPANY MARKETING PLANS
**CHAPTER 12** MARKETING PLANS FOR MANUFACTURING COMPANIES **CHAPTER 13** MARKETING PLANS OF INTERNET COMPANIES

# Chapter 10

# Retail/Coffee Shop Marketing Plans

**10: RETAIL/COFFEE SHOP MARKETING PLANS**

11: SERVICE COMPANY MARKETING PLANS

12: MARKETING PLANS FOR MANUFACTURING COMPANIES

13: MARKETING PLANS OF INTERNET COMPANIES

14. THE OPENING

15: SITUATION ANALYSIS

16: STRATEGY, TACTICS, AND IMPLEMENTATION

APPENDICES A, B, C, D

INDEX

Marketing Plan
H&R Trains
Pinellas Park, Florida

## Executive Summary

H&R Trains is a store known as the "model railroader's paradise." The 23-year-old store is more of a model railroad complex than just a store. It consists of several buildings with over ten thousand square feet of floor space dedicated exclusively to the model train in the Tampa/St. Petersburg area. The store has increased its sales level over 400 percent over the last 10 years through its efforts to build the hobby of model railroading. It helps develop, promote, and support model railroading enthusiasts through a wide variety of tactics including model railroading shows, classes, seminars, a wide inventory, and products designed to appeal to every age group.

H&R Trains has been successful in the past because it has worked to become not just a resource for model railroaders, but also the hobby's top promoter, marketer, and sales group in the Tampa/St. Petersburg area. H&R Trains plans on continuing its effort to both promote the hobby to new people and increase the enthusiasm of current model railroaders through a series of events and seminars and by continuing to improve its store layout to strengthen its image as a destination for a fun family weekend.

H & R Trains succeeds in part because it has chosen to focus on a customer need—a place to meet fellow hobbyists and to show off model train layouts.

## Marketing Objectives

1. To continue H&R Trains' steady sales growth in the year 2000. (*Note*: H&R Trains has confidential specific growth target that is not listed here, but is in their actual plan.)
2. To maintain the enthusiasm of model railroaders in the Tampa/St. Petersburg area.
3. To have the highest level of customer service and technical support of any train retailers in the Tampa/St. Petersburg market.
4. To create ample opportunities for people in the Tampa/St. Petersburg area to experience the joys of model railroading.
5. To continue to prove that model railroading is a still a viable hobby in the face of all the competition from new electronic games, the Internet, and other entertainment options.

## Current Situation

H&R Trains has been running event-based marketing programs for 23 years and it has a solid reputation in the market and it has continued to grow every year. The company has several model train retail competitors in the area but they don't offer the complete package of big events, weekly classes, and extensive store layout of H&R Trains. H&R Trains continues to be the clear market leader in the Tampa/St. Petersburg area.

### Major Marketing Concern

H&R Trains isn't overly worried about its competitors as it has a strong, loyal customer base. Its major concern is attracting new people to the hobby of model railroading. Of special concern is attracting children to the hobby prior to their getting involved in video games or other activities. H&R Trains plans on continuing to promote its Little Engineers Club and its line of children's train products from a wide variety of manufacturers. Getting children involved in model railroading also gets parents involved, and helps build the number of model railroaders in the Tampa/St. Petersburg area.

### Market Overview

There are approximately twenty thousand model railroad enthusiasts in the country with about two-thousand to twenty-five hundred living within a two-hour drive of H&R Trains. But there is a far larger number of people who are interested in the hobby and whom H&R targets with their large train shows every April and October. Anywhere from 8,000 to 20,000 people attend those shows depending on the weather, and H&R Trains believes that any of these attendees could turn into a model railroad enthusiast.

The number of people involved in hobbies, including model railroading, has been dropping over the last 10 years. Most people engage in hobbies as way of relaxing from the daily stress of their jobs, but increasingly people feel they have less and less time for hobbies. Many people in Florida are retired but even they have time constraints built into their busy lives.

One of H&R's main programs to address this trend is its Little Engineers Club. This club is for children as young as three years old and it brings together parents and children in a fun atmosphere where they can spend quality time together. All parents, and especially professional parents, are concerned about time together, and H&R Trains believes that model railroading is a perfect vehicle for extensive child-to-parent interaction.

Overall, the Tampa/St Petersburg area is growing fast with the population increasing over 20 percent over a 10-year period while jobs increased 30 percent over that same period. The

H&R Trains was way ahead of most marketers and has built its success on event-based marketing over the last 23 years.

H&R Trains pays lots of attention to every detail in their customer group, including little future engineers. A good tip from H&R Trains is to take nothing for granted. Your job is to keep your customers interested in your business.

economy of central Florida is booming and the area's residents have strong disposable income levels to support the costs of taking up model railroading.

## Market Trends and Opportunities

There are three trends in the market that are favorable for H&R Trains.

1. People are trying to set aside more time to relax and enjoy life. Companies are going to four-day work weeks and people are trying to take more time off to enjoy their families and hobbies.
2. There has been a tremendous push for parents to spend more on-on-one time with their children. One of the best ways for a parent and child to spend time together is with a hobby, whether it is hunting or fishing, or model railroading.
3. Disposable income levels are high at the moment, and especially high in Florida, meaning that most people who develop an interest in model railroading can probably afford to take up the hobby.

Helping parents spend time with their children is a market desire that might not be obvious to most model train stores. Smart marketers look for every opportunity to advance their business.

## Competitors

Benjy's Trains and Toys, Pinellas Park, Florida
Chester Holley Model Railroad, Tampa, Florida
Gulf Coast Limited Trains & Hobby, New Port Richey, Florida
Happy Hobo Trains, Tampa, Florida
Train Depot, Winter Park, Florida
Trains & Treasure, Clearwater, Florida
Whistle Stop Hobbies, Palm Harbor, Florida

## Customer Profile

Why would customers want to keep adding to their model train layouts? One reason is to show off at the H&R Train's semiannual events.

Experienced model railroaders have an older demographic profile, with a significant percentage being over 50. These people took up model railroading in their youth when it was a major hobby group nationwide, and have continued to enjoy the hobby throughout their adult years. These people are always adding new products and features to their model railroad layout. H&R Trains has built a strong relationship with these customers by giving them opportunities to show off their train layouts in the stores two big annual sales.

People who are new to model railroading can come in any age group from five to 95. There is not really any way to predict just who will be bitten by the model railroading bug, other than most people involved with the hobby are men. H&R Trains works to attract prospects by hosting two large annual events that receive tremendous newspaper, radio, and TV coverage in the Tampa/St. Petersburg area. H&R Trains then hosts weekly clinics and training sessions to help fledgling model railroaders develop an increased interest in the hobby, and to help them optimize their enjoyment of the hobby.

H&R Trains has relied on its shows, extensive store display, and Little Engineers Club to attract the attention of parents who want to spend more time with their children with a hobby they can both enjoy. H&R Trains will expand their outreach to this market by setting up field trips for young children and their parents, working with both schools and Cub Scout troops.

## Positioning Strategies

### Major Positioning Statement

1. H&R Trains is a place for people to come to relax, to have fun and to learn more about the hobby of Model Railroading.

### Secondary Positioning Statements

2. H&R Trains' store is an adventure, where kids, parents, railroading enthusiasts, and people wanting to know more about the hobby can get wide-ranging exposure to all facets of Model Railroading.
3. H&R Trains' Little Engineer Club is a great program for kids and their parents to play and have fun together.

Secondary positioning statements help balance your marketing program so it presents a total marketing approach to your customers.

### Competitive Position Statement

H&R Trains is the only true destination store in the Tampa/St. Petersburg area devoted exclusively to model railroading. H&R Trains wants everyone to have fun and its 30,000 square foot store can provide several hours of enjoyment for every visitor. Most of all, H&R Trains wants to work with established enthusiasts in the Tampa/St. Petersburg area to promote and attract new participants to the hobby of model railroading.

## Marketing Tactics

**Merchandise**. H&R Trains will continue its quality merchandise theme by continuing to performance-test all new products prior to stocking them, and putting each product it

H&R Trains sells fun and adventure, not model railroading equipment. Sales will come if you give customers what they want.

sells through a quality check before the buyer takes the product home. H&R Trains will continue to stock most new products available to the market that pass its performance testing.

**Store layout**. The store will be reviewed and changes made throughout the year to keep it fresh and exciting even for frequent visitors. The emphasis will remain on fun product displays where customers can see how the products will really work and look in their own home layouts.

**Advertising/publicity**. H&R Trains will continue to run a small Yellow Pages ad and a small amount of advertising. It will continue, as it has in the past, to run a major publicity program for all media outlets along with its two major shows in April and October.

**Model railroading shows**. H&R Trains will continue to run its two big shows in April and October. The shows are free to the public, and free to model railroad enthusiasts who display their layouts. Manufacturers of model railroading equipment also attend the show. There is no cost for anyone to attend the show and no one is allowed to sell products at the show other than H&R Trains. The show is held outside in an area next to the store in three big tents, one 60 feet by 120 feet, another 60 by 30, and a third tent 30 by 30. The cost of the show is covered by the products people purchase at the store during the show. The purpose of the show is not for H&R Trains to make money, but rather to generate interest and enthusiasm in model railroading as a hobby.

**Newsletters**. Two newsletters will be sent out to customers and past attendees of the model railroading shows. Each mailing goes out to more than twenty thousand people, and it contains information about new products, shows, upcoming classes, and the Little Engineers Club.

Give a short description of each tactic, so you and everyone else has an overview of what you are trying to accomplish.

**Publicity with Cub Scouts and schools**. H&R Trains will send announcements out to the volunteer coordinators of the Boy Scouts throughout the Tampa area. Every month each district (which contains 25 to 30 Cub Scout Packs) has a roundtable meeting where ideas for outings, den trips, and other organizational details are discussed. H&R Trains will also send a mailing to area preschools announcing that the store can accommodate visits from schools on field trips during 10:00 A.M. and 2:00 P.M. provided the school calls first for an appointment.

**Web page**. H&R Trains has a Web page at http://www.hrtrains.com. The site is maintained with up-to-date information regarding new products, shows, classes, meetings, and a variety of other information for H&R Trains' best customers. The site is maintained by H&R Trains and updated at least once a month.

**Classes/seminars**. H&R Trains will continue to run weekly classes on different aspects of model railroading. The classes will be hosted by either store personnel, manufacturers, or model railroading enthusiasts in the Tampa/St. Petersburg area. A schedule for new classes will be scheduled every quarter so it can be posted on the Web page and listed in the newsletter.

**Little Engineers Club**. This club is run for parents and their children and meets once a month throughout the year. Each meeting has a small program, and then a hands-on demonstration with time for the children to play with the trains.

**Service**. H&R Trains is continuing to expand its service levels, adding parts for repairing older model railroading equipment. The store will also continue its policy of providing free service for one year after an item is purchased, and will also continue to do free performance checks on all purchased equipment for one year after its purchase.

**Pricing**. H&R Trains is a full-service, high value-added store and will continue to sell most products at the suggested manufacturer's price. Occasional sales will be held on discontinued or overstocked merchandise.

← Always include a section in the plan on your pricing plan. It is an important part of your marketing strategy.

## Implementation Plan*

*Note*: The store's actual plan lists costs and the person responsible for making sure the activity occurs. They are deleted from the plan here because the information is confidential.

| DATE | ACTION | COST | PERSON RESPONSIBLE |
|---|---|---|---|
| 12/1/98 | Complete schedule of classes and seminars for first quarter 1999. | .... | ............. |
| 12/1/98 | Complete schedule of activities for Little Engineers Club for first quarter 1999. | .... | ............. |
| 12/15/98 | Determine advertising program for first quarter. | .... | ............. |
| 1/15/99 | Initiate publicity program to Cub Scouts and preschools. | .... | ............. |
| 1/30/99 | Initial announcement to manufacturers and potential exhibitors for the spring show. | .... | ............. |
| 3/1/99 | Begin initial contacts for publicity program of spring show. | .... | ............. |
| 3/1/99 | Complete schedule of classes and seminars for second quarter 1999. | .... | ............. |
| 3/1/99 | Complete schedule of activities for Little Engineers Club for first quarter 1999. | .... | ............. |
| 3/15/99 | Determine second quarter advertising schedule. | .... | ............. |
| 3/15/99 | Send out first newsletter announcing the spring model railroading show. | .... | ............. |
| 3/15/99 | Review store layout and decide on any modifications. | | |
| 4/20/99 | Start of spring show. | .... | ............. |
| 6/1/99 | Complete schedule of classes and seminars for third quarter 1999. | .... | ............. |
| 6/1/99 | Complete schedule of activities for Little Engineers Club for third quarter 1999. | .... | ............. |
| 6/15/99 | Determine third quarter advertising schedule. | .... | ............. |
| 7/30/99 | Initial announcement to manufacturers and potential exhibitors at the fall show. | .... | ............. |
| 8/15/99 | Evaluate store layout, make any modifications needed. | .... | ............. |
| 9/1/99 | Begin initial contacts for publicity program of fall show. | .... | ............. |
| 9/1/99 | Complete schedule of classes and seminars for last quarter 1999. | .... | ............. |
| 9/1/99 | Complete schedule of activities for Little Engineers Club for last quarter 1999. | .... | ............. |
| 9/15/99 | Determine fourth quarter advertising schedule. | .... | ............. |
| 10/15/99 | Fall show. | .... | ............. |

H&R Trains goes out to recruit customers. Don't wait for customers to find you.

Try to evaluate and, if necessary, freshen up your store layout at least every six months.

## Budget

*Note*: The store's actual plan lists budget numbers for its projected expenses. They are deleted here because the information is confidential.

| ITEM | BUDGET |
|---|---|
| Yellow Pages Advertising | . . . . . . . . . . . . . . . . |
| Other Advertising | . . . . . . . . . . . . . . . . |
| Web Page Hosting | . . . . . . . . . . . . . . . . |
| Web Page Updating | . . . . . . . . . . . . . . . . |
| Newsletter Printing | . . . . . . . . . . . . . . . . |
| Newsletter Mailing | . . . . . . . . . . . . . . . . |
| Publicity to Cub Scouts/Schools | . . . . . . . . . . . . . . . . |
| Publicity Materials for Show | . . . . . . . . . . . . . . . . |
| Spring Show | . . . . . . . . . . . . . . . . |
| Fall Show | . . . . . . . . . . . . . . . . |
| Little Engineer Club Activities | . . . . . . . . . . . . . . . . |
| Class and Seminar Costs | . . . . . . . . . . . . . . . . |
| Service Costs—New Products | . . . . . . . . . . . . . . . . |
| Service Costs—Warranty | . . . . . . . . . . . . . . . . |
| Miscellaneous Printing Costs | . . . . . . . . . . . . . . . . |
| **Total** | . . . . . . . . . . . . . . . . |

Company owners, marketers, and collaborators on marketing plan: Alice and Don Morris.

I prefer to break out the budget by the activity supported, rather than separate items by categories such as advertising.

**Marketing Plan 2000**
**Mighty Grounds Coffee Shop**
**Cottage Grove, Minnesota**

*Author's Note*: The retail space Mighty Grounds was going to rent effective January 1, 2000, was rented by another tenant before Mighty Grounds could actually open. As of the date this plan was written, the Mighty Grounds Coffee Shop had not found another suitable storefront.

## Executive Summary

### Business Description

Mighty Grounds is a coffee shop that will sell regular coffee, cappuccino, breakfast muffins, and desserts in the Cottage Grove, Minnesota area, which is a suburb of St. Paul. Cottage Grove is a town of approximately thirty thousand residents; about 50 percent of the families are professionals. Mighty Grounds is a for-profit coffee shop owned by members of a Lutheran church who wanted to have a "meeting place" coffee shop with a Christian focus in their community. The coffee shop will be located in a large 2,000-square-foot space in a strip mall, three doors down from one of Cottage Grove's largest grocery stores.

> Mighty Grounds had a concept for their shop: a meeting place with a Christian focus. Having a concept is a great marketing strategy.

### Situation

Cottage Grove is suburb of St. Paul, 14 miles from downtown, that is situated around Highway 61, which was one of the original trunk highways into St. Paul. The suburb had a small population through the 1970s and has some older retail establishments along Highway 61 from the 1960s. Since 1980, Cottage Grove has been growing rapidly as the outer ring suburbs of the Twin Cities expanded with rapid growth. Since Cottage Grove's main thoroughfare was an older highway, the suburb has a haphazard retail section that didn't provide any convenient community meeting locations. Mighty Grounds was conceived as a place that would function both as a full-service coffee house and a meeting place for small community groups.

### Marketing Strategy

Mighty Grounds has a two-prong strategy. In the morning it will offer coffee, cappuccino, and breakfast muffins and pastries to the morning commuters, 50 percent of whom are professionals. After 9:00 A.M., the coffee house will strive to become a meeting place for various community groups and residents, including a place for high school students to meet after school.

Mighty Grounds will have a part-time program director who will work with other churches and community groups to help facilitate community meetings and set up interesting forums and discussion groups and to provide games and other entertainment for high school students.

## Marketing Goals

Mighty Grounds' goal is to generate $500 per morning, or $3,500 per week, in traditional coffee house business, and average another $7,000 per week in business generated from a variety of community meetings or drop-in traffic throughout the day. Mighty Grounds' marketing goals include:

1. Have at least half of Cottage Groves' organized service groups, such as Lions Clubs move their meeting to Mighty Grounds by the end of 2000.
2. Average 20 organized meetings per week by the end of 2000.
3. Average attendance of at least one hundred high school students throughout the week.
4. Be perceived as the number one community meeting location and coffee house in the Cottage Grove area.

# Internal Audit

## Business Background and History

Cottage Grove is split in half by Highway 61. The original idea for Mighty Grounds came from a Lutheran church located just off the main road that leads from the west side of town to Highway 61. The church was overcrowded and needed more meeting space and a youth activity room. As the church was discussing the possibility of adding to its building, a 3,000 foot retail area in the strip mall that sat 100 yards from the church became vacant. One of the pastors of the church thought it might be a good idea for the church to rent the building and use it when needed. The rent was too high to justify that expense, but then a member of the church opened a coffee house with a Christian focus similar to one that had opened in Stillwater, Minnesota. It was decided to sell 20 shares in the coffee house for $2,000 each, hire a manager and proceed to open the coffee house in the front room of the building and the back room, which had no windows, would be converted to a youth room for the church. The decision was made to have a full-time employee manage the coffee house part of the business and a part-time program manager to arrange for meetings, forums, discussion groups and other activities. The part-time program manager would also be responsible for inviting and working with other churches in the area to ensure the coffee shop has an ecumenical focus.

When you choose a strategy, be sure to put in the resources, such as Mighty Grounds Program Director, to implement the strategy.

These objectives are measurable, which is a feature you want in your plan to judge performance.

## Concept

In this plan the organization history of the company explains the company's focus.

A "meeting place" coffee shop with a Christian focus that can act as (1) a meeting place for small church and community groups; (2) a facilitator for the formation of new small (or not so small) community groups such as parent groups, book reading groups, etc.; (3) a focal point where members of the community can come to see their friends; (4) an evening meeting place for young adults and teenagers; and (5) an overflow location for church groups, including youth Sunday School classes. The space Mighty Grounds is negotiating for is 3,000 square feet, about three times the size of a regular coffee house, and it will have tables that can be placed together to seat 16 to 20 people, or separated to hold a group of four. The church will furnish the back room that will be used as the middle school or senior high youth room.

## Coffee Shop

Marketing strategies and plans should constantly reinforce a company's business concept.

Mighty Grounds needs to be self-supporting and it will only do that by running a profitable coffee shop. Studies of successful coffee shops in the Twin Cities have pointed out these keys to success for a coffee shop.

You always want to spend more of your marketing dollars on your highest profit products.

1. The espresso machine contributes well over 50 percent to a coffee shop's revenue, and even more to its profits. High-quality espresso drinks that people will go out of their way to get are the secret to coffee shops that do more than $1 million per year. Mighty Grounds will purchase a new espresso machine for $45,000 and have four people—the manager and three people—on the organizing committee.
2. There was a tremendous difference in the quality of espresso drinks from different coffee cafés and coffee bars. The cafés and bars with the best tasting drinks did five to ten times the business of shops with average tasting espresso. Mighty Grounds members will do a quality check on their coffee every month.
3. Besides being sure the espresso tastes good, Mighty Grounds needs to market espresso in the coffee shop if the store wants to get its percentage of espresso drinks to over 50 percent of the drinks served. Mighty Grounds plans on setting up a separate espresso station, with an explanation of what makes an espresso taste so great, and detailed instructions on how to make a good espresso. Mighty Grounds also plans to give people a check slip at the espresso station that they use to pay at the dessert and coffee counter to ensure people get their espresso right away.
4. Mighty Grounds will not prepare any food on site to keep the emphasis on espresso. It will bring sandwiches in between 11:30 A.M. and 1:00 P.M., but otherwise will only offer desserts, muffins, and pastries. Pastries will be prepared both by women from the

church and the Bon Appetite's catering service, whose owner is a member of the Lutheran church.

5. The coffee shop will start with a cooler with soft drinks for teenagers, but will add a fruit smoothie station after six months.

Mighty Grounds will set its pricing approximately 25 percent below typical Starbucks' pricing. This is in keeping with the community oriented nonsecular image of the store.

No point in marketing your business is too small to plan out in advance.

## Focus and Mission

Mighty Grounds wants to work together with all the churches in Cottage Grove to offer small group opportunities for all church members in the community. Only 20 to 30 percent of the groups will be involving Christian themes, and all members of the community are welcome to attend any group. But the focus and mission of Mighty Grounds is to offer the community an interesting meeting point that is compatible with the values of the area religious groups. Fifty percent of Mighty Grounds, profits will be used to help fund community day care centers, after-school programs, summer programs for children, and other children-related programming.

## Types of Groups Mighty Grounds Will Facilitate

**Bible studies**. Breakfast, daytime, or evening sessions. They could be run by individual churches or be an ecumenical group.

Mighty Grounds has multiple investors. The plan is written to educate them about the company's mission.

**Card groups**. Bridge, pinochle, or other games. Studies indicate many retirees would like to have an opportunity to play cards with others.

**Games**. Trivial Pursuit, Monopoly, Gestures, and other games could be set up for teenagers, young singles, or young couples.

**Discussion groups**. Parent groups and any number of support groups such as people living with an elderly parent could all be helped at Mighty Grounds.

**Special interest groups**. Book reading groups, model airplane clubs, and any other group that might meet in the area.

**Community service groups**. Lions Clubs, Jaycees, and other community groups currently drive 12 miles to Hastings to meet. Mighty Grounds gives them a closer alternative.

## Sales Trends

Many coffee shops specializing in espresso are doing in excess of $1 million per year in the Twin Cities. Mighty Grounds is setting its budget based on $550,000 for the year, or about $1,500 per day. The average purchase at an espresso-oriented coffee café is $3 to $5 per day, so the coffee shop needs to average 350 visitors per day. Mighty Grounds is confident it can do that with the support of the area churches and with the high traffic that goes by the strip mall each day as people travel to Highway 61. Mighty Grounds, breakeven point is $225,000 per year.

## Strengths and Weaknesses

### Strengths

1. Connection to the churches in the area will quickly build wide exposure in the community and will help create a loyal customer base.
2. The railroad tracks west of Highway 61 are only crossed by four roads in Cottage Grove. Mighty Grounds sits on the most heavily traveled of the four roads.
3. The location is two doors away from the most popular grocery store in Cottage Grove.
4. Many church members are willing to help out at Mighty Grounds on a volunteer basis until the business is making money.
5. Church members involved in the construction industry are willing to volunteer their time to do much of the required remodeling tasks.
6. Much of the coffee shop's layout is based on two successful shops in the Twin Cities.

### Weaknesses

1. No one on the Mighty Grounds start-up team has experience running a coffee café.
2. The large number of owners doesn't leave someone fully in charge with a large vested interest in ensuring Mighty Grounds will succeed.
3. The rent for the store is high due to the shop's location and the larger than typical space.
4. Cottage Grove doesn't have as many office buildings, and it will have to attract commuters' business as they leave for work.

You need more detail in a plan to keep you on track as your strategy becomes more complicated.

Mighty Grounds depends on a high traffic site and a good marketing concept. It is a big mistake to think only one of the two traffic building strategies is enough.

The reason Cottage Grove doesn't have a coffee shop now is that it doesn't have office buildings. The lack of office buildings opened up the opportunity.

## External Audit

### Customer Information

Cottage Grove has had two major stages of development, one is the mid-1960s to mid-1970s, and one in the late 1980s and early 1990s. Its mid-1960s developments were smaller homes targeted at the workers of an adhesive and sealant plant of 3M's and a refinery in nearby St. Paul Park. The last wave of construction was for commuters into St. Paul and Minneapolis. Eighty-six percent of Cottage Grove residents live in homes, and 14 percent live in multifamily dwellings.

Fifteen percent of the area's homes are owned by retirees, and the rest are working families, about 65 percent of whom still have children at home, and Cottage Grove has a fairly even age distribution among its residents. Cottage Grove is an average income suburb with homes selling in the $90,000 to $150,000 range. About 40 percent of Cottage Grove's thirty thousand residents are members of a church.

Cottage Grove doesn't have a community center and the lack of a central gathering point, together with the impact of Highway 61 and the railroad tracks dividing the town, have resulted in the town's not having a strong community focus. People do most of their shopping in the two nearby towns of Woodbury and Hastings, and when they do go out to eat they typically go the local fast-food restaurants, or to town.

Based on the results of informal studies of residents, it appears that they would like a neighborhood gathering place where the town could develop a greater sense of community, and where residents could meet other residents with whom they have common interests.

Local residents don't have any coffeehouses in the area, and most aren't espresso aware. They typically don't go out to expensive restaurants, and for the most part don't spend a great deal of money on entertainment. This could be a result of few entertainment options, or a result of people preferring to stay home. Cottage Grove has not had restaurants or coffeehouses open and fail, but instead there just haven't been any that opened.

### Target Customer

Residents of the Cottage Grove/St. Paul Park area who are receptive to a meeting place/coffeehouse with a Christian focus. These are primarily people who already attend local churches or who have considered joining churches. Mighty Grounds will reach out to the broader community with its bulletin board of upcoming community events and by giving residents opportunities to meet like-minded people, but the core customer group is still members of local churches.

Cottage Grove is an average income suburb, which is another reason Mighty Grounds' pricing is 25 percent lower than Starbucks'.

The plan responds to the uncertainty of residents paying for espresso drinks by including a part-time program manager.

This customer group is more varied than H&R Trains' target customer group, which makes it more difficult to predict their behavior.

## Competition

There aren't any coffeehouses or coffee shops in the Cottage Grove area. There is a Dunkin' Donuts and the convenience stores in the area do sell coffee, cappuccino, donuts, and muffins. St. Paul Park, which is about two miles away, has a small coffee shop just off its downtown area. The shop is small and is really not designed in the "meeting house" style, and it does not heavily promote its espresso and cappuccino products.

Competitors don't have to be just like you, they just need to serve the same customer need.

# Positioning Strategies

## Positioning Statements

1. Mighty Grounds has great-tasting specialty espresso and cappuccino products.
2. Mighty Grounds is the meeting place of the community with room for groups from four to 30 members.
3. Mighty Grounds has regular meeting of a wide variety of special interest groups.
4. Mighty Grounds is a meeting place with a Christian focus.

## Rationale for Positioning Statements

The most critical positioning statement for Mighty Grounds is that has great-tasting specialty drinks. For Mighty Grounds to be successful, it needs to attract 350 customers per day. The meeting place environment of Mighty Grounds will give the business exposure and customer awareness, but Mighty Grounds can't succeed with just people attending meetings. It needs people to stop in at various times throughout the week for a dessert or muffin and cappuccino. This won't happen unless they enjoy Mighty Grounds' espresso and cappuccino drinks.

Mighty Grounds' success depends on the product being great. Success always counts on a quality product that meets people's needs or desires.

Mighty Grounds also wants to attract people in the community who aren't members of a church to its meetings, and it wants Mighty Grounds to be known as a meeting place, rather than as a Christian meeting place. The coffee shop's name captures its Christian emphasis, and many of the groups meeting there will have a Christian focus, and members of churches are its core customer group. Mighty Grounds needs to also work to position itself as a community meeting place and not just a church meeting location.

## Competitive Positioning

Mighty Grounds is the only coffee shop in the Cottage Grove area with great-tasting specialty coffee drinks. It is also the only business in Cottage Grove with a meeting place focus, where groups can sit around and meet for an hour or two and the only place in Cottage Grove where people can find groups of like-minded people meeting on a regular basis.

## Marketing Tactics

### Product

The key to Mighty Grounds is the merchandising and taste of its specialty drinks, which involves not only having the right coffeemaker and coffee, but also having people who understand the art of making good coffee. Mighty Grounds is purchasing a high-end cappuccino coffeemaker that has a shiny copper and bronze exterior that can be set out in a separate station to attract interest to specialty coffees. Three church members who are great fans of specialty coffees are being trained, along with the manager, in the proper technique of making specialty coffee drinks. The three church members will also help out as "quality control" inspectors, checking to be sure the product maintains its high quality. Specialty regular coffees will also be available.

If your product depends on quality, try to include independent quality audits in your plan.

### Displays

The espresso/cappuccino coffee machine will be stationed next to a post that will have a triangular display explaining the different types of drinks available, how each is made, and what they taste like. The dessert display will be along the wall where the cash register and regular coffee machines are located.

### Pricing

Pricing will be set about 25 percent below the standard Starbucks' coffee pricing in downtown St. Paul and other St. Paul suburbs.

### Bulletin Boards

The store location has windows across the front, and a few windows across the south side of the coffee shop. The north side of the store abuts against another store and it has a solid wall. The store will have three bulletin boards up: one for community events, one for upcoming events at Mighty Grounds, and one that lists upcoming events of the area churches.

### Programming

Mighty Grounds has a programming/sales person identified who has been active in local school and civic groups. This would be a part-time position and the job would entail encouraging local groups to hold meetings at Mighty Grounds, create new groups to match the interests of the community, and work with other local churches to help sponsor Mighty Grounds. This person is scheduled to be hired November 1, 1999, two months before Mighty Grounds is scheduled to open.

## Publicity

The local community paper publishes a weekly calendar of events and the paper has already indicated that it would carry the announcements. Other local churches have also indicated that they might post a Mighty Grounds' schedule and announcements in their churches.

Every business has publicity opportunities, and it is smart marketing to exploit those opportunities.

## Church Alliances

Mighty Grounds will only succeed if it is viewed as a cooperative effort of all the neighborhood churches. The original investors come from four of the six churches, but the pastors of the various churches are not completely sold on the concept. One reason the program director has been hired two months before the store opens is to elicit additional support from other churches. The other pastors do like the idea of posting their church activities at Mighty Grounds so they have shown some interest in the concept.

## Recruiting Community Groups

Lions Clubs, Jaycees, and the Cottage Grove Little League are just some of the twenty-some community groups that meet more that four times per year. The program director will also be encouraging those members to come to Mighty Grounds for their meetings. The Lutheran church will also be surveying their members to see which members belong to certain organizations. They will be recruited to help make the right contacts at each group.

Alliances can be set up with a small investment, and they have an enormous return.

## Promotions

On February 15 Mighty Grounds will send out coupons to churches and community groups offering a 25-percent-off coupon for people attending a church meeting at Mighty Grounds prior to June 1, 2000.

## Teenage Programming

Two members of the high school's youth group will be recruiting six additional high school students from other churches to be members of a youth advisory group to help establish what programming high school students would like for both afterschool activities and Friday and Saturday night games or entertainment.

## Store Signs

Mighty Grounds' location is at the south end of a strip mall. Mighty Grounds will have a standard sign on the front of the building as approved by the mall management. But the mall will also approve big banners 6 feet by 20 feet on the south side wall of the building, which faces the main road out of the west side of Cottage Grove onto Highway 61.

Signs are a critical part of every retailer's marketing strategy.

## Implementation Plan 2000

*Note*: Code for person responsible: Org. Com. = Organizing Committee; PD = Program Director; MGM = Mighty Grounds Manager.

| DATE | ACTION | COST | PERSON RESPONSIBLE |
|---|---|---|---|
| 11/1/99 | Hire part-time program director | $20,000 | Org. Com. |
| 11/30/99 | Hire full-time Mighty Grounds Manager. *Note*: Salary in operating budget. | | Org. Com. |
| 12/10/99 | Receive triangular display. | 4,000 | Org. Com. |
| 12/15/99 | Have rough store layout in place, including the setup. | | MGM |
| 12/15/99 | Complete initial schedule of events for January. | | PD |
| 12/15/99 | Release to local newspaper an announcement about the Mighty Grounds opening and upcoming events. | | PD |
| 12/15/99 | Purchase banner for side of building announcing that Mighty Grounds' is now open. | 300 | MGM |
| 1/3/00 | Official opening. | | MGM |
| 1/15/00 | Release to local newspaper an announcement about the Mighty Grounds upcoming events. | | PD |
| 1/15/00 | Send announcements to local churches about next month's activities. | 20 | PD |
| 1/30/00 | First meeting with youth advisors to decide on youth programming. | | PD |
| 2/1/00 | Initiate bulletin board system that needs to be checked and updated every week. | | PD |
| 2/15/00 | Provide each church in the area 25-percent-off coupons for any church meeting held at Mighty Grounds prior to June 1, 2000. | 100 | MGM |
| 2/15/00 | Provide each community group in the area 25-percent-off coupons for any group meeting held at Mighty Grounds prior to June 1, 2000. | 100 | MGM |
| 2/15/00 | Release to local newspaper an announcement about the Mighty Grounds' upcoming events. | | PD |
| 2/15/00 | Send announcements to local churches about next month's activities. | 20 | PD |
| 2/28/00 | Cost of coupons for February. | 1,500 | MGM |
| 2/28/00 | Programming aids. | 500 | PD |

Different people can be responsible for different tasks. What's important is that they know they are responsible, and commit to getting the job done.

Keeping people apprised of upcoming activities helps make them a success.

# Retail/Coffee Shop Market Plans

| DATE | ACTION | COST | PERSON RESPONSIBLE |
|------|--------|------|--------------------|
| 3/15/00 | Release to local newspaper an announcement about the Mighty Grounds' upcoming events. | | PD |
| 3/15/00 | Send announcements to local churches about next month's activities. | 20 | PD |
| 3/15/00 | Have a minimum of four planned groups (i.e. book reading clubs) ready for grand opening. | | PD |
| 3/15/00 | Purchase grand opening banner for side of building. | 300 | MGM |
| 3/30/00 | Cost of coupons for March. | 1,500 | MGM |
| 4/1/00 | Grand opening. | 1,000 | MGM |
| 4/1/00 | Begin youth programs. | 500 | PD |
| 4/15/00 | Release to local newspaper an announcement about the Mighty Grounds' upcoming events. | | PD |
| 4/30/00 | Cost of coupons for April. | 1,500 | MGM |
| 4/30/00 | Programming aids. | 500 | PD |
| 5/05/00 | Revise triangular display | 500 | PD |
| 5/15/00 | Send announcements to local churches about next month's activities. | 20 | PD |
| 5/15/00 | Release to local newspaper an announcement about the Mighty Grounds' upcoming events. | | PD |
| 5/15/00 | Form an additional four more special interest groups to meet at Mighty Grounds at least once per week. | | PD |
| 6/1/00 | Announce summer youth programming. | 500 | PD |
| 6/15/00 | Release to local newspaper an announcement about the Mighty Grounds' upcoming events. | | PD |
| 6/15/00 | Send announcements to local churches about next month's activities. | 20 | PD |
| 7/15/00 | Release to local newspaper an announcement about the Mighty Grounds' upcoming events. | | PD |
| 7/15/00 | Send announcements to local churches about next month's activities. | 20 | PD |
| 7/30/00 | Programming aids. | 500 | PD |
| 7/30/00 | Replace triangular display. | 500 | PD |
| 8/15/00 | Release to local newspaper an announcement about the Mighty Grounds' upcoming events. | | PD |
| 8/15/00 | Send announcements to local churches about next month's activities. | 20 | PD |

Carefully planned displays reinforce your marketing message.

Be sure to put in money for the aids you need to execute the plan.

| DATE | ACTION | COST | PERSON RESPONSIBLE |
|---|---|---|---|
| 8/30/00 | Announce fall youth programming. | 500 | PD |
| 9/1/00 | Programming aids. | 500 | PD |
| 9/15/00 | Release to local newspaper an announcement about the Mighty Grounds' upcoming events. | | PD |
| 9/15/00 | Send announcements to local churches about next month's activities. | 20 | PD |
| 10/15/00 | Release to local newspaper an announcement about the Mighty Grounds' upcoming events. | | PD |
| 10/15/00 | Send announcements to local churches about next month's activities. | 20 | PD |
| 11/15/00 | Release to local newspaper an announcement about the Mighty Grounds' upcoming events. | | PD |
| 11/15/00 | Send announcements to local churches about next month's activities. | 20 | PD |
| 12/15/00 | Release to local newspaper an announcement about the Mighty Grounds' upcoming events. | | PD |
| 12/15/00 | Send announcements to local churches about next month's activities. | 20 | PD |

Local papers will keep publishing releases as long as you have newsworthy events.

## Marketing Budget

| ITEM | COST |
|---|---|
| Training on Espresso/Cappuccino Machine | $ 3,000 |
| Program Director | 20,000 |
| Banners | 600 |
| Triangular Display | 5,000 |
| Announcements to Churches | 240 |
| Promotional Programs | 6,200 |
| Programming Aids, Youth & Adult | 3,000 |
| Grand Opening Costs | 1,000 |
| Miscellaneous Costs | 1,000 |
| Total | $40,040 |

Plan Collaborator, Pastor Craig Pederson, All Saints' Lutheran Church, Cottage Grove, Minnesota.

## Final Comments

Both plans concentrate on serving customers' needs as a basis for their core strategy. Each plan has a concept based on their customers and markets and their strategies flow from that concept. This is the marketing approach you want to follow. Most small businesses I've worked with start with the opposite approach. They decide what type of business they want to open, and then try to figure out a way to market their business to customers. Effective plans for those businesses are typically much more difficult to write, because the core concept of the business isn't based on customer desires. If your business didn't start with a customer orientation, stop and take the time to create a strategy that is customer based and then move your company's operations to that new customer-oriented concept.

Note that these marketing plans have detailed actions and schedules built in. Many small business marketers tell me they keep their marketing plan in their head. Those companies aren't executing their strategies nearly as effectively as they would with a plan. Dates for a program can sneak up fast and, without an implementation plan, marketers will often not have the groundwork done in time to successfully implement a tactic. Listing implementation tactics also helps you ensure that you have the resources you need to launch the plan. Mighty Grounds originally thought that the store manager could handle programming duties. Once the planning committee laid out the work that needed to be done, they realized they also needed a program manager.

The main point is that a marketing plan is not a task to shuffle through. The planning process creates an effective strategy and gives you the tools you need to implement that strategy. Many times companies have to readjust their strategy because they don't have the resources to execute all their tactics. Companies also have to readjust their plans because they have too many tactics occurring at the same time. I firmly believe that companies that go through a formal marketing plan process operate at a much higher level of effectiveness than companies that don't. There is no point going through all the trouble of creating a great marketing strategy if you aren't willing to take a little extra time to write a plan that will allow you to execute that strategy.

Be sure and write a new plan every year.

> You need a plan, so you can be sure to do the initial steps to implement each tactic on time.

Basic marketing strategy of customers forms always come first, no matter how innovative a tactic might be.

## Key Starting Points

Both plans point out several key starting points of a good plan. I've listed those points here. Check if your strategy and plan meet these requirements. If not, you should go back and re-evaluate them.

|  | YES | NO |
|---|---|---|
| 1. Is your business based on a customer-focused concept? | _____ | _____ |
| 2. Does your plan list all of the details of your upcoming activities? | _____ | _____ |
| 3. Does part of your strategy call for going out into the market to reach out to potential customers? | _____ | _____ |
| 4. Do you have the resources, both manpower and financial, to implement your strategy? | _____ | _____ |
| 5. Do you have a well defined customer group that has somewhat predictable behavior? | _____ | _____ |

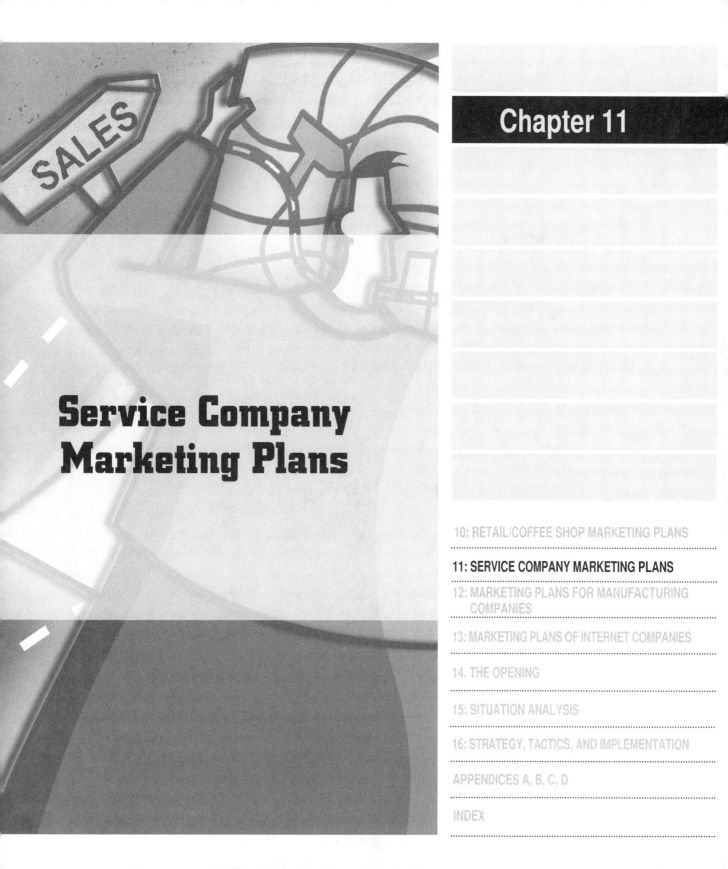

# Chapter 11

## Service Company Marketing Plans

10: RETAIL/COFFEE SHOP MARKETING PLANS

**11: SERVICE COMPANY MARKETING PLANS**

12: MARKETING PLANS FOR MANUFACTURING
    COMPANIES

13: MARKETING PLANS OF INTERNET COMPANIES

14. THE OPENING

15: SITUATION ANALYSIS

16: STRATEGY, TACTICS, AND IMPLEMENTATION

APPENDICES A, B, C, D

INDEX

**Marketing Plan
Resnick Associates
Harrisburg, Pennsylvania**

## Background

Resnick Associates is a life insurance brokerage firm that specializes in estate and business succession planning. It concentrates on owners of successful businesses that are interested in keeping their companies intact when they pass on the business to their heirs, co-shareholders, or partners. Resnick Associates is composed of three brothers, Terrance, Leon, and John who took over their father's 35-year-old firm over a decade ago and refocused its strategy on business succession and estate planning. The company's original office is in Harrisburg, Pennsylvania, and five years ago the company opened a second office in Kansas City, Kansas.

The Resnicks have focused their marketing efforts on educational seminars, informative articles on issues related to estate and succession planning, and a patient approach to sales. This approach has worked well in the past, as the owners of the business are take-charge businesspeople who prefer an approach where they make the final choice. The Resnicks' initial approach to marketing is typically to work initially through business associations with a high percentage of private owners, such as the trucking industry, where the association welcomes presentations on business planning. The Resnicks then follow up with interested parties, typically with a series of six or more meetings, which often include the client's attorney and accountant. Succession plans are then finalized anywhere from three months to one year after the initial presentation. The Resnicks also mail out articles and other items of interest to people who've expressed interest, but aren't quite ready to begin the planning process.

Marketers should have a clear focus, or concentration, on a particular aspect of their customers' needs or desires.

### Growth History and Goals for 2000

When the Resnicks took over the firm, the new partners did not want to have a traditional life insurance agency, and instead decided to focus on estate planning and business succession. The firm's overall approach has been very successful, and the firm wants to keep its approach and philosophy of providing the best service it can to its target market. The firm adds anywhere from 20 to 25 new customers per year and has a substantial client base throughout the country. The Resnicks want to maintain its current client base and growth rate. Their objective for next year is to work on succession plans of higher net-worth individuals, particularly owners of large private businesses.

## Company's Previous Marketing Approach

Resnick Associates has developed its business through presentations at associations with a high percentage of wealthy owners and by writing columns for national business magazines, local papers and association newsletters regarding succession planning, insurance due diligence, and buy-out plans. This strategy has both enhanced the firm's credibility and produced a steady stream of prospective clients for the firm. To improve its position as a leader in estate planning and business succession the firm has also co-founded the Elizabethtown College Family Business Center in Elizabethtown, Pennsylvania, and has been involved with the Family Business Program at the Wharton School of the University of Pennsylvania. A last major initiative of the firm has been to coordinate presentations with CPA and law firms that also specialize in business succession planning.

The Resnicks succeed in part by helping associations provide meaningful information to their members.

A partial list of the associations where the firm has made presentations include:

Missouri Motor Carrier Association
Wisconsin Motor Carrier Association
Missouri Petroleum Marketers Association
Maryland Ready Mix Concrete Association
Illinois Movers' and Warehouseman's Association
IGA Successorship Institute
Sheet Metal and Air Condition Assn. of PA
Kansas Motor Carriers Association
Pennsylvania Bus Association
Missouri Association of Convenience Stores
Pennsylvania Restaurant Association
Pennsylvania Distributors Association
Pennsylvania Movers Association

Credibility building tactics should be a key component of every service business.

A partial list of articles that have appeared in *Nation's Business* and Kansas City and Harrisburg newspapers and business journals include:

"Firms Fail to Plan for Succession"
"Preparing for a Shift in Ownership"
"Estate Tax Proposal is Altering the Meaning of Repeal"
"Plan Helps Family Business Survive"
"Buying Insurance Calls for Caution and Clear Goals"
"Preserving Years of Work Demands Careful Estate Planning
"Beware of Universal Life Insurance"

"Financial Gains Often Emerge Through Charitable Giving"
"Business Needs Plan for Naming Successors"
"Survival Strategies for Family-Owned and Closely Held Broker Organizations"
"Politicians Give New Meaning to the Word Repeal"

**Often you can work with other groups and associations to promote your service cost effectively.**

While the newspaper articles have strengthened the firm's credibility and exposure and allowed the firm to establish a competitive advantage, it is uncertain that the papers will continue to publish a steady stream of articles on a topic of interest to only a small percentage of readers. Resnick Associates needs to increase its exposure to associations with a high percentage of individual business owners and improve its ability to generate referral business from current accounts.

## Strengths and Weaknesses

### Strengths

- Access to policies from a wide number of insurance companies guarantees the firm can produce a cost-effective plan for every situation.
- Strong credibility due to published articles, association presentations, and support of Family Business Centers at Universities.
- Patient sales tactics match customers' preferred buying behavior.
- Satisfied customers and good working relationships with CPAs and attorneys.
- Strong focus on target customer group.

### Weaknesses

**Competition from a large number of small competitors is only noteworthy if you haven't differentiated your company.**

- Many insurance competitors offer estate planning and succession planning.
- Prospective clients occasionally go to their CPA or lawyer first for estate planning advice.

## Market Analysis

### Environment

There are many people involved in estate and business succession planning, including lawyers, accountants, and other insurance agencies. In the past many insurance agents worked closely with accountants and lawyers to build a client base. Under that scenario the client was often steered toward an insurance agency by an accountant or attorney. As a result the client didn't always end up with the best product for his or her needs. Resnick Associates took a radically different approach when they decided business owners like to make their own independent decisions based on their knowledge of the facts. Resnick Associates has based their whole marketing approach on putting the actual decision in the hands of their client, and then helping the client understand his or her needs so they can choose the best product for them. This strategy frequently requires six or more meetings, and often requires three months to a year before the client is satisfied they have the best plan for their situation. But the client ends up much more satisfied as they then have a product and plan that they have chosen.

Customers want to be in charge of an important decision. Pushing for a quick sale often has negative results.

## Competition

Both Kansas City and Harrisburg have a large number of insurance agents who offer insurance packages for estate and business succession planning. Some of these agents have a strong customer base due to length of time in the industry and network of contacts. They can generally offer a similar package of products to the customers. Resnick Associates has two competitive advantages. One is that it creates demand with its presentations, creating interest in potential clients before its competitors have a chance to talk to them. The second advantage is that Resnick Associates has set up its sales process to cater to the desires of its clients selecting estate or business planning through an informed decision-making process. While there are many other insurance agencies, none of them operate in the same information-providing format as Resnick Associates.

## Customer Profile

Resnick Associates targets the owners of prosperous companies that have a net worth of seven or more figures. These customers have several characteristics:

1. These customers are not looking for choices. They are looking for customized solutions—something that fits them. Two of the goals of the firm's marketing and sales strategy are first, to show they truly are experts in the field, which is done through articles and presentations, and second, to take the time to get to know the client so that a program can be written to meet the client's needs.

Marketers should always determine not only what customers want, but how they like to be sold.

2. The Internet has caused an explosion of decision-making data for investment decisions, and business owners are no longer comfortable just accepting someone else's recommendation.
3. The business owners are value oriented, and it is important that they understand the value of the products they buy.

4. Wealthy business owners want to take the time to be sure the product they buy is the best one available. They will buy from several vendors if needed, and prefer dealing with a firm like Resnick Associates that offers a large number of products from a variety of customers.

5. Wealthy clients expect to hear both the benefits and pitfalls of each alternative.

6. Demographic data: (From *U.S. News & World Report*, April 14, 1997)

   A. There are 3.5 million households in America with a net worth of over $1 million.

   B. Two thirds of the millionaires are self-employed entrepreneurs in small businesses.

   C. Fifty-nine percent of the wealth of the richest 1 percent of the people in the country is concentrated in unincorporated businesses.

   D. The average age of millionaires is 57.

   E. Ninety-five percent are married and they have an average of three children.

   F. Only 20 percent of millionaires had rich parents.

   G. Millionaires tend to be frugal; more own Fords than any other car; they take home income of just $131,000 per year and live in homes with an average value of $320,000.

> The high percentage of millionaires who are entrepreneurs played a key role in the Resnicks' marketing strategy.

## Positioning Tactics

Resnick Associates is positioned as a leading source of information and expertise in the area of estate and business succession planning, and it is positioned as a firm that works carefully with clients to develop a plan that is right for them.

> Often service companies differentiate themselves by what they have done, rather that who they are.

Resnick Associates' competitive advantage is all the articles its personnel have written, and the work they've done at associations and Family Business Centers to establish themselves as experts in the field.

## Strategy for 2000

The firm plans on expanding its presence in the marketplace by aggressively approaching new associations for presentation opportunities, and increasing its referral business by offering its current clients Resnick Associates information folders that they can share with their friends. Resnick will be approaching the Pennsylvania, Kansas, and Missouri chapters of the following organizations with a high percentage of high-income owners to set up new presentations. The firm will also be targeting associations in two new states in the Midwest. The firm's goal is to start a relationship with at least four new organizations in 2000.

State Advertising Federations
Ready Mix Concrete Association
Association of Builders & Contractors

Association of General Contractors
Automotive Recyclers Association
Brick Industries Association
National Association of Home Builders
International Builders Exchange Executives
North American Equipment Dealers Association
National Automotive Dealers Association
Building Owners and Managers Association
Independent Business Association
American Foundrymen's Society
National Asphalt Pavement Association
Construction Management Association
American Electronics Association
State Grocer Association
Manufactured Housing Institute
American Petroleum Council
National Tooling and Machining Association
State Restaurant Association
Service Station and Convenience Store Association
National Soft Drink Association
American Moving and Storage Association
American Trucking Association
National Utility Contractors Association
National Electrical Contractors Association
National Federation of Independent Business
National Lumber & Building Materials Dealers
National Association of Plumbing, Heating, and Cooling Contractors
Surface Mount Technology Associates
Manufacturing Associations

← Try to keep expanding your alliances and partnerships every year.

## Tactics

**Product**. Resnick Associates will continue to take advantage of its independent broker status to offer the most cost-effective policies from a wide variety of insurance companies.

**Pricing**. Resnick Associates will continue to take its standard commission on products sold and to provide its services to customers at no cost other than the cost of the insurance product.

**Advertising.** The firm won't do any advertising. It will be listed in the Yellow Pages, but not with an ad.

**Association contacts/publicity.** Resnick Associates will establish contacts with state chapters of national associations. It will offer to do presentations and also provide articles for the associations' newsletters and magazines. Resnick's goals are to start a meaningful relationship with at least four associations in 2000, and to have published six to eight articles in industry association publications.

**Presentations.** The goal for 2000 is a minimum of twelve presentations to key industry groups throughout the year.

**Sales strategy.** The firm will continue its to use its patient "go slow" sales strategy to ensure that every client is certain they are getting a plan and product that is right for them.

**Direct mail.** Resnick doesn't direct mail to cold prospects, but it does send out articles and information to people who have attended past presentations and expressed interest in their products and services. Resnick plans three mailings next year, in March, June, and September.

**Referral folders.** The firm will put together their past articles, along with other information related to estate and business succession planning, into a special folder or booklet that Resnick's clients can pass out to their friends.

**Publicity articles.** The firm will continue to place information articles in local newspapers to gain publicity and credibility. The goal is to get eight articles published during the year 2000. Resnick Associates will continue to do all the publicity work on their own.

**Customer service.** Resnick Associates provides continuous service to all its clients, and the person who set up the initial plan continues to work with the client each year to ensure the plan and products are still right for the customer's needs.

**Market expansion.** Resnick Associates already has a client base that extends throughout the United States. The firm will be working to expand its presentations into a minimum of two new states in 2000. Resnick still has more than enough opportunities to expand its client base in the markets it now serves.

Alliances with associations are much more cost effective than advertising for many small companies.

You always want to send periodic mailings to prospects when they have a slow decision-making process.

## Implementation Plan

*Note*: Company did not want actual cost numbers disclosed.

| DATE | ACTION | COST | PERSON RESPONSIBLE |
|---|---|---|---|
| 1/25/00 | First presentation to an association. | .... | ............ |
| 1/30/00 | Publicity article published. | .... | ............ |
| 2/15/00 | Set up an appointment with a new association for presentation or news article. | .... | ............ |
| 2/15/00 | Second presentation to an association. | .... | ............ |
| 2/28/00 | Publicity article published. | .... | ............ |
| 3/15/00 | Third presentation to an association. | .... | ............ |
| 3/15/00 | Have referral book completed. | .... | ............ |
| 3/15/00 | Send out direct mail to people who've indicated an interest. | .... | ............ |
| 4/15/00 | Fourth presentation to an association. | .... | ............ |
| 4/15/00 | Print referral book. | .... | ............ |
| 4/30/00 | Publicity article published. | .... | ............ |
| 5/15/00 | Set up an appointment with a new association for presentation or news article | .... | ............ |
| 5/15/00 | Fifth presentation to an association. | .... | ............ |
| 6/15/00 | Sixth presentation to an association. | .... | ............ |
| 6/30/00 | Publicity article published. | .... | ............ |
| 7/15/00 | Seventh presentation to an association. | .... | ............ |
| 7/15/00 | Send out direct mail to people who've indicated an interest. | .... | ............ |
| 7/30/99 | Publicity article published. | .... | ............ |
| 8/15/00 | Set up an appointment with a new association for presentation or news article. | .... | ............ |
| 8/15/00 | Eighth presentation to an association. | .... | ............ |
| 9/15/00 | Ninth presentation to an association. | .... | ............ |
| 9/30/00 | Publicity article published. | .... | ............ |
| 10/15/00 | Tenth presentation to an association | .... | ............ |
| 10/15/00 | Set up an appointment with a new association for presentation or news article. | .... | ............ |
| 10/30/00 | Publicity article published. | .... | ............ |
| 11/15/00 | Send out direct mail to people who've indicated an interest. | .... | ............ |
| 11/15/00 | Eleventh presentation to an association. | .... | ............ |
| 11/30/00 | Publicity article published. | .... | ............ |
| 12/15/00 | Twelfth presentation to an association. | .... | ............ |

← I've found that marketers are twice as likely to accomplish tasks when they give themselves deadlines.

← The articles the Resnick's publish also add credibility when they are included in the referral and presentation folders.

# Budget

*Note*: Actual budget withheld at company's request.

| ITEM | | BUDGET |
|------|------|--------|
| Travel | . . . . . . . . . . . . . . . . . | . . . . . . . . . . . . . . . . |
| Entertainment | . . . . . . . . . . . . . . . | . . . . . . . . . . . . . . . . |
| Direct Mail | . . . . . . . . . . . . . . . . | . . . . . . . . . . . . . . . . |
| Referral Books | . . . . . . . . . . . . . . . | . . . . . . . . . . . . . . . . |
| Sales Materials | . . . . . . . . . . . . . . . . | . . . . . . . . . . . . . . . . |
| Training | . . . . . . . . . . . . . . . . | . . . . . . . . . . . . . . . . |
| Presentation Materials | . . . . . . . . . . . . . . | . . . . . . . . . . . . . . . . |
| | Total | . . . . . . . . . . . . . . . . |

Resnick Associates partners, marketers, and collaborators on plan: Terrance and Lee Resnick.

**Marketing Plan/2000**
**Southwest Painting**
**Pennsville, New Jersey**

## Executive Summary

Southwest Painting is a small painting firm that paints home interiors and exteriors and decks in the Southwestern section of New Jersey. The company has targeted as its best customer group people who live in expensive new bedroom communities in Southwest New Jersey. These new homes have basic paint jobs and the owners are ready for an upper-echelon paint job after two years when settlement cracks appear throughout the house. Southwest Painting has specialized services for these target customers, including re-nailing, spackling, and re-taping throughout the homes as required. The company's biggest advantage is that it has specialized equipment to apply the new Multispec Special Effects paints, which are a replacement for wallpaper. The result is the owners end up with a superior interior look, which is perfect match for the value of the homes.

Southwest Painting's goal in 2000 is $250,000 in revenue, which equates to repainting part of the interiors, or decks, of 40 to 60 homes in the target area. The company plans on doing this by use of a referral network of current customers, publicity in local papers, and through alliances with a carpet store chain, caterer, and with home a interiors multilevel marketing organization in Southwest New Jersey.

> Identifying the best target customer is a great marketing tactic for any business.

## Situation Analysis

### Internal Audit

**Company Background and Description.** Wayne Mills, the company owner, has been a painter for painting contractors for almost 20 years, painting a wide variety of jobs including commercial and residential work. In the mid-1990s, Mills worked extensively at the Hotel Dupont, an elegant hotel in Wilmington, Delaware, and a national historical landmark. Mills made all the repairs related to painting and wall coverings, including spackling, painting, and wallpaper repair. The Hotel has a high standard for maintenance that is well known in Southwest New Jersey.

While working at the Hotel, Mills made contact with a few residents of some newer housing developments in his area who wanted to repaint their homes so that they would stand out when they entertained their friends. These contacts wanted a special look, but they also were

> Mills's background was a key factor in his success in lining up alliance partners, as well as in establishing himself as a premium supplier.

demanding that every detail in their home be perfect. These new homes had natural settlement cracks in the walls and numerous other small defects from the original wallboard installation and subsequent paint jobs. Mills painted both the interiors and decks of these homes, and the owners were thrilled with the high quality of the work.

Mills continued to get occasional part-time work from the neighborhood on a referral basis, from people who wanted the interiors of their homes to be reflective of the home's overall value. His customers appreciated Mills's fastidiousness, and his ability to apply Mulitspec Special Effects coatings in a way that highlighted a room.

Many of Mills's original customers loved to entertain and they started to redecorate their homes every two years just to get a new look. As more and more new expensive bedroom communities were built in the area for Philadelphia commuters, Mills realized that the market was now large enough to go into business on his own.

The company has always differentiated itself from competitors through its concentration on what it calls "upper-echelon" interiors. The Multispec paint jobs it does are the center point of conversation for its customers, and the company has over 15 satisfied customers in the area who have had major jobs done by the company. The company wants to focus its attacks on high-end neighborhoods where construction is two to four years old and where settlement cracks have developed, often causing some wallboard nails to loosen and tape joints to show.

**Sales Trends.** Southwest Painters has been a part-time business through 1999, and 2000 will be its first year of full-time business.

## Company Strengths/Weaknesses

### Strengths
1. Company has a strong base of referral business in its targeted neighborhoods.
2. All the company's work is done by the founder, guaranteeing high-quality work on all jobs.
3. The company is the only painter in the area that specializes in the new Multispec-type coatings. It is also one of the only painting contractors in the area with the special high-volume, low-pressure equipment (versus airless spraying) that works best with Multispec coatings.
4. The company is the only one in the area that doesn't also do commercial buildings and other work that doesn't require the same attention to detail that Southwest Painting's customers require.

Marketers always benefit from having a special product, because it differentiates their business and gives them something to talk about to customers.

Special equipment reinforces the message that Southwest Painting is a premier supplier of upper-echelon paint jobs.

### Weaknesses

1. Few new or untrained painters can handle the detailed work required by the target customer group. That limits the number of customers the company can take on.
2. The company doesn't have an office person to handle paperwork, phone calls, and sales work.
3. The company is unknown outside of its small group of core customers.

## Customer Information

**Target Customers.** People who have moved into new high-end bedroom communities in Southwest New Jersey, particularly Swedesboro, Piles Grove, and Mullica Hill, over the last two to four years who want to upgrade the basic paint and decorating schemes that the contractor provided with the new home.

### Customer Profile

1. Desire a spectacular, innovative home interior.
2. Like to entertain.
3. Are professionals and have income over $100,000.
4. Decorate frequently, typically every two to three years.
5. Live in the newer bedroom communities of Swedesboro, Piles Grove, and Mullica Hill.
6. Are willing to pay a premium for an upper-echelon painting service.

**Customer Buying Pattern.** While some of Southwest Painting's customers have been trendsetters, willing to pay $5,000 to $8,000 for a new look, the bulk of its business will come from people who will only buy after they are comfortable that the new look will work in their home. They need reassurance and referrals before stepping out with the Multispec look in their home. They also need to see that Southwest Painting's repair of raised nails, spackling, and repairing of stress cracks returns the home into like-new condition. Southwest Painting needs to reinforce the comfort level of its target audience looking to purchase an extensive interior repainting project before they will buy.

## Industry Profile

**Industry Trends.** The small-to-midsize painting contractor industry has traditionally relied on commercial buildings—either industrial factories, office buildings, government buildings—apartments, new home construction, and retail stores for the bulk of their business. Some contractors have painted home exteriors, power-washed aluminum siding, or have done interior paper and wallpapering. Most of the interior decorating of homes has been done by small

Characterizing target customers to the detail of people who love to entertain increases referrals because they will have many people over to their homes.

People will pay a premium price when you give them what they want.

companies that specialize in wallpaper installation. Painting contractors handled only a small percentage of the work in upper-echelon decorating jobs.

New paint systems that have come out such as the Multispec Special Effects Coatings have challenged wallpaper's dominance in the market. The coatings act like seamless wallpaper, and are more durable, longer lasting, and more easily cleaned than wallpaper. Additionally, people are wallpapering less and painting more as more open home styles become popular.

New home contractors in Southwest New Jersey are still painting new homes as if they will be wallpapered. They use wallboard nails rather than screws, which can easily come out as the house settles in the first year or two. They use basic paint, and a minimal amount of joint compound over the taped joints. The paint job is fine when the house is first built, and also works well if the homeowner decorates with wallpaper. The flaws in the walls start to show when the house settles and the homeowner has to decide whether to have the home wallpapered or repainted.

Market knowledge allows marketers to fine-tune their marketing strategy.

### Competitor Audit

There are about 20 competitors in the Southwest New Jersey area. They include:

R & R Custom Paint
Pro Spec Painting
Industrial & Commercial Painting
Regal Custom Paint and Wallpaper
Brennan Painting

These competitors will all paint homes, but none of them market their Multispec-type coating expertise, nor do any of them concentrate exclusively on upper-echelon interior painting. These firms are all larger than Southwest Painting, and all have additional employees. Southwest Painting stresses its "tender loving care" approach to each home, and its small size and special painting capabilities set it apart in the market.

## Positioning

### Positioning Statements

1. Southwest Painting is the premier upper-echelon painter in Southwest New Jersey.
2. Southwest Painting's attention to details in finishing a wall before painting, and its specialty paints and techniques produce the finest looking home interiors in the area.

3. Southwest Painting's use of Multispec paint as an accent decoration in entertaining rooms guarantees a spectacular room that will impress virtually every visitor.

## Rationale for Strategy

1. Southwest Painting's target neighborhoods have large upper-end homes. The home owners want their homes to have interiors that are as impressive as their exteriors.
2. Southwest Painting's target customers like to entertain and want a spectacular entertaining environment.
3. Southwest New Jersey's sandy soil on top of a clay base leads to extensive settling in most homes. This creates problems with the finish of the walls.
4. The company wants to turn its small size into an asset rather than a liability. The attention to detail, special coating capability, and entertainment focus all set it apart from its competition.

# Marketing Tactics

## Product

The company will continue to focus on decks and the entertaining areas of home interiors. While the company does paint all of a home's interior, it will continue to concentrate on the areas that are most important to its target customers, which are all areas in or around the home that play an important role in entertaining.

A service company that knows about marketing creates services based upon its customers' desires.

## Pricing

The company will continue to set its pricing based on the Dodge Blue Book. These prices are for painting contractors and are about 20 percent to 30 percent higher than some local individual painters charge. The Blue Book prices work well as they reinforce Southwest Painting's image as a supplier of upper-echelon paint jobs, while still having industry standard pricing for union-quality paint jobs.

## Signs

Southwest Painting has 20 signs that it can post at its best customers during work and for a short period after the job is completed. Many of Southwest Painting's clients entertain neighbors frequently and signs in their yards act as an endorsement for the company's services. The signs can also be placed on the yards of the company's Home Decorator alliance partners.

## Brochures/Flyers

Southwest Painting will be printing a brochure on its computer that will show a series of home interiors in the Southwest New Jersey area that it has painted. The brochure will establish the dramatic looks that Southwest Painting can achieve as well as reinforce its image as the premier painter for the new high-end homes in the Southwest New Jersey area. This flyer will be used primarily for direct mail.

The company will also print a simple black-and-white flyer for referrals that will emphasize Southwest Painting's status as the premium supplier of upper-echelon paint jobs in the Southwest New Jersey area.

## Referral Strategy

Southwest Painting will keep past clients supplied with referral flyers and business cards that they can pass out to their friends. The flyers will help customers point out to their friends that they hired the best painter in Southwest New Jersey. The flyer will let customers look like a trendsetter to their friends, and allow Southwest Painting to reinforce its image as the market leader in innovative home interiors.

Southwest Painting will also offer a 10 percent discount to customers with homes in prominent locations provided it can leave its sign in the front yard for two months.

Marketing tactics don't have to be complicated to be effective. A simple referral in this case is worth thousands of dollars of advertising.

## Publicity

Multispec Special Effects Coatings is a new type of paint that is a great substitute for wallpaper. It also isn't well known by consumers. Southwest Painting will line up several homes as samples and then arrange for publicity stories in the *Gloucester County Times* and Vinewood daily papers. The article will feature different ways for homeowners to decorate their homes, but it will also mention that Multispec coatings are a specialty of Southwest Painting, and also refer to Southwest Painting in the pictures of the homes.

## Home Decorating Alliances

The Southwest New Jersey area has about twenty franchisees of Home Decorating, Inc. This is a network of part-time designers who have home parties and sell various things people can use to decorate their homes. In return for selling supplies, the franchisees receive free merchandise for themselves. These home decorators will recommend Southwest Painting and its Multispec coatings to their friends and clients. Southwest Painting will pay the home decorators a $100 finder's fee for every job it receives from one of their recommendations. Southwest Painting will also paint the home decorator's family rooms for a 25 percent discount once one of their recommendations results in a paid project for Southwest Painting. The company will prepare an informational folder for each representative including flyers, information about finder's fees, and flyers showing the options of the Multispec coatings.

## Catering Alliance

Southwest Painting's primary target customers enjoy entertaining. The company has arranged to paint the reception area of Italian Kitchens, a leading Southwest New Jersey caterer, in Multispec coatings at a reduced price. In return the caterer will allow Southwest Painting to put up a sign as well as leave its referral flyers and business cards in the reception area.

Marketers can greatly increase their influence when they look beyond the obvious alliance partners.

## Carpet Store Alliance

Southwest Painting has agreed to paint part of the interiors of 10 carpet stores with the Multispec system at a slightly reduced rate. In return the stores will keep flyers on Multispec coatings and Southwest Painting readily available in each store.

## Direct Mail

Southwest Painting will do a direct mailing in the two- or three-block area around a home that it is painting. The letter will mention that the company is painting the home of one of its neighbors, and include a brochure of some of the work it has done in the past, as well as a copy of the articles that will be printed in the local papers. The letters will be passed out to the homes in the area, or the owners' names and addresses can be looked up in the Cole's Directory and a letter sent to each home owner.

Direct mail program's targeted at specific neighborhoods work well when you have a job in the area.

## Implementation Plan

| DATE | ACTION | COST | PERSON RESPONSIBLE |
|------|--------|------|--------------------|
| 1/15/00 | Prepare brochure with photos of actual painted homes with the Multispec finish. Done on company computer. | $1,500 | WM |
| 1/31/00 | Prepare a referral brochure that can be passed out to clients. | 500 | WM |
| 1/31/00 | Purchase signs to be placed in clients' yards. | 400 | WM |
| 2/1/00 | Distribute referral flyers and cards to past clients. | | WM |
| 2/15/00 | Direct mail around current clients' homes. | 50 | WM |
| 2/25/00 | Redecorate the customer lobby of the caterer for the cost of Multispec paint. | | WM |
| 3/1/00 | Acquire photos and prepare several articles for local papers. | | |
| 3/15/00 | Direct mail around current clients' homes. | 50 | WM |
| 4/1/00 | Complete publicity story and contact writers to see what other information they may need. | | WM |
| 4/15/00 | Prepare an information folder for the Home Decorating representatives. | 200 | WM |
| 4/15/00 | Direct mail around current clients' homes. | 50 | WM |
| 5/15/00 | Direct mail around current clients' homes. | 50 | WM |
| 5/15/00 | Complete training of multilevel marketing company for home décor products. | | WM |
| 6/15/00 | Direct mail around current clients' homes. | 50 | WM |
| 7/15/00 | Direct mail around current clients' homes. | 50 | WM |
| 8/15/00 | Direct mail around current clients' homes. | 50 | WM |
| 9/15/00 | Direct mail around current clients' homes. | 50 | WM |
| 10/15/00 | Direct mail around current clients' homes. | 50 | WM |
| 1115/00 | Direct mail around current clients' homes. | 50 | WM |
| 12/15/00 | Direct mail around current clients' homes. | 50 | WM |
| | | Total $3,150 | |

Effective marketers have to constantly generate activity that will interest prospective customers.

## Budget Summary

| ITEM | BUDGET |
|---|---|
| Brochure/Flyer | $2,000 |
| Signs | 400 |
| Direct Mail | 550 |
| Information Folders for Home Decorators | 200 |
| | **Total $3,150** |

Plan collaborator: Wayne Mills, owner of Southwest Painting.

You can have a big marketing strategy on a small marketing budget. Finding a key customer characteristic often allows you to deliver high-value, high-profit programs to customers.

# Final Comments

"I don't have any money to do marketing" is a comment I frequently hear from small business owners. These two plans have very modest budgets, but that doesn't mean they have a modest marketing program. They both have well conceived strategies and effective implementation plans. The only thing they don't have is a high expense budget. Small companies really can't afford a big budget, so they need to be more creative in their strategies. I chose these two companies because on the surface they are similar to thousands of other small businesses, but in reality they have implemented effective marketing programs that have set them apart in the marketplace.

There are several other points of note in these two plans. First, notice how both companies searched for that one special nugget of customer information that allowed them to penetrate the market. Resnick Associates discovered that customers want to have a slow and easy sales cycle with plenty of information. Southwest Painting learned that its best prospects like to entertain. That little nugget is all marketers need to set their business apart. Southwest Painting's strategy is especially impressive. It captures a unique high-value strategy that allows the company to charge premium prices while still differentiating its business. Discovering this one key marketing fact doesn't come from just a cursory evaluation of the market. It comes from talking to many potential customers with an open mind and listening to just what they are telling you.

Second, note both companies' use of alliances. Alliances, partnerships, cross promotions, and any other sort of cooperative marketing program are far and away the most cost-effective way to get new customers. Plus they will get you the most customers. Small business marketers simply can't afford the high costs of advertising and should do everything possible to form partnerships to cut their marketing costs.

Finally, notice the efforts these companies have taken to make themselves special in the marketplace. Resnick Associates has helped sponsor family-business units at university entrepreneur programs, and Southwest Painting purchased special equipment to emphasize its capabilities in creating an upper-echelon paint job. Neither effort probably has a direct payoff. But each one helps its company create an indelible image in the minds of its prospects—an image that will produce a steady stream of customers over the next few years. That sustained market relevance is exactly what every marketer should strive for in each year's marketing plan.

## Marketing on a Tiny Budget

Contrary to popular opinion, you don't need a huge marketing budget to do an effective marketing job. You just need to be creative. First, find that one special customer characteristic you can focus on, and then use a variety of low-cost tactics to reach customers. Marketers with small budgets may need to spend more time on their strategy to find the right combination of positioning tactics to succeed, but it can be done no matter how small your budget is. Use this checklist below to see if you've done your homework to succeed with a low cost marketing budget.

> If you don't have the money, you need to spend more time setting up marketing alliances and referral networks. The benefit is that you will create a low-cost and highly effective marketing program.

| | YES | NO |
|---|---|---|
| 1. Have you discovered a key customer characteristic that will set you apart from your competition? | _____ | _____ |
| 2. Have you done at least one or two things, or do you have one or two special features, to help you stand out from the competition? | _____ | _____ |
| 3. Do you have a comprehensive referral program to take advantage of the customers you do have? | _____ | _____ |
| 4. Have you considered and approached all types of alliance partners including alliances with companies that: | | |
| a. Have complementary products (i.e., carpet stores for Southwest Painting)? | _____ | _____ |
| b. Could sell your products for a commission or finder's fee (i.e., the multilevel marketing organization for Southwest Painting)? | _____ | _____ |
| c. Focus on the same target customer (i.e., the catering company for Southwest Painting)? | _____ | _____ |
| d. Can give you access to your target customer (i.e., the associations that Resnick Associates works with)? | _____ | _____ |

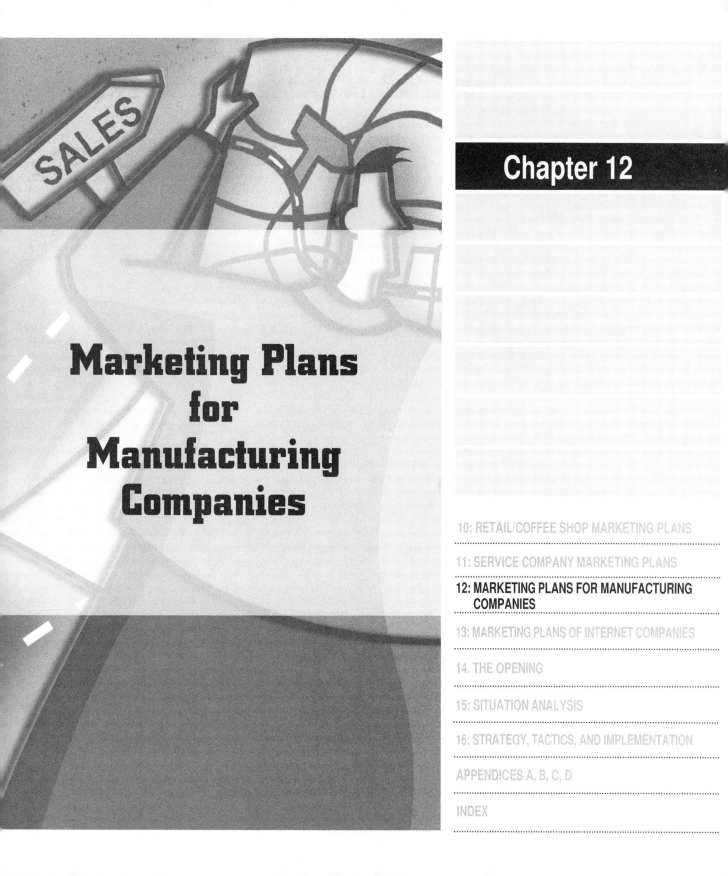

# Chapter 12

# Marketing Plans for Manufacturing Companies

10: RETAIL/COFFEE SHOP MARKETING PLANS

11: SERVICE COMPANY MARKETING PLANS

**12: MARKETING PLANS FOR MANUFACTURING COMPANIES**

13: MARKETING PLANS OF INTERNET COMPANIES

14. THE OPENING

15: SITUATION ANALYSIS

16: STRATEGY, TACTICS, AND IMPLEMENTATION

APPENDICES A, B, C, D

INDEX

Marketing Plan 2000
Safeplay Systems, Inc.
Marietta, Georgia

Prepared by Robert Gredys
President

## Executive Summary

*Author's note*: This plan doesn't contain actual sales and budget numbers because the company considers that information proprietary. The original plan does contain this information.

### Background

Safeplay Systems is a nine-year-old multimillion-dollar company that sells playground equipment primarily to day care centers. Its target market includes day care centers associated with churches, private schools, and small day care chains. The company has a full product line that focuses on equipment for younger children from two to five, although it is adding equipment for infants (age 12 months) and toddlers (age 18 months) in order to better serve its day care market.

The company's major competitive advantage is that its equipment is made from recycled materials and sold under the EcoPlay brand name. The company markets its products through four outside company salespeople and a network of 30 representatives nationwide. Its primary nationwide marketing effort is through trade shows that are well attended by day care providers.

### Problems and Opportunities

Targeting the specific market of day care centers allows Safeplay to produce the products that day care centers desire.

Safeplay has traditionally focused on the day care market, which is much less competitive than the park and recreation market. More competitors are coming into the young children market (two to five years old) as day care centers continue to increase. Currently, 20 million preschool children are in day care centers, and that number is expected to continue to grow. Safeplay's major competitors include large competitors such as Little Tykes Commercial Division, which is owned by Rubbermaid. Safeplay's EcoPlay product line is well received by churches, which make up 21 percent of the day care market, and it provides one of the top product lines for young children. Its emphasis on children younger than five also improves its position in the day care market, as it is a product category some of the larger competitors are not concentrating on.

The two problems that Safeplay Systems will be attacking this year are: first, the problem that purchase decisions for many churches and employer-connected day cares are made by people who have a limited amount of knowledge about the products available on the market; and second, that its representative network is not as strong as many competitors'.

Safeplay's plan is devised to adjust for two problems that are limiting the company's success.

## Year 2000 Strategies

Safeplay will continue to expand its line for young children, increase its presence in directories, especially construction directories, improve its representative network by introducing a representative advisory council and representative referral program, and emphasize at major trade shows the fact that its products are made out of recycled plastic.

# Market Conditions

## Market Segments

The overall playground market can be broken into several segments: (1) schools, (2) park and recreation playgrounds, (3) residential market, (4) large customer commercial market (i.e., playgrounds at McDonald's), and (5) day care centers. Safeplay Systems has chosen to compete in the day care market because it is the least competitive of the markets, and it is a market where customers value, and will pay for, products that better meet the needs of their users. Safeplay also chose the day care market because there was, and still is, not much equipment for infant to two-year-old children, who are most important to day care providers.

## Day Care Market Segments

According to *Child Care News*, the 100,000 licensed day care centers are divided into these categories:

| | |
|---|---|
| Independents | 26% |
| Church Affiliated | 21% |
| Public/Private Schools | 20% |
| Head Start | 7% |
| Employer Based | 4% |
| Chains | 3% |
| Other | 19% |

Small company marketers should look for product areas that major competitors are avoiding.

Safeplay Systems' main markets are independents, church affiliated, and private schools. These markets have smaller purchases and aren't pursued quite as vigorously by big competitors, and they are interested in buying top-quality equipment with the best features. Safeplay Systems' products are competitively priced, but staying with smaller, quality-conscious buyers helps Safeplay avoiding bidding wars from its larger competitors.

## Competitive Analysis

Safeplay has four major competitors in the day care market that are well established and have strong distribution networks of manufacturers' representatives. These competitors also compete in the park and recreations and school markets. They are:

**Gametime, Inc.** Fort Payne, Alabama. Gametime is one of the largest playground equipment suppliers in the United States. They have been in business since 1929, and are the number one supplier of community-built playgrounds. They offer fund-raising help for communities, generate 3-D drawings so communities can see what their playground will look like, and have introduced TotTime systems, which are geared toward both the park and recreation and day care market. They are just starting to target the day care market, but their size makes them a formidable competitor. Gametime has 375 employees and sales between $20 and $50 million.

**Landscape Structures**, Delano, Minnesota. This company is the leading innovator in the market, consistently producing innovative designs that kids like. One of the top two competitors in equipment for children two to five, and they also have products aimed at younger children. They also serve school and park and recreation markets. The company has a strong network of representatives and a strong presence throughout the country. Landscape Structures has 300 employees and sales between $20 and $50 million.

**Little Tykes Commercial Play Systems**. This is a division of Rubbermaid, and Little Tykes also sells playground equipment for residential, as well as playground, school, and day care use. The company has an established group of representatives; in many cases the current representatives had fathers who were the original Little Tykes representatives. The company is well-funded, well-known, and a major competitor. Little Tykes has 600 employees and sales in the $50 to $100 million range.

**Playworld Systems, Inc.** This competitor has a well designed product line, places a heavy emphasis on day care and younger children systems, and also has a strong representative network. This company is smaller that the other competitors and is also working hard to establish a pre-eminent national position in the day care market. Playworld has 150 employees, and sales of $10 to $20 million.

There are also two catalogs that target day cares that offer playground equipment. One is **ABC**, and the other is **Kaplan**. Both companies offer a broad array of products and are popular

---

Smart marketers choose market segments in which they can make money.

---

Gametime uses a value-added strategy for playgrounds, offering fund-raising help and 3-D drawings to build community support.

---

Safeplay has strong competitors that are considerably larger, but Safeplay still has plenty of opportunities to find its place in the market.

with day cares. They have their playground equipment made by outside manufacturers that otherwise are not in the playground market. Their sales in playground equipment aren't known, but they are significantly larger than Safeplay's.

## Market Trends

Currently 20 million preschool children and 24 million school-age children spend time in 100,000 licensed day care facilities. According to *Child Care News* there is a 20 percent growth rate in the number of licensed day care centers as the number of working mothers increases both from two-parent working families, and from mothers who are moving off of welfare. Many of the new children entering day care are from poor families leaving welfare, and the one group picking up much of this day care load are churches, which is one of the best markets for Safeplay Systems.

The other major market trend that benefits Safeplay is the trend toward playground equipment for infants and toddlers. This market is new and Safeplay has already placed several products into this market. Some large competitors are slower introducing infant and toddler products and this delay gives Safeplay an opportunity to increase its share of the add-on market, which are purchases day care centers make to add to their playground.

# Situation Analysis

## Product Line

Safeplay has a full product line for children from infants to 13 years old. The emphasis of its product line is on children under five. Safeplay plans to continue to offer its full product line, but places special emphasis on infant and toddler lines of equipment that are currently a strong seller among day care centers. Safeplay frequently custom-designs systems to meet the needs of day care centers, but it also offers a standard product line, which includes:

> **The Charlestown Totville**. A small tower and slide set designed for toddlers.

> **The Peachtree Center**. Larger system with two slides, a store front, tower, and under-deck play area. For children two to five.

> **Sand & Fun Play Islands**. Shaded play area that combines with a variety of options including slides, crawl tubes, spiral climbers, tree climbers, and learning panels. Ages two to five.

Small companies can move fast and seize new market opportunities before larger competitors can react.

**The Georgian Tower**. Has a spiral slide, fun climbers, and many learning panel options. Ages two to five.

**The Ascot Twin Towers**. Includes a slide and a clatter bridge with two shaded towers and many climbing options. Ages two to five.

**Cartersville Fun Center**. Two towers with lots of slides and a crawl tube. Ages two to five.

**Crabapple Funville**. Three towers, tic-tac-toe panels, clatter bridge, crawl tubes, and the option of adding many climbers and learning panels.

**Toss and Fun Ball**. A large receptacle that adjusts to different heights that kids throw balls though.

**Fun & Activity Center**. Ground-level activities for toddlers and infants. Swings, benches, and other standard playground items are also available.

## Competitive Positioning

Safeplay Systems is the only manufacturer of playground systems that are made from recycled plastic. Plastic has major advantages over wood and metal because maintenance costs are eliminated, a major concern of day care centers which often have only minimal custodial help. Safeplay's EcoPlay line is the only one on the market that is made from recycled plastic. The environmental savings that EcoPlay represents is a major selling point to day care centers associated with churches.

## Marketing Strengths/Weaknesses

Safeplay's major strengths are that its EcoPlay system offers a major benefit that is important to its target customers, day care centers associated with churches. It also offers a strong product line that is safe, maintenance free, and backed up with sales and service. The product line is somewhat well known to day care providers through the company's attendance over the last ten years at two key trade shows: the National Association for the Education of Young Children and the National Childcare Convention.

The company's weaknesses include its small size, poor representative coverage in some areas, and their lack of name recognition. The last point, name recognition, is important because in many cases their target customers will have people buying equipment who may only buy it once or twice. This is especially true at churches where the people on a day care centers board

**Safeplay has fun names for its products, which emphasizes that they are fun to play on.**

**When all their competitors are large, small companies have to make sure they have a strong distinguishing feature.**

will change every few years. Contributing to the company's name recognition is the fact that it doesn't have a prominent position in many key directories and doesn't attend park and recreation trade shows that its competitors attend. Safeplay Systems doesn't attend those shows because it doesn't target that highly competitive market.

## Distribution

Safeplay has four company salespeople located at its headquarters in the Atlanta area as well as having 30 representatives, seven to ten of whom do an excellent job. Safeplay has a unique approach with its representatives. It sets a price that it charges the representatives and then allows the representatives to set their own sales price. The representatives are really acting as distributors, and they are responsible for billing and collecting from customers.

This approach has two benefits for the representative. First, it allows the representative to earn more money. Second, and more important, the system allows the representatives to offer, and charge for, the value-added services its customers want. The representatives are free to charge for installation, yearly maintenance checks, and assistance in designing the playground area. These services are highly valued by day care centers that purchase playground equipment infrequently. The value-added services also allow representatives to keep closer contact with day care customers.

While some representatives do an outstanding job, others don't. Part of the problem is that there is not a good communication system between representatives. In the year 2000, Safeplay will be setting up a representative Advisory Council to help provide direction to the company, and to act as mentors with poor performing representatives.

Always look for ways to improve the quality of your distribution network.

## Pricing

Safeplay is not able to compete in competitive pricing situations such as McDonald's, large chains of day care centers, and park and recreation, and public school programs where the equipment is let out for bid. Instead it has focused on smaller day care accounts, especially those that are associated with churches, where its pricing is competitive, and its feature of being made out of recycled plastic is especially prized by customers. The other benefit of Safeplay's target market is that churches want the value-added installation and maintenance service that Safeway's representatives provide. Competitors constantly go after the big dollar sales at public schools and parks, and don't spend the time delivering value-added installation and planning services to their customers. Competitors also do a poor job of follow-up and customer service after a sale has been made.

## Company Trends

Safeplay Systems has had steadily increasing sales over the last years. Originally it had a retail store and concentrated on sales in the Atlanta area. The company has steadily increased its sales anywhere from 5 percent to 25 percent per year and has developed a national sales base. It has added representatives that concentrate on the church, private school, and small chain day care market niche. The company has focused on this market segment and has designed its product line and sales strategy to meet this market's needs. With this focus in place the company plans on fine-tuning its sales and distribution strategy to expand sales in its chosen market niche.

## Problems/Opportunities

### Problems

1. Most buyers of day care equipment only purchase an original setup once or twice. They aren't well informed of their choices and they may go to a well known brand or be swayed by a referral either from another day care, or a park and recreation department.
2. Safeplay has a much smaller base of customers than other day care playground suppliers. This limits its ability to generate add-on business when a day care decides to add to its playground.
3. Only about 25 to 30 percent of Safeplay's representative network is doing a good job marketing its product.
4. Safeplay has a much smaller marketing budget than many of its major competitors.

### Opportunities

1. Safeplay does have a few highly motivated representatives who want to help the company succeed.
2. Safeplay's EcoPlay product line is the highest quality line on the market made of recycled plastic.
3. Smaller buyers such as day care centers associated with churches and private schools place a premium on buying the best available equipment. These buyers typically aren't looking for the lower price, and the fact that EcoPlay is made from recycled plastic is often an important feature to this market.
4. Safeplay is a leader in getting out infant and toddler playground equipment that is no more than 16 inches from the ground. Day cares are buying this equipment, as the young child is too small and is not fully physically developed enough to play on equipment built for children two to five.

5. Safeplay hasn't been listed in construction directories such as the Blue Book. These directories are often the first source of information for new day care centers where buyers are unfamiliar with the market. Safeplay can get in these directories for a modest sum.

## Strategy for 2000

### Positioning Statement

Safeplay produces the playground of the future, 100 percent made from recycled plastic geared toward the needs of church and private school–affiliated day care centers. Products are designed for children from one to 13, with most products geared to children from one to five. Safeplay Systems' products meet all safety specifications, are easy to install and maintain, and are the perfect product for day care centers with minimal custodial support.

### Major New Activities in 2000

1. Set up a Representative Advisory Council composed of the top Safeplay representatives. Representatives will provide guidance to the company, plus offer suggestions and mentoring to poor performing representatives. The members of the Representative Advisory Council will receive a 1.5 percent override for three years on all additional sales made by the representatives they are mentoring. Safeplay will offer a 2.5 percent override for three years for new representatives who are recruited by members of the Representative Advisory Council.
2. Increase its listings in key directories that are used by day care centers, especially the Blue Book.
3. Increase attendance at local and regional shows through its representatives, such as the Minnesota Association for the Education of Young Children (MNAEYC) convention and the regional shows.
4. Put a new Web site online that can be accessed through a variety of different Internet sources, including the Blue Book for people searching for ideas.
5. Put out a small booklet on the Internet site, and also make it available in print format, discussing how to choose equipment for infants and toddlers.
6. Concentrate on obtaining government GSA business.
7. Seek other applications for EcoPlay outside of the playground business.

When you are a small competitor, specialize in something important to your customers, even if it is just a small part of what they buy.

Improving distribution can have a dramatic impact a on small company's sales.

Little information is available about what type of playground equipment works best for infants and toddlers.

## Marketing Tactics

### Product

Safeplay plans on introducing several new products aimed primarily at younger children, with at least one or two of the products being for infants and toddlers. Several low-height learning panels for infants and toddlers will be included. The emphasis will continue to be EcoPlay and its recycled plastic feature, which is unique to Safeplay Systems.

### Pricing

A good marketing plan keeps emphasizing the company's key advantages.

Safeplay Systems will continue its current pricing policies, which offers competitive pricing for independent day care centers and church-affiliated day cares. Safeplay won't try to match the discounts for larger customers such as day care chains or fast-food chains like McDonald's. Safeplay will also keep its policy of selling its product to its representatives for a set cost and then allowing them to set their own final price. This allows the representatives to react to pricing from small local suppliers, drop prices at key accounts to penetrate a new market, and more important, to offer and charge for value-added installation services that can be key in selling individual day care accounts.

### Representative Advisory Council

Getting input from your top representatives typically motivates them to work harder on your line.

The company will start a Representative Advisory Council effective January 1, 2000. In the past the company has met with several of its top representatives to gain advice on market conditions, sales tactics, and product innovations. The representatives provided key information and they genuinely appreciated being asked for input. This year the company will formalize the Representative Advisory Council to gain better information, but more importantly to help the company convert more of its representatives in the field into top producers. The company will offer a small commission override on sales to encourage the top representatives to assist poor performing representatives. Safeplay will also offer its top representatives an override commission on any representatives they recruit to fill open territories.

### Directory Listings

Safeplay Systems will be listed in the Blue Book Construction Directory in the year 2000. This directory includes products in a wide variety of categories including playground equipment. The Blue Book also has an excellent, easy-to-use Web site. It is one of the first resources people use when looking for equipment that they don't buy frequently. All of Safeplay's major competitors are in the Blue Book. Safeplay will also be in the directory published by *Early Childhood News* and will look into other directories as they become known.

## Web Site

The Company has started work on its Web site and it will be on the Internet in 2000. It is a basic site that is geared toward day care operators. The company has budgeted money to finish its site and to upgrade it over the next year.

## Domain Name Site Registration

The company will maintain the domain names: safeplaysystems and ecoplay.

## Publicity

The company will put together at least one article for *Early Childhood News* regarding playground equipment for children through 18 months old. The company will use an expert in the area to talk about what equipment works best, and then have references to its equipment throughout the article. The article will also be put into a pamphlet and made available through a variety of Web sites targeted at day care providers. The pamphlet will emphasize Safeplay's position as a leader in products for young children. It will also help generate additional leads for Safeplay, especially with new day care centers that may not have heard of Safeplay. The company also hopes to make a presentation at the MNAEYC Conference.

You should have an active publicity program when you aren't sure what customers will be buying in the next year.

## Advertising

Safeplay Systems limits its advertising to directories in *Early Childhood News*, which is widely read by day care providers.

Safeplay Systems will also hire a local Atlanta company specializing in setting up interlinks to other Web pages geared toward day care providers. This company will be hired once the free pamphlet on playgrounds for young children is ready.

## Direct Mail

The company will not do any direct mail this year.

## Trade Shows

Safeplay will attend the National Childcare Convention and the annual convention of the National Association of Young Children. Through its Representative Advisory Council the company will also be working to encourage its representatives to attend state and regional shows.

## Printed Informational Materials

Safeplay will publish a pamphlet covering the topic of designing playgrounds for very young children. The article will include the publicity article written about Safeplay products as well as other articles written on the topic that have already been published.

When you're up against big competitors, free informational pamphlets on an important topic is typically a better investment than advertising.

## Implementation Plan 2000

*Note*: The store's actual plan lists costs and the person responsible for making sure the activity occurs. They are deleted here because the information is confidential.

| DATE | ACTION | COST | PERSON RESPONSIBLE |
|------|--------|------|--------------------|
| 12/01/99 | Register domain names and *www.ecoplaysystems.com*. | . . . . | . . . . . . . . . . . . . |
| 1/1/00 | Introduce Representative Advisory Council Program. | . . . . | . . . . . . . . . . . . . |
| 1/10/00 | Locate freelance writer for article on toddler and infant playground equipment. | . . . . | . . . . . . . . . . . . . |
| 2/15/00 | Locate articles from past magazine issues on infant and toddler playgrounds. Acquire the rights to reprint articles in a pamphlet. | . . . . | . . . . . . . . . . . . . |
| 3/10/00 | First Representative Advisory Council meeting. | . . . . | . . . . . . . . . . . . . |
| 3/15/00 | Send articles to magazine for publishing in May or June. | . . . . | . . . . . . . . . . . . . |
| 3/15/00 | Assign top representatives to mentor poor performing representatives. | . . . . | . . . . . . . . . . . . . |
| 4/15/00 | Publish a schedule for representatives that lists all the state and regional shows that representatives will be attending. | . . . . | . . . . . . . . . . . . . |
| 4/15/00 | Complete Web page and go onto the Internet. | . . . . | . . . . . . . . . . . . . |
| 4/15/00 | Hire Web site consultant to locate and establish other sites with interlink connections. | . . . . | . . . . . . . . . . . . . |
| 4/15/00 | National Childcare Convention. | . . . . | . . . . . . . . . . . . . |
| 4/15/00 | Introduce new products for infants and toddlers at National Childcare Convention. | . . . . | . . . . . . . . . . . . . |
| 5/15/00 | Sign up for listing in Blue Book Directory. | . . . . | . . . . . . . . . . . . . |
| 6/1/00 | Complete and print pamphlet on playground equipment for young children. | . . . . | . . . . . . . . . . . . . |
| 6/15/00 | Place directory advertisement in *Child Care News*. | . . . . | . . . . . . . . . . . . . |
| 9/15/00 | Second Representative Advisory Meeting. | . . . . | . . . . . . . . . . . . . |
| 10/10/00 | Introduce new products for the November Convention of the National Association of Young Children. | . . . . | . . . . . . . . . . . . . |
| 11/1/00 | Review representatives' performance and target territories where representatives need to be replaced. | . . . . | . . . . . . . . . . . . . |
| 11/15/00 | National Association of Young Children Convention. | . . . . | . . . . . . . . . . . . . |

◄— Stories written by freelance writers will be oriented more toward giving readers information. This orientation will increase your chances of getting the article published.

◄— You get cost-effective exposure when you introduce products at major trade shows.

Marketing Plan 2000
Schulco
Clear Lake, Minnesota

## Executive Summary

### Company Description and Background

Schulco is a small manufacturer of closed loop non-ferrous casting equipment for the manufacturer of aluminum castings. A closed loop system is one that carries out a significant part of the manufacturing process automatically with minimal to no labor involvement. Schulco has the only closed loop system available for the manufacture of small to midsize quantities of aluminum permanent mold production, and it is an ideal product for small to midsize foundries as well as independent and end user–owned machine shops.

A prototype of the Schulco 2000 has been in use for nine years at its Clear Lake, Minnesota, plant, producing hundreds of thousands of parts. Schulco has machined the castings into final parts for its customer base of machine and equipment manufacturers. Schulco has started to sell its Schulco 2000 to other foundries in late 1999, and is planning a full-fledged marketing effort in 2000.

### Target Market/Benefits

Schulco's target market are the 500 to 600 foundries with 50 or fewer employees and the 8,000 small machine shops in the country. The Schulco 2000 offers two benefits to the foundries. First it cuts cost by eliminating labor for a significant part of the operation; and two it helps the foundries overcome the severe worker shortage that currently exists for foundries. The major benefits for machine shops, which normally wouldn't cast any of their own parts, is that they will gain a competitive cost advantage in bidding out jobs by adding a Schulco 2000 to their facility. The machining industry is very competitive, and bringing castings in-house cuts the price significantly. The Schulco 2000 is also an ideal piece of equipment when a machine shop helps small outsourced vendors set up their own casting operations.

Not all customer groups can be segmented into well defined groups. You still need to do your best to define your customer.

### The Product/Operation

In a typical casting operation of small parts, an operator has to use a ladle to place molten metal into the mold. After three to five minutes the part is extracted from the mold and placed in a bin. Another person has to cut off the extra material or flashing that is around the part, and one of these two people then has to return the extra metal to the furnace to be used again. In the case of the Schulco 2000, all of these steps are completed in the closed loop system without any labor. The parts are then cleaned and sent off for machining in both the Schulco and conventional systems.

In addition to cutting labor costs, the Schulco 2000 also yields over 75 percent (weight of completed castings divided by weight of initial metal) compared to about 65 percent for conventional casting methods of small parts. Employee safety is another feature of the Schulco 2000, as foundries typically have high workmen's compensation rates due to injuries. Another feature of the Schulco 2000 is that it can run 24 hours a day, seven days a week with only minor monitoring to help companies deliver big orders. There is also no lost time due to employee breaks, mistakes, or other lost time.

The Schulco 2000 sells for $50,000, and a complete system, including a furnace and robotic arm, for about $85,000. The Schulco 2000 was patented in 1998, and has patent protection until 2018.

## Marketing Objectives

Schulco intends to sell thirty Schulco 2000s this year, primarily through the use of an aggressive publicity program, card pack advertising, and the addition of several manufacturers' representatives. Total sales, including the robotic arm, will be $2.0 million. Schulco plans on coordinating with the already existing network of manufacturers' representatives of a furnace company to sell Schulco 2000 systems throughout the country. Schulco's goal is to have full representative and technical service support of the Schulco 2000 in the Midwest at the end of the year 2000.

← There can be no doubt about whether or not you meet a plan's goals when they are stated this clearly.

## Situation Analysis

### Company Description

Schulco is a manufacturer of non-ferrous machined parts for a variety of manufacturers. About 10 years ago Schulco developed the initial models of the Schulco 2000 in order to offer better pricing for its customers on machined parts that required extensive machining. At the time Schulco had only one employee, was run as a part-time business, and the closed loop casting system offered Schulco the ability to offer lower pricing, take on midsize orders, and continue operating with a small number of employees on a part-time basis. With the patent awarded in 1998, Schulco went to full-time operations, has added two employees, and is prepared to hire more as Schulco 2000 sales develop. Since 1998 Schulco has completed the engineering documentation and sourced all required parts for production. Initial market tests have shown that about 75 percent of the foundries contacted had interest in adding a closed loop system. An informal market survey with people experienced in the machining industry indicates about 10 to 15 percent of the machine shops will have an interest in adding a closed loop system that could significantly improve their bidding position.

Schulco was unable to determine common characteristics of interested customers. This would force the company to rely on representatives to find interested companies.

## Labor Savings from Equipment/Competitive Advantage

| MACHINE CHARACTERISTIC | ACTIONS ELIMINATED |
|---|---|
| Built-in pockets for use with the forklift and pallet jack | Jacking and blocking the machine when moving it |
| Automatic gating block closure | Closing the mold before pouring |
| Automatic and consistent timing of cooling cycle | Opening the mold early |
| Automatic degating | Manual degating |
| Returning gating system waste to furnace while hot | Cold returns |
| Automatic casting removal | Manual casting removal |
| Automatic die air-blast cleaning | Manual die air-blast cleaning |
| Automatic ejector pin lubrication | Manual ejector pin lubrication |
| Automatic tilt cylinder pulsing | Manual monitoring and resetting of tilt angle |

## Company Strengths and Weaknesses

### Strengths

1. Company has the only automated closed loop system for midsize production runs of permanent mold non-ferrous castings.
2. Product delivers three key customers' desires: lower cost, ability to attract more business, and operating with fewer employees.
3. Prototype version has been operating for several years without any problems. Yields, quality, and scrap rates have all exceeded industry norms.
4. Furnace manufacturers also benefit from the Schulco 2000 and may provide ideal alliance partners.

### Weaknesses

1. Company doesn't have an established name or performance record in the market.

Schulco emphasizes its advantage by using the technical term "closed loop system."

2. Gene Schultz, company president and the Schulco 2000 inventor, doesn't have a network of contacts in the market and doesn't have past employment history with an established molding manufacturer.
3. Company doesn't have an established distribution network.
4. Company needs to complete field testing of three or four units to better document the Schulco 2000's performance.

Schulco will have trouble succeeding without an alliance partner to help find viable prospects.

## External Audit

### Market Assessment

The aluminum castings market is a $35 to $40 billion market. The market is broken into several markets, including:

**Sand Castings**–Approximately 55 to 60 percent of the market. These are castings made of sand that have a shorter life cycle, but are ideal for larger parts where permanent tooling is prohibitively expensive. Projected to grow 100 percent in total over the next four years, primarily due to the increased number of aluminum automotive castings.

**Die Castings**–Approximately 15 to 20 percent of the market. High-pressure, high-volume, low-cost method of castings for high-volume production. Projected to grow 3 to 5 percent over the next four years.

**Low-Pressure Molding**–About 5 percent of the market. A bottom-loading molding system used to gain certain metallurgical advantages. Slow growth projected over next four years.

**Investment Castings**–Less than 5 percent of the market. High-cost manufacturing method used when close tolerance parts with complex shapes are required.

**Permanent and Semi-permanent Molding**–Approximately 15 to 20 percent of the market. Used for smaller to midsize parts with high production capacity. Projected growth 40 percent in total over the next four years. This is the Schulco 2000's target market. There are approximately 975 aluminum foundries doing permanent and semi-permanent molding in the United States.

Small companies will generate higher sales by concentrating on one market segment.

Aluminum castings are just the first step in a finished aluminum part. After casting, the parts are then machined to achieve close tolerances and to produce a satisfactory finish. As a rule on small parts the cost of the castings is about 35 to 45 percent of the final product cost, the machining is 35 to 45 percent of the final product cost with the remainder of the cost being miscellaneous expenses. Foundries are job shops for the most part, making castings to order for either end users or machine shops. In many cases, the foundry also performs machining to deliver a final product, which is typically used in the automotive, industrial machinery, transportation equipment, construction materials, and electric power generator markets. Very few foundries have proprietary products that they market directly to the end user. They are dependent on low-cost production to win bids.

## Competitor Audit

> Customers are always concerned about cost when they live in a cost-competitive world.

The major competitor in the market is Stahl Equipment Company, a $50 to $100 million manufacturer of aluminum castings and a wide assortment of products including molding equipment, control units, furnaces, mold equipment, mold components, and foundry supplies. Casting equipment represents 15 to 20 percent of Stahl's sales. Stahl basically has built the permanent mold aluminum casting business on its own and is still the market leader. Stahl has always kept the interest of foundries as its top priority and has a solid industry reputation. Stahl's biggest drawback is that it insists that foundries need to use tilt pour units versus a direct gravity feed on all parts, when many applications don't require a tilt pour system, which do a better job of avoiding voids in the molds.

The Schulco 2000s major advantage over Stahl is that it is a complete closed loop system. People may be able to configure Stahl equipment into a closed loop on their own, but Stahl's equipment doesn't come in a complete package like Schulco's. Stahl's pricing tends to be higher than other competitors.

Other smaller competitors include:

CMH Manufacturing Co., Cambridge, Massachusetts, over $5 million in sales
Loma Machine Co., Gorham, Maine, over $5 million in sales
Economy Industrial Corp, Ambridge, Pennsylvania, over $1 million in sales
Horst Continuous Casting, Somerville, New Jersey, over $1 million in sales
Raustmeal, USA, Bristol, Rhode Island, over $1 million in sales
George Fischer, Holly, Michigan, over $25 million in sales
M.A.S., German manufacturer, sales over $1 million in the United States

## Pricing

Pricing for somewhat comparable systems

- Stahl Specialty Company: $56,430. *Note*: No automatic gating cut-off or return of discarded material to the furnace. Die sizes up to 12 x 18.
- CMH Manufacturing: $34,660. *Note*: No gating cut-off, no return of discarded material, manual fill, manual tilt. Die sizes up to 12 x 18.
- Schulco 2000: $50,000. Includes automated die preheat and temperature maintenance, mold opening, gating system separation, casting system removal, casting removal, die air blast, mold closure, ejector pin lubrication. Die sizes up to 12 x 18.

One last competitive factor is that many foundries will buy components and build their own equipment. The cost is about one half to two thirds of buying new equipment. These home-made systems do not have the automated features of the Schulco 2000 and typically produce parts at a significantly higher per-piece price than the Schulco 2000.

## Complementary Products

One avenue open to Schulco is to form an alliance with a seller of complementary products. One of the best possible alliances is with companies that supply crucible furnaces, which are the furnaces that melt the aluminum prior to its being placed into the permanent mold. Some of the major companies in these areas are:

Palmer Manufacturing & Supply, Springfield, Ohio, sales over $1 million.
Thermtronix, Adelanto, California, sales over $5 million.
ABB Metallurgy, North Brunswick, New Jersey, sales over $50 million.
Dynarad Corp., San Leandro, California, sales over $5 million.

Schulco would be better off selling an entire system to its customers and it can only do that by joining with a furnace company. This partnership would also give Schulco access to the furnace company's manufacturers' representative network.

## Customer Information

The Schulco 2000 will run 24 hours per day, seven days per week unattended. Aluminum ingots need to be added to the furnace periodically, but for the most part the equipment runs without an operator. This saves foundries money, and it lessens their need for employees. But it also adds another feature that makes the product ideal for small machine shops and foundries with machine shops. A part takes about three minutes to cast, but only about a minute to machine. Running the Schulco 2000 allows the casting process to keep pace with the eight hour per day machining operation, which cuts inventory needs and simplifies production planning.

Schulco's customers are the 950 aluminum foundries that do permanent mold castings and 15,000 machine shops throughout the country. Each of these customer groups has different requirements that the Schulco 2000 helps meet.

**Foundry Market.** Foundries needs include: high quality, low cost, and high yield, which allows foundries to win more bids from its customers. These are the very qualities that the Schulco 2000 delivers. There is one factor regarding foundries that will make the product difficult to sell. Foundries will set up two to six manual molds of smaller parts for an operator, which means they need two to six castings systems. Often that means that they have a significant

---

Getting more orders is a much better feature than lower cost. Try to introduce revenue building features into your products.

---

Small companies often benefit by tying into another company's existing distribution network instead of spending the money to create their own.

---

Coordinating casting time to machining time is a unfamiliar feature to customers. This might make it a difficult feature to market.

investment in process equipment, which they aren't anxious to drop. Many foundries will keep operating this equipment. Schulco's only sale will be to companies that are expanding sales or having trouble hiring personnel. Schulco does have a big advantage with the 40 to 50 percent of the foundries with machine shops where the foundry can coordinate casting production and machining production into an in-time inventory and production system.

Schulco's target customers are small to midsize foundries, with or without machine shops, that want to set up closed loop production systems either to cut costs or to reduce the need for new hires.

**Machining Market.** The machine shop market, which includes machining centers at companies, as well as independent machine shops, is also a job shop business. The companies compete on price, quality, and delivery, and in many cases the machining center will order castings to complete the job. Machine shops are need to be cost competitive in order to obtain business. The Schulco 2000 offers them the opportunity to set up a closed loop system to produce castings that they need for machining parts. They can take advantage of this opportunity without having to make a major space or resource commitment to a foundry operation. Schulco expects that 2 to 5 percent of small to midsize machine shops might be interested in adding a small foundry operation.

**Outsourced Vendors.** Castings for the most part are sent to machine shops, either independent shops, foundry machine shops, or machine shops at companies. They complete the part with machining. One other customer group to target would be tool regrinders and sharpeners. Frequently these are one- or two-man businesses that have close ties to many machine shops in their geographic region. They could easily set up a small foundry operation to service their machine shops. These entrepreneurs are always looking for profit-making opportunities, they have access to the management at machine shops, and they have the mechanical aptitude to run a foundry operation.

Sharpening is a very labor intensive service, and the sharpener's income is restricted by how much time they have available to perform work. The sharpeners are interested in any service that can make them more money and they will appreciate the ability to increase their income with a minimal amount of their own labor. There are approximately eight hundred independent sharpeners who do extensive work resharpening tools for machine shops. These people are easily reached through their main vendor, Foley Belsaw in Kansas City, through their trade magazine, *Sharpeners Report*, and through their annual trade show. Larger sharpeners have anywhere from $25,000 to $100,000 in equipment, and would be able to purchase or arrange a lease for a $60,000 package of products.

---

One of the reasons that Schulco uses the term "closed loop" is that it attracts the attention of the innovators Schulco needs to buy its equipment.

Schulco looked for customers in a nontraditional market because the product produces small parts, while foundries were more interested in large parts.

Sharpeners are a target customer group that is easy to find and can be reached through direct mail and sharpeners' magazines.

## Positioning Strategy

### Positioning Statements

For foundries: The Schulco 2000 is the market's only complete closed loop, gravity fed casting system that is ideal for small to midsize parts. The Schulco 2000 automates every casting manufacturing step prior to cleaning, cutting both labor and material costs.

For machine shops: The Schulco 2000 offers machine shops a way to offer lower priced products on midsize production runs by producing lower cost castings, which are about 40 percent of the total cost of an aluminum part.

For sharpeners: The Schulco 2000 offers an attractive money-making opportunity for selling castings to the sharpeners; existing customer base—machine shops. The Schulco 2000 offers sharpeners a closed loop system that requires only minimal oversight while producing parts twenty-four hours per day.

You should have a different positioning statement for each target customer group because each group has different needs.

### Strategies for 2000

1. Establish an agreement with a small furnace manufacturer to provide sales representative support on leads for the Schulco 2000 system, which includes a furnace, robotic arm, and a Schulco 2000.
2. Offer those representatives commission on sales of the Schulco 2000.
3. Run an extensive publicity program in foundry, machining, and metalworking magazines.
4. Run a coordinated program with *Sharpeners Report* to convey the income possibilities of having a Schulco 2000 system.

### Rationale for Strategy

Schulco is a small company with a limited marketing budget, no name recognition, and limited sales support. To overcome these problems, and still meet its goal of 30 units in the first year, the company needs to combine with a company with a sales representative network in place. The best candidate for this is a manufacturer of crucible furnaces, which are an integral part of the Schulco 2000 system. Some of the smaller crucible manufacturers may be interested in picking up an additional 30 to 40 furnaces per year. Having the leads funneled through the furnace company representatives will help the furnace company increase sales and give the representatives the opportunity to make an extra $5,000 commission on the $50,000 sale of a Schulco 2000. Without the support of another company and its representative network, it will be hard for Schulco to develop and support its sales base. The furnace representatives will also help generate referral customers in their area after they are able to sell their first system.

Setting up a distribution system from scratch is both expensive and time-consuming.

The next phase of Schulco's strategy is an extensive publicity program to a wide range of machining and metalworking magazines. Schulco can't effectively market its product to all the foundries due to its limited budget. It can however generate a significant amount of free publicity in foundry, machining, and metalworking magazines. Companies responding to the press releases should be receptive to a closed loop system in their facility. Publishing ten to 12 press releases should generate enough leads to interest a furnace company in working cooperatively with Schulco.

The third major program will be to first have the *Sharpeners Report* run a major story on how sharpeners can put together an automated closed loop casting system to increase their income. The focus of the story would be on how sharpeners can develop additional business with their already existing customer base. The inherent lower cost of castings from the Schulco 2000, along with the low overhead of the sharpeners, should allow them to bid competitively on many small to midsize parts.

## Marketing Tactics

### Brochures

Schulco needs to prepare slightly differing brochures for each market. The brochure can have much of the same content, with just the front page and some of the headlines different. The three brochure variations will be:

1. Foundry market
2. Machining market
3. Sharpener market

Schulco will not have a requirement for a large number of brochures, and rather than have the brochures printed, they will be stored on Schulco's computer and printed out as needed. The brochures will be customized to each of the three markets.

### Publicity Campaign

Schulco will be sending out press releases three times during the year to the following magazines:

*American Fastener Journal*, McGuire Fasteners, Inc., 293 Hopewell Drive, Powell, Ohio
614-848-3232

One of the problems small companies have trying to market to different customer groups is that they need multiple strategies.

New printer technology allows marketers to actually customize brochures for every prospect.

*American Machinist*, Penton Media, Inc., 1100 Superior Ave., Cleveland, Ohio, 216-696-7000

*Automatic Machining*, Screw Machine Publishing Co., Inc., 1066 Gravel Road, Suite #20, Webster, NY 14580-1769, 716-787-0820

*Canadian Machinery & Metalworking*, Maclean Hunter Publishing Ltd., Maclean-Hunter Building, 777 Bay St. Fl. Toronto ON M5W 1A7 Canada, 416-593-3193

*Casting Source Directory*, American Foundrymen's Society, Inc., 505 State St., Des Plaines, IL 60016-2267, 847-824-0181

*Cutting Tool Engineering*, CTE Publications, Inc., 400 Skokie Blvd., Ste. 395, Northbrook, IL 60062-7903, 708-559-4444

*Foundry International*, Argus Business Media Ltd., Queensway House, 2 Queensway, Red Hill, Surrey RH1 1QS, England

*Foundry Management & Technology*, Penton Media Inc., 1100 Superior Ave., Cleveland, OH 44114-2543, 216-696-7000

*Home Shop Machinist*, Village Press, Inc., 2779 Aero Park Drive, Traverse City, MI 49686-9100, 616-946-3712

*Metalworking Digest*, Cahners Business Information, 301 Gibralet Drive, PO Box 650, Morris Plaines, NJ 07950-3409, 973-898-9281

*Metalfax Magazine*, Adams Business Media, 29100 Aurora Road, Suite 200, Solon, OH 44139-1855, 440-248-1125

*Modern Application News*, Nelson Publishing, 2504 Tamiami Trail, N. Nokomis, FL 34275-3482, 941-966-9251

*Modern Castings*, American Foundrymen's Society, 505 State St., Des Plaines, IL 60016-2267, 847-824-7848

*Modern Machine Shop*, Gardner Publications, Inc., 6915 Valley Ave. Cincinnati, OH 45244-3029, 513-527-8800

*Tooling and Production Magazine*, Adams Business Media, 29100 Aurora Road, Ste. 200, Solon, OH 44139-1855, 440-248-1125

Magazine stories typically attract three to four times the number of leads as a third- or quarter-page ad.

Schulco will also arrange for a story regarding extra profit possibilities for sharpeners to be included in the Sharpeners Report.

## Distribution

Rather than set up a separate distribution system, Schulco plans on teaming up with an already existing distribution system from one of the furnace companies. Schulco will use the leads and the furnace company can offer complete system. This will help sales of the Schulco 2000 and it will help the furnace company partner create a differential advantage over its competitors. Schulco will run its publicity program first, and then after it has lead potential, approach furnace manufacturers.

Establishing a distribution network is Schulco's most important marketing task.

## Sharpener Approach

In July, once the distribution channel has been established, Schulco will work with the *Sharpeners Report* to explain the program. The product will be offered through the furnace representatives who can help install the equipment for sharpeners.

## Sales Support Package

Schulco will prepare a sales support package for the representatives with detailed product information, along with customer benefits, cost savings, and maintenance requirements. Package will be a one-page binder that representatives can use with sales prospects.

## Implementation Plan

| DATE | ACTION | COST | PERSON RESPONSIBLE |
|------|--------|------|--------------------|
| 1/1/00 | Complete brochure layouts for printing. | $2,000 | Gene Schultz |
| 1/15/00 | First press release mailing. | 100 | Gene Schultz |
| 2/15/00 | Make initial contacts with furnace companies. | 200 | Gene Schultz |
| 3/15/00 | Prepare a report on money-making potential of the Schulco 2000 for *Sharpeners Report.* | 250 | Gene Schultz |
| 3/15/00 | Complete sales representative sales package. | 1,500 | Gene Schultz |
| 4/15/00 | Second press release mailing. | 100 | Gene Schultz |
| 4/15/00 | Finalize arrangement with furnace company to have its representatives call on leads. | 500 | Gene Schultz |
| 5/15/00 | Complete article for the *Sharpeners Report.* | 100 | Gene Schultz |
| 7/1/00 | *Sharpeners Report* article releases. | | Gene Schultz |
| 9/1/00 | Third press release mailing. | 100 | Gene Schultz |

Don't take representatives for granted. You must give them the tools they need to succeed.

## Budget Summary

| ITEM | BUDGET |
|------|--------|
| Brochure Printing | $ 2,000 |
| Press Releases | 300 |
| Mailing | 1,500 |
| Travel | 4,000 |
| Sales Book Packages | 1,500 |
| Sharpeners Market | 250 |
| Furnace Company Contacts | 700 |
| **Total** | **$10,250** |

Plan collaborator Gene Schultz, president of Schulco.

Don't overlook travel costs in your budget if you need to visit customers or alliance partners.

## Final Comments

Both Safeplay Systems and Schulco are small companies that are up against large competitors. Safeplay Systems has been able to find a niche that is significant to a certain segment of the market: products for infants and toddlers geared toward the church-oriented day care market. Safeplay has even added a feature—products made of recycled plastic—that allows it to be come a preferred supplier to many church-oriented day care centers. Schulco, on the other hand, is trying to introduce a new type of product to a conservative industry. Although it offers significant benefits to its customers, the customers did not see the need for a closed loop system for small to midsize parts before the product was introduced. That makes it more difficult to identify the best target customers, and makes the job of marketing the product much more difficult. It is always much easier to market a product to customers who already perceive that they have a need, than to try to create a demand for a product prospects aren't aware that they want.

This does not mean that Schulco is doing a poor marketing job. It has a sound strategy for its market. The problem is that the foundry and machine shop market is more difficult to market to than the church-affiliated day care center market. Schulco's market is conservative, has different buying habits determined primarily by the owners' business orientation, and requires a great deal of hands-on product support to close a sale. The primary underlying problem is that each machine shop and foundry makes different parts that may have different equipment requirements. As a result, the market is fragmented, and it is hard to define and find target customers who are ideal for any product. Because Schulco is already in that market, it has to make the best of the situation. If you are not in business already, try to look for markets in which customers groups can be easily defined, and will make purchases for similar reasons. You will have the best chance to succeed in those markets.

Small companies don't have to be afraid of markets that have big competitors. All they have to do is find a small niche that other companies are overlooking and create the right product for that niche. Small companies should also create a specialized feature that is important to

> Try to introduce products where prospects feel they have a need rather than trying to create a need or demand for a new product.

the customer and then promote that feature repeatedly, so the market begins to remember the company for that specialized feature. Safeplay Systems repeatedly emphasizes that their products are made from recycled plastic. The company even uses the name EcoPlay to help customers remember this feature. Small companies can do well against anyone when they can execute this strategy.

One last point is that these two plans emphasize is the importance of distribution. Customers won't buy products that they are unaware of, or that aren't presented to them properly. The biggest mistake many new manufacturers make is assuming that distribution will not be a problem. Distribution is by far the most difficult part of marketing a manufactured product. It takes time, effort, and money to set up the distribution network, and for most small manufacturers, it is an area that always needs improvement. Manufacturing companies need to spend 25 to 30 percent of their marketing budget improving distribution.

Marketing against big competitors is a challenge because they have far larger marketing budgets and much better distribution systems. But it is not an insurmountable obstacle for marketers who take advantage of their small size by finding new niches that they can serve better than any other competitor, large or small.

> Small companies compete by funding new niches that they can serve better than larger competitors.

Small companies not only need to move fast, they also need to anticipate market trends.

## Are You Fast?

Small companies succeed against larger competitors when they capitalize on new opportunities and trends in the market, or when they find under-served market niches. Of course, small companies can only be first if they have their antennae up in order to pick up market information early. Check to see if you are doing everything you can to keep market intelligence at a high level.

|  | YES | NO |
|---|---|---|
| 1. Do you re-evaluate your breakout of market segments at least once per year? | _____ | _____ |
| 2. Do you assign the responsibility of keeping up with new market trends and opportunities to any one employee? | _____ | _____ |
| 3. Do you attend industry conferences or other roundtables to see what other people see as developing trends? | _____ | _____ |
| 4. Do you have a network of key industry contacts whom you talk to regularly about what is happening that will affect the future of your market? | _____ | _____ |
| 5. Do you have a mechanism to receive suggestions about new products from your sales force, distributors, and customers? | _____ | _____ |
| 6. Do you follow up on special requests or other unusual customer requests to discover the underlying reason behind the request? | _____ | _____ |

# Chapter 13

# Marketing Plans of Internet Companies

10: RETAIL/COFFEE SHOP MARKETING PLANS

11: SERVICE COMPANY MARKETING PLANS

12: MARKETING PLANS FOR MANUFACTURING COMPANIES

**13: MARKETING PLANS OF INTERNET COMPANIES**

14: THE OPENING

15: SITUATION ANALYSIS

16: STRATEGY, TACTICS, AND IMPLEMENTATION

APPENDICES A, B, C, D

INDEX

Marketing Plan 2000
BHD Corp.
Santa Clarita, California

## Executive Summary

### Company Description

The BHD Corp. is a collection of Web sites that provide financial advice to stock market investors and banner advertising to financial Web site owners. Although the company is not a broker or media company, it provides financial information and banner advertising to thousands of investors over the Internet on a daily basis. The company has four basic products:

1. The Financial Ad Trader itself–a financial Web site banner exchange program
2. Short Term Stock Selector–a short-term stock advisory service
3. Mutual Fund Magic–a short-term mutual fund advisory service
4. Doh.com–an award-winning Web site that offers free stock picks

The company has two distinct core technologies. The first is a set of neural networks that predicts short-term movements in stock and mutual funds, and the second is a proprietary banner exchange program that manages advertising on over four hundred Web sites. A neural network is an advanced computer hardware and software system that can predict behavior from a large number of indicators based on past results. The neural network is also capable of adapting its predictions based on the most current market events. The BHD Corp.'s core long-term business strategy is to sell the results of its neural network stock projections over the Internet to people who invest in stocks.

The company's guiding principle has been content first, and then commerce will follow. The Web site doh.com is an award-winning stock site that offers investors a wide variety of free services. It is the information core of the company's business and it attracts over twenty-five thousand hits per day. The doh.com Web site and financial banner ad trader services are designed to steer investors to the Mutual Fund Magic and Short Term Stock Selector Web sites, the company's two money-making Internet sites. The company also produces income by selling banner ads for its Web sites and ad trader network.

Banner exchange programs are a low-cost effective tactic for bringing people to your Web page.

## Situation Analysis

When the company was formed in 1996, it faced two main obstacles: investors were not familiar with the concept of picking stocks with a neural network; and most investors were not familiar with the concept of buying and holding stocks for less than seven days. To overcome these obstacles the company has given away stock picks with both its doh.com and Short Term Stock Selector Web sites to establish credibility. The company has picked winners 60 to 67 percent of the time on the Short Term Stock Selector site and its return on its mid-term stock picks on the doh.com site have averaged of 63.97 percent in 1999 versus a Standard & Poor's 500 return of 10.88 percent (as of November 24, 1999). The company has successfully positioned itself as a key information source with its doh.com Web site and has impressively proven the viability of its neural network technology.

The company has developed product lines for different types of customers. Mutual Fund Magic is for investors who want to take advantage of short-term market positions but who do not want to be involved in day-to-day investment activities. The Short Term Stock Selector is targeted at people who want to make their own final investment choices. BHD Corp. has established a firm foothold on the Internet and is now prepared to expand its product line and increase its penetration of the target market.

One of the great features of the Internet is that you can give something away and it won't cost you anything.

## Marketing Goals

The company's major goals in 2000 are:

1. Receive a brokerage license so that it can start and manage its own mutual funds based on its neural network technology.
2. Expand its customer base in Mutual Fund Magic by adding products, and capitalizing on the success of the doh.com Web site.
3. Increase publicity of the neural network approach of the company's financial market conditions.
4. Increase the number conversion rate to customers of people who receive free picks in the Short Term Stock Selector Fund.

Try to limit your marketing goals to an achievable number that will significantly impact your business.

## Situation Analysis

### A. Internal Audit

**Company Description and Background History.** Robert Hessler, Hayden Mitchell, and Dan Kraft, the three original company partners met in the fall of 1996 via the Internet. Ever since then, the partnership has been running the company about 99.5 percent via e-mail. The three have only met face to face one time, in the summer of 1998. The company started not as a company, but as a partnership with a series of Web sites. The company doesn't identify with a single Web site, in fact the partnership does not even have an official name. Some of our customers know the company as the Financial Ad Trader, some know it as the Short Term Stock Selector, some know it as MFMagic, and some know it as Webthemes (Webthemes is the name under which it handles credit card processing and payment). The partners refer to themselves as "The Partnership." (*Author's Note*: The company is referred to as BHD Corp. in this plan as it is a name they have considered using.)

#### The Partnership Team
1. Robert Hessler–Visionary & Neural Network Expert
2. Hayden Mitchell–Marketing Expert
3. Daniel Kraft–Programmer #1 & Stock Expert
4. Lajoo Motwani–Programmer #2 & New Web Site Developer

Partner #1, Robert Hessler: The roles he plays in the partnership are:

- Chief Brainstorming Officer
- Neural Net expert & system builder
- Webmaster for the Short Term Stock Selector
- Webmaster for the Financial Ad Trader
- Webmaster for Mutual Fund Magic

Partner #2, Hayden, Mitchell, became one of the Internet's first experts in Web site promotion when the Web was first formed. He quickly established himself and his own personal Web site (not part of the partnership), Webthemes.com, back in 1994. The roles he fills for the group are:

- Chief Marketing Officer
- Chief Financial Officer
- Handles Web promotion and marketing for all of the Web sites on an ongoing basis
- Processes all orders and takes care of the financials for the group

This plan lists the partners' functions because the company may want to form alliances in the near future.

Partner #3, Dan Kraft, is a software engineer/avid stock market enthusiast. Previously he has worked for Broderbund Software, Dun & Bradstreet, and PeopleSoft. The areas/roles that he fills for the group are:

- Chief Technical and Investment Officer
- Handles the engine and the database for the Financial Ad Trader
- Maintains numerous custom made applications used by the partnership
- Webmaster for doh.com
- Stock picker for doh.com

Partner #4, Lajoo Motwani, is an engineering consultant and programmer who joined the group a little over a year ago. He is currently working to implement ideas that the partnership has had in the past but never had time to do.

**History of Web Sites.** The Short Term Stock Selector Web site was initiated in 1996. The site only offered free stock picks first for two reasons. One, because search engines will place sites offering free services before sites that charge money when doing a Web search. Second, the company wanted to prove that the neural network method of picking stocks had distinct advantages over more traditional stock selection advice. To take advantage of the traffic at the Short Term Stock Selector site and earn money in this period, the company started the Financial Ad Trader, which is a banner ad exchange program. Sites that have financial Web sites agree to place banner ads from other members of the network on their site. For every two ads that the site runs, it receives credit to run one of its ads on another Web site. The second ad belongs to the Financial Ad Trader in return for its management of the banner program. The company sells some of that banner ad space to other companies, and uses the other ads to promote its own Web sites. This arrangement has allowed the company to be profitable from the first year of its existence. This banner ad exchange has been very popular, and today 424 Web sites are members and about 200,000 banner ads per day are placed through the network. The difference between the Financial Ad Trader program and other banner exchange programs is that it is restricted to financial sites only while most other programs are for all Web sites.

In the beginning of 1997, the company started a service for $150 per quarter for people who wanted to receive stock picks every night, rather than receiving the picks free at noon the next day. This service has expanded to the point where over a thousand people have purchased the ability to get the next day's stock pick selection at night. In 1998 the company started its Mutual Fund Magic program. This program moves shares in Rydex, a large mutual fund manager, from one fund to another every night. Rydex offers a wide variety of sector funds, such as a technology fund, a manufacturing fund, and energy fund as well as many others. Rydex

> The company has concentrated on generating traffic through a magnet Web site and a banner exchange program.

> Internet marketers need to understand the rules of search engine placement in order to succeed.

allows its customers to switch from one fund to another as often as they like without any fee. The Mutual Fund Manager informs Rydex every day what fund its clients should be moved to. Clients' money is moved to whatever fund the company's neural network predicts will do best the next day. The company started its high growth mutual fund service in late 1998, its high safety mutual fund service in early 1999, and its NASDAQ fund service in late 1999. The company charges an annual fee of three-quarters of 1 percent of the money it moves for a client, and in 1999 the company's customers had given it the right to move over $7 million per day. The company is not licensed to sell or manage people's money, and only acts as their agent when moving the client's money from one fund to another.

While the company used the banner ads it picked up from the Financial Ad Trader to drive traffic to its two sites, it also wanted to establish itself as an expert in the field of picking stocks, and as one of the leading resources for financial information on the Internet. So in 1998 the company added the doh.com Web site, which was a site offering free stock advice and a wide variety of other information. The site has received 11 awards as a top financial Web site. To promote its site the company takes advantage again of the search engines' protocol that lists sites with free stock picks first during an Internet search. It also promotes the site through its Financial Ad Trader Network, and doh.com has as its two top links the Short Term Stock Select and Mutual Fund Magic Web sites.

**Sales Trends.** All three of the company's three main products have produced consistent sales growth.

1. The Financial Ad Trader has about two hundred thousand banner placements per day, of which 50,000 belong to the company. It sells about 20 percent of those sites to a variety of companies for $10 per thousand exposures and 1.82 percent of the people who see the company's banner click on it to go to the corresponding site. (The remaining exposures primarily feature the company's doh.com Web site.) The company also sells banner pages on a commission basis. For example the Investor's Business Daily pays for every trial subscription received through a banner ad with the Financial Ad Trader network.
2. Mutual Fund Magic revenues are based on a percentage of the money the company is authorized to move among Rydex's mutual funds. That sum has increased steadily to over $7 million, and is expected to continue to grow with the addition of several new funds.
3. The Short Term Stock Selector is also expected to continue its growth, especially as the market stabilizes and investors need to look harder for growth opportunities.

Once the company started to charge for its services, it needed to offer a new site with free stock picks to attract investors to their for-pay sites.

A 1.82 percent is a great click-through rate on a banner ad. Most ads have a request rate of far less than 1 percent.

## Company Strengths and Weaknesses

### Strengths
1. Company's Web experience makes it a top listing on many investor Web searches.
2. Company's neural network technology has been tested for four years.
3. Company has the number one banner ad trading program for financial Web sites.
4. Company doh.com Web site is a recognized leader in free stock selection advice.
5. Company has always been profitable.
6. Company's management team has a strong entrepreneurial background, which will help it launch new products on the Internet.

### Weaknesses
1. Company does not have the backing of a well established financial newsletter or brokerage house to add to its credibility in predicting the movement of stock prices.
2. The advantages of the company's neural network technology are not well understood by investors.

← Internet companies can make money but they need a sophisticated marketing program that knows how to attract visitors.

## Customer Information

**Target Customer Profile.** BHD Corp.'s target customers are investors who want to maximize their return by taking advantage of the short-term trends in the stock market. These investors can be big or small, and can use any type of brokerage for actually buying and selling stock. The company targets investors who want to make and follow their own stock selections with the Short Term Stock Selector Web site, and it targets people who don't want to follow the market that closely with its Mutual Fund Magic service and Web site.

A recent study by the Securities Industry association and the Investment Company Institute (Time magazine, Nov. 1, 1999, page 116) points out several customer characteristics that are favorable for the company's long-term growth.

1. Seventy-eight million Americans own stock or stock funds, up from 42 million in 1983.
2. Sixty-four percent of stockholders rely on advisors to tell them when to hold and when to sell.
3. Seventy-seven percent of stock-fund holders buy and sell through some sort of advice filter.
4. Nearly half of all stock owners are baby boomers, with an average time to retirement of eleven years. This market should be anxious to maximize its short-term gains.

← A key customer characteristic is most of them want advice. That desire is the underlying reason that the company's Web sites are popular.

5. In employer stock funds, the typical account has only 61 percent in stock. People under 65 should have 70 to 85 percent of their assets in stock.

The study points out three significant factors for long-term growth of the company.

1. There are a large number of investors.
2. They tend to be conservative in their investment decisions primarily because they are not confident in their investment knowledge.
3. There is a huge untapped market for people in company sponsored retirement plans for advice on what mutual fund sector they should be in. The company's success with Mutual Fund Magic is a natural lead into this market.

The conservative nature of investors is why the company added Mutual Fund Magic to supplement the Short Term Stock Selector site.

While the company started with the Short Term Stock Selector, that product is focused on people who want to make their own stock selections. People in this market are not overly loyal, which is why the company is moving away from this market. The company is instead focusing on people who want someone else to make their day to day investment choices. The Mutual Fund Magic product line is geared toward those people, as is the company's new managed fund, which will be introduced in 2000 once the company is fully licensed. The company may also offer free advice on switching sector funds in employer retirement funds on doh.com with the eventual aim of adding a for-fee service on an additional Web page.

E*Trade's average investor is thirty-nine years old and has $25,000 in his or her trading account (Source: *Business Week*, Feb. 22, 1999, page 113). This is younger than the average trader, with a smaller amount to invest. Merrill Lynch's average customer, as example, is fifty-two years old and has an average of $200,000 in household assets (Source: *Business Week*, Feb. 22, 1999, page 113). The company's doh.com Web site is designed for younger Internet users, with entertaining graphics, and a more irreverent tone than expected for a financial information site, in order to appeal to the younger Internet trader. The programmer for this Web site is 24 years old, which also helps to keep a more youthful look to the site.

The company adjusted its Web site content to appeal to the more youthful Internet stock trader.

**Key Customer Desire.** Customers want to raise their returns without raising their risk. The company meets this desire by allowing people to choose their own long-term risk range—by choosing the type of stocks or funds they want to buy, and then maximizing their return by taking advantage of short-term market trends that favor one sector or stock type over another. The company's neural network technology is designed to predict the best performing sector fund over a five-to-seven day period. Taking advantage of these short-term trends can raise an investors yield substantially over a one-year period.

**Customer Buying Criteria.** Credibility, trustworthiness, track record, safety, cost, and proprietary stock selection are some of the major criteria that concern investors when they determine where they will obtain stock selection advice. Credibility, trustworthiness, track record, and safety all involve an investor's fear of losing their hard-earned money. The company has worked hard to establish these four factors in its business, first, by giving its products away for an extended period, and by offering its doh.com financial news Web site free to all comers. But realistically the company can't make the customer feel as comfortable doing business with them as they might with a financial planner who is a personal friend, or a large brokerage with an impeccable reputation.

*Your marketing plan should always be geared toward providing customers the information they want before they decide to buy.*

The one criterion the company does excel in is proprietary stock selection criteria. Many investors are just like Gordon Gecko in the movie Wall Street. They want to know information that no one else knows in order to outperform the market. People often think of special "insider information," but in fact the market considers people like Warren Buffet to have uncanny insights into what companies will do best in the long run and they treat his choices as proprietary information.

BHD Corp. sells a different type of proprietary stock section criteria. Rather than using "uncanny insights and intuition," it relies on advanced programming tactics first, to identify what market factors and events affect short-term stock movement and, second, to further identify what market sectors and stocks are most likely to benefit from the current market conditions.

*The company's neural network is a specialty in the market that no one else either has or promotes*

**Major Customer Obstacle.** Investors have heard for years that investing for the long term has a better return than short-term investments, primarily because commission fees eat up whatever profits an investor might gain. Reinforcing that image are the negative articles on day trading that have stated that only a small percentage of day traders actually make money. The message of the dangers of short-term trading has been repeated for years, and many investors have a negative reaction to moving stocks over the short term.

The situation in investment has changed radically over the last few years. Fidelity Investments, as an example, will charge investors as little as $14.95 to trade 1,000 shares on-line, while it charges up to $140 to do the same service over the phone (Source: *Forbes* magazine, June 15, 1998, page 261). Some aggressive investors realize that buying and selling stock with a short-term outlook is much more profitable now than it has been in the past. The company will work with its doh.com Web site to get this message out, but it will also prepare a study on short-term investing results that it will release to major media outlets in the country.

*Changing customers' perceptions is always a difficult marketing challenge.*

**Customers' Buying Patterns.** Investors increasingly are turning toward the Internet for both financial information and for on-line trading. Some of the facts that support the Internet's momentum with investors are:

1. At Vanguard, 37 percent of its shareholders used the Web to get information about an investment in the first quarter of 1999. This was up from 20 percent in the first quarter of 1998 (Source: *New York Times*, Aug. 1, 1999).

2. At Charles Schwab, 45 percent of all transactions were on-line in mid-June 1999, up from 25 percent in June of 1998, and 16 percent at the start of 1998 (Source: *New York Times,* Aug. 1, 1999).

3. In 1998, 14 percent of all equity trades were conducted online, up 50 percent since 1997 (Source: *Business Week,* Feb. 22, 1999, page 113).

4. The on-line industry doubled its assets to $420 billion and doubled the number of accounts to 7.3 million in 1998 (Source: *Business Week,* Feb. 22, 1999, page 113).

5. Eight percent of Paine Webber's accounts have opened on-line accounts, and 30 percent said they planned to do so in 1999 (Source: *Business Week,* Feb. 22, 1999, page 113).

6. At the beginning of 1997 only 30,000 accounts of Fidelity Investments were doing transactions on-line. Fourteen months later the count was over 1 million accounts (Source: *Forbes,* June 15, 1998, page 261).

7. In early 1997, 7 percent of Fidelity's commissionable trades were done on-line. In early 1998 the number was over 60 percent (Source: *Business Week,* Feb. 22, 1999, page 113).

8. In May of 1998, a survey by RelevantKnowledge found that 57 million people in the United States were on-line (Source: *Editor & Publisher,* May 9, 1998).

> People are buying more and more on the Internet, but financial advice is still primarily garnered through print media. This has opened up the opportunity that BHD is working to exploit.

The company has developed credibility over the last three years and it is well situated to take advantage of the major market moves toward investors conducting research and executing trades on the Internet.

## Industry Profile

### Current Trends.

The six trends that are dominating the industry are:

1. The majority of investors are going on-line to both learn about stocks and invest.

2. The stock market's period of rapid growth is slowing up and investors will be looking at new ways to increase the value of their stock holdings.

3. People are no longer tied to just one investment route, they are exploring many different ways of investing. No one system, whether it is on-line, brokerage house, or stock funds, is clearly winning over other methods.

4. The commissions for trading stock on-line have dramatically declined, to the point where more frequent trading is cost-effective.

5. The free flow of information about competing sources of information and stock trades has driven the price for investment services down.
6. The number of firms offering on-line brokerages, mutual funds, and investment advice is increasing rapidly.

**Competitive Audit.** BHD Corp. provides investment advice. There are literally thousands of other competitors offering advice to investors. They range from powerful brokerage houses like Morgan Stanley and Merrill Lynch, to on-line brokerage houses that offer more limited service to the thousands of investment newsletters that are available from a wide variety of sources. Most newspapers as well as many business magazines also offer columns that include investment advice. Finally there are thousands of financial planners throughout the country, many of whom manage their clients' investment decisions.

The company can't worry about all those competitors and has decided instead to pursue its unique positioning strategy of maximizing returns by using neural network programming to establish short-term market trends. Nevertheless, the company is aware that it competes with all other companies in two distinct ways. The first is appealing to investors' needs and desires, and the second is each company's ability to cost effectively attract prospects to their business.

There are several factors that play heavily into investors' minds when they make a decision. They are credibility, trustworthiness, track record, safety, cost, and proprietary stock selection criteria. The company has worked hard to establish a base of credibility over the last three years, a time when it has shown repeatedly that its neural network stock selection technology does produce many more winning than losing stock selections. The company has also been in business three years, produced a profit every year, and is in the market for the long term. The company has established that it has proprietary stock selection criteria that work and is positioned as a viable choice for investors looking for investment advice.

What elevates BHD Corp. above all competitors is its unique cost advantages in attracting prospects to look into its products. This is an extremely large advantage in a market with thousands of competitors where it is very difficult for marketers to break through the clutter of marketing messages. The company has created this advantage with two methods: first, by setting up the Financial Ad Trader where the company currently owns about fifty thousand banner ads per day, and uses about forty thousand of those banner ads to promote its own Web sites. At a click-through rate of 1.82 percent, these ads bring over seven hundred visitors per day to its sites in return for maintaining and operating the banner exchange program.

The second factor that cuts the BHD Corp.'s marketing cost is the doh.com Web site. An award-winning site that has gathered wide ranging publicity for its ease-of-use and clever graphics, the doh.com site acts an entry point into the company's fee-based sites, which are the first

BHD Corp. differentiates its advice by gearing it toward the younger on-line investor and through its use of its neural network technology.

The Internet has created a new marketing challenge, how to bring prospects to your site.

two links listed in the site's link section. Doh.com has also been designed so that it is an early placement in the Internet search results for most of the major search engines.

The company reinvests these cost savings for its customers, first, by maintaining high quality information at its doh.com site, and second, by keeping its prices and fees to consumers below the industry average for small to midsize accounts. The company's groundwork over the last three years makes it difficult for competitors to dislodge the company from its favorable marketing positioning. The company's major advantage lies in its ability to cost effectively attract prospects to its site, which is why it has maintained its name as the Financial Ad Trader.

# Positioning

## Positioning Statements

1. BHD Corp. has created a proprietary neural network technology that helps investors maximize their overall return by taking advantage of short-term market trends. The company's proven performance with its neural network lies in its ability to choose the relevant market indicators based on the past three to five years, and the past one to five months, to predict future performance.
2. The company's products are ideal either for people who want to do their own trading (Short Term Stock Selector) or who want someone else to monitor the day-to-day activity of the account (Mutual Fund Magic).
3. BHD Corp. has set up a long-term sustainable cost advantage in its marketing program with the dominance of its Financial Ad Trader network, and the creation of its award-winning doh.com Web site.

You want to bring customers to your site every day or at least once a week. Otherwise your customers might latch onto another site.

## Rationale for Positioning Statements

1. Company needs a differential advantage for investors to succeed in a very crowded market. Offering a new stock picking technology offers investors a different perspective than they might otherwise have for their investments. Neural network technology is created to give investors another tool to maximize their stock market return.
2. There are two groups of investors, those who want to control their own investments, and those who want advice from other people. The first group is smaller, but also trades more frequently. The second group is much larger, but wants to trade less. The company has products for both groups.
3. The third positioning statement, regarding the company's long-term strategic marketing advantage, is important because the company may work toward establishing strategic alliances with other firms to help build its credibility when it moves to establish

itself as a money manager. The company's strategic marketing advantage should be appealing to many of its potential partners.

## Marketing Strategy

### Strategies for 2000

1. Receive brokerage registration and start a stock fund based on the company's neural network technology.
2. Generate additional publicity stories in traditional media regarding neural network technology and the results it has gotten to date.
3. Continue to expand and promote the doh.com Web site on the Internet. The goal is to make it the most visited independent financial Web site on the Internet.
4. Add to the doh.com site information for people in retirement funds regarding which funds or sectors should do best over the next week, 30 days, and six months. This service would be free this year, and possibly spun off next year into a fee-based service.
5. Continue actively promoting the Financial Ad Trader Network to new financial sites as they come onto the Internet.
6. Initiate advertising of the doh.com Web site in various business publications such as the Investor's Business Daily in a barter arrangement for banner ads in the Financial Ad Trader banner exchange program.

## Marketing Tactics

### Products

The company will be adding a stock management fund in 2000 once its brokerage registration is in order. The company will also be offering additional free services through its doh.com Web site to gauge interest for products in subsequent years.

### Pricing

The company will continue to set its pricing at about 50 percent of the cost of similar services offered off-line to small to midsize investors. For Mutual Fund Magic the management fee will be three-quarters of 1 percent of the managed assets. The quarterly fee for the Short Term Stock Selector will continue at $150 per quarter, which is about 35 percent of the cost of most established investor newsletters. The banner ads will continue to be sold at $10 per thousand exposures.

Traffic to your site has been proven to be the most important marketing tactic for on-line companies without a major off-line presence.

Being an award-winning site has generated significant publicity for doh.com.

## Publicity

The company will put together several press release articles about the use of neural networks, how they were developed, their evolution from the evaluation of R&D research results, and how they are used today. This would not be an article featuring the company's neural network technology, but the company would be prominently listed in the article.

The company will also put out publicity to company newsletters, business magazines, and investment oriented publications regarding new features it adds to doh.com, especially features related to retirement accounts. Sector switching is a high demand topic for company accounts as many retirement accounts are tied into a family of mutual funds. Long term this strategy can be used to set up roll over accounts when people leave a retirement account.

## Advertising

The company will continue to use the banner ads it acquires from the Financial Ad Trader to promote its Web sites. It will also trade some of its banner ads with print publications that have Web pages to advertise its new managed fund once it becomes active. The company plans on devoting 20 percent of its banner page advertising to this barter exchange for remnant ads. It will approach financial advertisers through e-mail to set up the barter program.

Trading ads with print media will gain the company exposure to new customers at a very low cost.

## Sales

The company will continue to approach new financial Web sites about the possibility of joining the Financial Ad Trader. The new brokerage houses, financial newsletters, and other sites coming out on the Web should lead to an increase of at least 100,000 banner ads in the year 2000. Sales to Short Term Stock Selector and Mutual Fund Magic will continue through their Web sites with investors inquiring through the Web and being sold through the Web.

## Contests

To help launch the new stock fund, the company will run a contest that can be heavily promoted on the doh.com Web site and banner ads. The company will offer winners $1,000 in stock, and five years of half-price fund fees for their initial investments. To enter the contest investors need to just list what new feature they would like to see added to the doh.com site. The winners will be drawn randomly, but the doh.com site will add the most requested features to the site.

The ability of Web sites to take surveys from a large number of people has proven to be a valuable publicity generating tool.

A second contest could be run in the latter part of the year if the fund needs a boost. The contest could include an entry for who is the most admired, and least admired businessperson in America. Again the contest could offer a small amount of stock in the new fund, or reduced fees depending on how successful those incentives were in the first contest.

## Implementation Plan/2000

*Note:* Costs and person responsible for each action withheld at company's request.

| DATE | ACTION | COST | PERSON RESPONSIBLE |
|------|--------|------|--------------------|
| 1/15/00 | Initiate work on press releases for business publications regarding neural network technology. | .... | ............ |
| 2/28/00 | Send out press releases to business publications on neural network technology. | .... | ............ |
| 3/15/00 | Add features on www.doh.com for people in retirement plans relating to sector switching. | .... | ............ |
| 3/15/00 | Complete a plan for ensuring that the new stock fund comes out early in search placements. | .... | ............ |
| 3/30/00 | Initiate new stock trading fund. | .... | ............ |
| 4/15/00 | Send out press releases on new features on doh.com to business magazines. | .... | ............ |
| 4/15/00 | Start using 20 percent of the banner ad space for the new stock fund. | .... | ............ |
| 4/15/00 | Place the new fund prominently on the site. | .... | ............ |
| 5/15/00 | Start contest to promote the new stock fund for the company. | .... | ............ |
| 6/15/00 | Post the results of the contests for most requested features. | .... | ............ |
| 6/30/00 | Send out press releases to business publications with the results of the survey from the contest. | .... | ............ |
| 7/16/00 | Put together the results of the first six months of the neural network investment advice and post it on the doh.com sites. | .... | ............ |
| 7/30/00 | Add an additional major service to the doh.com site based on the results of the contests. | .... | ............ |
| 8/30/00 | Start second contest to attract interest in the new stock fund. | .... | ............ |
| 9/15/00 | Add an additional fund to Mutual Fund Magic. | .... | ............ |
| 10/15/00 | Put together the results of the survey relating to the contest and issue a press release to business publications. | .... | ............ |
| 11/15/00 | Put together stock performance for all of the neural network picks during the first nine months of the year. Post the results on the doh.com site. | .... | ............ |

Plan prepared in collaboration with Hayden Mitchell.

New Web sites have become major advertisers in traditional media because it is difficult today to build traffic on the Internet with Internet-only tactics.

The company needs an active program to continually promote its differential advantage—neural network technology.

You need to offer a steady stream of new features and site changes to keep up your on-line momentum.

**Marketing Plan**
**Oil-N-Gas, Inc.**

Contact: Jerry Capehart
PO Box 642
Grand Prairie, TX 75053

Telephone: 972-988-1191
e-mail: info@oil-n-gas.com

## Executive Summary

### Company Summary and Product Description

Oil-N-Gas, Inc., is an Internet start-up company whose goal is to create an interactive Web site offering information regarding oil and gas investment opportunities, as well as general information regarding oil and gas investments. The site's two primary customer groups are the 3.5 million U.S. accredited investors (investors with a net worth of $1 million or more) and the 7,500 oil and gas companies that on occasion offer a direct participation investment in oil or gas wells. The company generates revenue in four ways, selling individual memberships to accredited investors, selling Internet postings to oil and gas production companies, selling books and other informational products to investors, and selling advertising on its Web site.

Oil-N-Gas was formed to provide a service that investors *and* oil and gas companies want, but is not available.

### Marketing Objectives

Oil-N-Gas, Inc. was conceived in 1995, and its Web page is now up and operational, but the program has not yet been actively marketed to investors or oil and gas companies. In the fall of 1999 Oil-N-Gas began signing up oil and gas drilling companies to list their investment opportunities on the Internet on a free trial basis. Internet investors will not be signing up unless gas and oil property investment opportunities are listed. Starting in year 2000 the Company's investment objectives are:

Clear objectives are the best way to have every employee working toward the same goal.

1. Sign up 25,000 accredited investors for $39 annual memberships.
2. Post 1,000 oil and gas investment opportunities at an average price of $175.
3. Sell books and other information to a minimum of 25 percent of its members.
4. Generate $50,000 in ad revenues.

## Three Year Dollar Sales Objectives

|  | 2000 | 2001 | 2002 |
|---|---|---|---|
| Membership Fees | $ 975,000 | $ 7,800,000 | $15,600,000 |
| Posting Fees | 175,000 | 1,750,000 | 3,750,000 |
| Product Revenue | 125,000 | 900,000 | 2,500,000 |
| Advertising Revenue | 50,000 | 225,000 | 600,000 |
|  | $1,325,000 | $10,675,000 | $22,450,000 |

## Mission Statement

Oil-N-Gas strives to provide a comprehensive source of information on oil and gas production and investments. The site is exclusively for the accredited investors (millionaires) who are allowed to invest in the high risk/high return world of oil and gas production investments and who can benefit from the tax benefits from those investments provided by U.S. law. The company's original target market will be current investors in gas and oil investments, but eventually it will target all accredited investors.

# Situation Analysis

## Market Size

Twenty-five thousand to 35,000 wells in the United States are drilled per year with a peak of 90,000 in 1981 and a low of 18,000 in 1995. Worldwide market for upstream production and exploration cost in 1997 was $80 billion with a minimum of 15 percent of that number being U.S. activity. A significant percentage, in the range of 15 to 20 percent, are financed privately through the sale of direct participation investment programs to individual investors. In addition to new activity, the market includes sales in a variety of investments in oil and/or gas well drilling and production operations such as existing production royalty streams, offsets to exiting production, infield developments, re-entries, horizontal/directional drilling activity, seismic shoots, secondary recovery, tertiary recovery, and a variety of other special programs.

The number of investment opportunities provided by the 7,500 oil and gas production companies operating in the United States is large, estimated to be at least 15,000 opportunities per year. The number of accredited investors in the United States is 3.5 million households, and while we can't predict the exact potential market size for an information service, we know that it can be very large. We expect that the Internet listing of Oil-N-Gas, Inc. can significantly expand the market as it will both increase the number of people investing in gas and oil opportunities, as well as

Designing your product to meet a market need is a traditional marketing strategy that still works in an on-line world.

expand the number of opportunities offered to accredited investors. Right now the market size is limited by the lack of free flowing information regarding investment opportunities.

## Market Need

Gas and oil well developers routinely try to sell opportunities to investors. The problem in the market currently is that it is inefficient, with gas and oil producers routinely having to cold call themselves, or have a broker cold call in order to raise money. It is common for producers to spend four to six months to raise the money, which delays the start of oil wells, as well as taking up an excess amount of management time. Investors are also shortchanged by the current sales techniques because they have access to only a limited number of potential investment opportunities. They can't know whether or not they are getting the best deal on the market.

A second problem is that only a small number of the 3.5 millionaires in the country are fully aware of the opportunities that oil and gas investments offer. Most investors are in oil and gas producing states and most new investors to the gas and oil industry don't have an independent, non-broker source of information. The result is that only a percentage of the nation's accredited investors know enough about oil and gas investments to get started in the market.

The current inefficient system is not adequate to handle potential increases in business from two favorable market conditions. The first trend is the higher cost of oil and natural gas, which makes it economical for oil and gas producers to open a greater number of wells in the United States. In the first half of 1999 oil prices rose 30 percent, making all producing wells much more profitable, and opening up opportunities for many formerly unprofitable wells. The second trend is the apparent leveling off of the stock market. Investors selling stock to lock in profits are prime candidates for oil and gas investments, especially with the special tax benefits offered to oil and gas investors.

## Target Customer Profile

*Accredited Investors.* There are 3.5 million households in America with assets (less liabilities) of over $1 million (*U.S. News and World Report*, April 14, 1997). Their average age is 57, and 26 percent of their assets are invested in passive investments like stocks, bonds, and oil and gas investments. Most of these individuals are clearly in a position to invest in oil and gas operations.

According to a survey by *Trusts & Estates* magazine, wealthy people do not like a hard sell on potential investments, which is the technique commonly used by most oil and gas producers. Instead they prefer information, lots of alternatives, and a solution they feel is tailored to their needs. An Oil-N-Gas membership allows wealthy investors to view information about selecting

---

Oil-N-Gas wants to offer new investment opportunities as the stock market levels off.

---

Federal law requires companies that sell private placements to sell only to accredited investors.

the right oil and gas investment, see many alternative investments, and then choose which oil and gas producers to contact for more information.

*Oil and Gas Producers.* The majority of the companies selling oil and gas investments are small companies that are not listed on a major exchange. They fund projects either by soliciting investors, or borrowing from banks and other financial institutions. When raising money for a project the companies can either pay a broker a commission of 2 to 5 percent, or have the company make direct mailings or phone calls to accredited investors who must invest a minimum of $25,000 in a project. Companies feel fund raising is a major obstacle for most projects, and they are receptive to any program that helps raise money.

The Oil-N-Gas Web site is geared towards investors' preferred buying process.

## Oil and Gas Investment Benefits

Oil and gas investments buy part ownership in a project that will produce (hopefully) a future revenue stream. The project also has significant tax benefits. Oil and gas investments have two components. The first is working interest, which includes drilling costs and all other costs associated with operating the well. These costs are typically 75 percent of the initial investment, and all of these costs can be written off as a tax loss. The other costs of a project, which include tangible assets, can be written off over a three-to-five-year period. Oil investments have particular appeal to most accredited investors at the moment because they can offset profits from stocks today, and take their hopeful profits from the oil and gas well later once the well starts operating.

## Oil-N-Gas Benefits to Investors
1. Low cost of $39.95 per year is small when compared to a typical minimum investment of $25,000.
2. Access to many more oil and gas investment opportunities.
3. Easy identification of different types of investments as they are grouped by category.
4. The best available market information from books, Oil-N-Gas newsletter, and other data posted on the Web site.
5. Quick links to other related sites.
6. Discounts on a wide variety of services.
7. ROI software is discounted to members.

An information site is particularly useful when the topic is as complex as oil and gas investments.

## Oil-N-Gas Benefits to Production Companies
1. No monthly fees.
2. People companies would not normally be able to reach will review their investment opportunities.

Oil-N-Gas has identified significant unmet customer needs for investors and for oil and gas producers.

3. Oil-N-Gas's Internet Web site is by far the lowest priced marketing program available to oil and gas producing companies.
4. Direct links to other gas companies like HIS Energy Group, allowing quick verification of geological data.
5. Oil and gas companies' members can list that fact in their literature.
6. Oil-N-Gas is listed on over 1,550 search engines, and your listing guarantees potential investors can find you quickly.
7. Oil-N-Gas owns over one hundred domain names related to oil and gas production. This helps ensure that investors will come to the Oil-N-Gas Web site when searching for virtually any oil and gas related term.

## Competition

Your site will come up in the first group of matches in a search when there is a direct match between a search request and an on-line site's name.

There are several Internet sites that also list acquisition and divestiture opportunities for the gas and oil industry, including sites sponsored by Amoco and Exxon. These sites aren't for individual investors, but instead are for complete purchases or sales by independent oil and gas producers. Individual producers may also have a Web site where they try to market their own investments. There are not any sites similar to Oil-N-Gas, which is simply a clearinghouse of information for investors. One step Oil-N-Gas has taken to minimize competition is to obtain over one hundred domain names that consist of every conceivable term associated with oil and gas investments. This will lead people directly to the site for many Internet searches.

## Oil-N-Gas Strengths and Weaknesses

### Strengths

The company has found an unmet need that no one else is addressing.

1. Only known clearinghouse for oil and gas investments.
2. Attractive pricing for investors and producers when compared to the size of typical investments.
3. High information content is ideal for novice oil and gas investors.
4. Price comparison between different options helps ensure investors they are getting a fair price.
5. Company founder has extensive experience in the gas and oil investment business.
6. Company Web page is complete and up and running and ready for marketing effort.
7. Site doesn't push any products other than memberships and postings. It is simply an information source, which is what investors are looking for. The company doesn't profit from any eventual investments. It is an investor's choice to contact the gas and oil producer.

### Weaknesses

1. Oil-N-Gas is a new company and not related to an up-and-running brokerage with an established reputation.
2. Oil-N-Gas is a new start-up that needs to build a base of both investors and postings so the site will have value to users.
3. Oil-N-Gas doesn't have its entire staff in place yet to maintain and monitor the activity level on the site.

## Market Trends

Oil prices hit a low in 1995 causing a drop-off in drilling activity. But since then prices have stabilized, before jumping 30 percent in early 1999. Salomon Brothers expect the market to keep increasing at a 14 percent per year growth rate, although the latest increase in oil prices could create a much stronger rise in drilling activity. In addition, improved techniques of oil recovery make more existing wells profitable that are not currently operating.

← The market for oil and gas investments is on a strong upward trend.

# Marketing Strategy and Positioning

### Strategy

Oil-N-Gas's goal is to be the complete, all-inclusive information site for people and companies interested in buying or selling oil and gas investment opportunities for accredited investors. Once it establishes that reputation the company will be able to add additional sites such as Oil-N-Gas Investment Trust. The key elements of this strategy are:

← To increase traffic to its site, Amazon.com has an active program to form alliances with special interest sites.

1. The site is only open to accredited investors. Oil-N-Gas will screen investors prior to accepting their membership to ensure they are accredited. This feature is important to producers who don't want to waste their time with people who aren't qualified to invest.
2. An alliance with Amazon.com has given Oil-N-Gas access to over six hundred titles regarding oil and gas investments.
3. Links to other sites offer producers access to key geological data that they need when preparing investment opportunities.
4. The information nature of the site places the burden for the actual sale and necessary securities documentation onto the producer and investor. This keeps the amount of legal jargon on the site to a minimum.

5. Oil-N-Gas has deliberately tried to acquire as many oil and gas related domain names as possible. To date it has acquired over one hundred names. Those names are currently in search engines and lead to the Oil-N-Gas Web site.
6. Oil-N-Gas wants to establish a dominant market position before any competitor can enter the market.

Oil-N-Gas's strategy is based on its desire to be the first place that investors come when they seek information about an oil and gas investment. Investors want a good informational source, and producers want access to a large pool of potential investors. Oil-N-Gas's strategy is based on four factors: one, be first into the market; two, provide a complete information site; three, be a neutral site by avoiding any direct involvement with selling securities; and four, make it difficult for competitors to enter the market.

> Being first in the market with a major presence is more important in on-line marketing than in any other marketing arena.

## Competitive Positioning

Oil-N-Gas has the only comprehensive Web site for oil and gas investments on the Internet. It is also the only site that doesn't have a vested interest in trying to sell securities to investors. Its only goal is to help investors understand what their investment opportunities are, and to give producers a low-cost method of posting their investment opportunities to a large group of potential investors.

# Marketing Tactics

> Internet companies need to generate revenues in as many ways as possible to become profitable.

### Product

Oil-N-Gas will produce revenue from four different products:

1. Memberships for investors. The introductory price is $39 per year, which gives investors access to all the information on the site as well as discounts on a variety of services.
2. Posting options for oil and gas producers. The options vary based on the amount of information that producers want on the sites. Postings will be categorized by type of investment and location.
3. Sales of information products through an alliance with Amazon.com, which is already in place.
4. Sale of advertising for banner pages and resource listings.

## Pricing

Oil-N-Gas's profitability depends on having a large number of investment members, rather than depending on a high price per member. The membership dues of $39 are set low to encourage investors to sign up, if for nothing else, just to learn more about oil and gas investments. To encourage more investor memberships, Oil-N-Gas wants to have as many postings of investment opportunities as possible. Prices for its postings start at $249, which represents a one-time fee. Since investments typically are in increments of $25,000 and up, the $249 fee is easily covered if just one investor buys a share in a producer's product. The books and informational products will be furnished by Amazon.com and sold to members at full retail pricing. Advertising on the site will be based on the number of hits the site obtains while the ad is running, probably $10 to $20 per thousand exposures.

On-line marketers need to employ traditional marketing tactics such as sign-up awards to encourage customers to buy.

## Web Site

The company's Web site is now up and running. It is a basic site that operates well, but the company has budgeted $280,000 to upgrade its site over the next year. The goal is to improve the site's interactive nature for investors.

## Initial Sign-up Awards

To initiate a rapid start for the site, Oil-N-Gas will put in place several initial sign-up programs.

1. For members. Charter members (those who invest in the first six months) can renew their membership for the first three years at the same $39 yearly membership fee.
2. For producers. Free basic listings on the Oil-N-Gas Web site if they post the listing within the first three months of the program. Upgrade options are available for just the upgrade charge, with the basic listing still being free.

## Domain Name Site Registration

To date the exclusive rights to over one hundred domain names have been obtained by Oil-N-Gas, and the company is working to obtain as many additional names as possible. There are two goals in obtaining as many domain names as possible. First, it helps Oil-N-Gas come up early in any Internet search related to oil and gas investments. Search engines typically pull up in the first 10 items any domain names that match the questionnaire's search inquiry. The second reason for registering names is to prevent competitors from easily entering the market.

Registering domain site names is effective when people are likely to enter very specific search terms.

## Publicity

Publicity remains an effective tactic for every type of business.

Fortunately there are a large number of magazines targeted at both investors and oil and gas producers. Oil-N-Gas will run an extensive publicity program with industry and investment oriented magazines to include both short product announcements, and feature length stories. Oil-N-Gas will hire a company to prepare and send out press releases and to coordinate the follow-up to generate as much publicity as possible. The targeted magazines are listed here.

INVESTMENT ORIENTED MAGAZINES
*The Investment Reporter*
*Bull & Bear Financial Report*
*Financial Product News*
*Futures Magazine*
*Better Investing*
*Texas Banking*
*Energy in the News*
*Oklahoma Banker*
*Oil and Gas Investor*
*Personal Investing News*

OIL AND GAS INDUSTRY MAGAZINES
*AAPG Bulletin*
*Oil & Gas Petroleum Equipment*
*Gas Industries*
*Well Servicing*
*Drilling Contractor*
*Journal of Petroleum Technology*
*Oil & Gas Journal*
*SPE Drilling and Completion*
*SPE Production and Facilities*

## Advertising

On-line companies are increasingly using a wide mix of marketing tactics to build traffic to their sites.

Oil-N-Gas has a $2.5 million advertising budget targeted at investors, and a $250,000 budget targeted at oil and gas producers. The company plans to front end load these advertisements into the first four months of 2000 to generate immediate registrations. Periodical advertising will continue through the year to increase membership.

Oil-N-Gas will also hire a company specializing in the placement of Web page advertising to promote its site to investors on other sites where accredited investors are likely to visit.

## Direct Mail

Direct mail will be sent to key individuals at the 7,500 oil and gas producing companies. Eighty percent of the budget of $400,000 will be budgeted for the first quarter. Oil-N-Gas will hire an outside direct-mail agency to prepare an elaborate mailing that will be much more than just a letter or postcard. We anticipate that each item mailed will cost $3, but also that the item will have enough emphasis to be sure it's opened and read by oil and gas producers. The cost for the mailing is high, but the company can justify it because over 50 percent of the recipients (oil and gas producers) will be soliciting investments in the year 2000.

No direct mail will be sent to investors as they already receive too much mail and it is unlikely it would be opened and read. A more elaborate program, such as the one to oil and gas producers, isn't cost effective for investors because the company can't isolate investors who are most likely to invest in an oil and gas property.

## Trade Shows

Oil-N-Gas will attend several shows that are targeted at gas and oil producers. Those shows include:

SPE (Society of Petroleum Engineers) Production Operations, March 26–31, 2000
SPE Annual Exhibition, October 1–4, 2000

## Alliances/Partnership

Oil-N-Gas has already established an alliance with Amazon.com Internet bookstore. Customers from Oil-N-Gas can order books related to gas and oil investing from Oil-N-Gas, which will then have those products shipped by Amazon.com Oil-N-Gas receives a 25 percent commission on each order shipped.

# Implementation Plan Fall 1999/2000

A public relations firm will be able to generate a great deal more publicity than the company can get on its own in major business magazines.

The Internet has become so crowded that a company needs to use every Internet tactic. Companies need to hire either an experienced on-line marketer or a consultant.

To keep traffic high, regular Web site upgrades need to be scheduled every four to six months.

Use separate tactics for reaching each targeted customer group.

| DATE | ACTION | COST | PERSON RESPONSIBLE |
|---|---|---|---|
| 10/30/99 | Select firm for sending out publicity on Web site to both trade and investment magazines. | $10,000 | . . . . . . . . . . . . |
| 10/30/99 | Select advertising agency for advertising program. | 5,000 | . . . . . . . . . . . . |
| 11/31/99 | Have in place all applicable domain name registrations. | 2,000 | . . . . . . . . . . . . |
| 12/31/99 | Release publicity program. Finalize publicity schedule. | | . . . . . . . . . . . . |
| 12/31/99 | Finalize and release advertising schedule for the year. | | . . . . . . . . . . . . |
| 12/31/99 | Select Internet consultant for setting up low-cost links, selecting spots where Oil-N-Gas should advertise, and solicit advertising from appropriate sources. | 10,000 | . . . . . . . . . . . . |
| 1/15/00 | Initiate new interactive changes for Web page. | 150,000 | . . . . . . . . . . . . |
| 1/15/00 | Web page designs and updated. | 20,000 | . . . . . . . . . . . . |
| 1/15/00 | Publicity releases. | 40,000 | . . . . . . . . . . . . |
| 1/15/00 | Advertising, directed at investors. | 300,000 | . . . . . . . . . . . . |
| 1/15/00 | Advertising, directed at producers. | 40,000 | . . . . . . . . . . . . |
| 1/30/00 | Direct mail. | 100,000 | . . . . . . . . . . . . |
| 2/15/00 | Web page designs and updated. | 20,000 | . . . . . . . . . . . . |
| 2/15/00 | Publicity releases. | 40,000 | . . . . . . . . . . . . |
| 2/15/00 | Advertising, directed at investors. | 500,000 | . . . . . . . . . . . . |
| 2/15/00 | Advertising, directed at producers. | 80,000 | . . . . . . . . . . . . |
| 2/28/00 | Direct mail. | 100,000 | . . . . . . . . . . . . |
| 3/15/00 | Web page designs and updated. | 20,000 | . . . . . . . . . . . . |
| 3/15/00 | Publicity releases. | 40,000 | . . . . . . . . . . . . |
| 3/15/00 | Advertising, directed at investors. | 500,000 | . . . . . . . . . . . . |
| 3/15/00 | Advertising, directed at producers. | 80,000 | . . . . . . . . . . . . |
| 3/20/00 | SPE Production Operation Show. | 15,000 | . . . . . . . . . . . . |
| 3/30/00 | Direct mail. | 100,000 | . . . . . . . . . . . . |
| 4/15/00 | Web page designs and updated. | 20,000 | . . . . . . . . . . . . |
| 4/15/00 | Publicity releases. | 40,000 | . . . . . . . . . . . . |
| 4/15/00 | Advertising, directed at investors. | 300,000 | . . . . . . . . . . . . |
| 4/15/00 | Advertising, directed at producers. | 10,000 | . . . . . . . . . . . . |
| 5/15/00 | Web page designs and updated. | 20,000 | . . . . . . . . . . . . |
| 5/15/00 | Publicity releases. | 40,000 | . . . . . . . . . . . . |
| 5/15/00 | Advertising, directed at investors | 200,000 | . . . . . . . . . . . . |

# MARKETING PLANS OF INTERNET COMPANIES

| DATE | ACTION | COST | PERSON RESPONSIBLE | |
|------|--------|------|--------------------|---|
| 5/15/00 | Advertising, directed at producers. | 5,000 | . . . . . . . . . . . . | ← |
| 6/15/00 | Web page designs and updated. | 20,000 | . . . . . . . . . . . . | On-line mar- |
| 6/15/00 | Publicity releases. | 40,000 | . . . . . . . . . . . . | keters need to |
| 6/15/00 | Advertising, directed at investors. | 100,000 | . . . . . . . . . . . . | keep their |
| 6/30/00 | Direct mail. | 5,000 | . . . . . . . . . . . . | momentum high |
| 6/15/00 | Advertising, directed at producers. | 20,000 | . . . . . . . . . . . . | with a steady |
| 7/15/00 | Web page designs and updated. | 20,000 | . . . . . . . . . . . . | year-long mar- |
| 7/15/00 | Advertising, directed at investors. | 100,000 | . . . . . . . . . . . . | keting effort. |
| 7/15/00 | Advertising, directed at producers. | 5,000 | . . . . . . . . . . . . | |
| 8/15/00 | Web page designs and updated. | 20,000 | . . . . . . . . . . . . | |
| 8/15/00 | Advertising, directed at investors. | 100,000 | . . . . . . . . . . . . | |
| 8/15/00 | Advertising, directed at producers. | 5,000 | . . . . . . . . . . . . | |
| 9/15/00 | Web page designs and updated. | 20,000 | . . . . . . . . . . . . | |
| 9/15/00 | Advertising, directed at investors. | 100,000 | . . . . . . . . . . . . | |
| 9/15/00 | Advertising, directed at producers. | 5,000 | . . . . . . . . . . . . | |
| 9/30/00 | Direct mail. | 40,000 | . . . . . . . . . . . . | |
| 10/1/00 | SPE Annual Exhibition. | 20,000 | . . . . . . . . . . . . | ← |
| 10/15/00 | Web page designs and updated. | 20,000 | . . . . . . . . . . . . | Trade shows are |
| 10/15/00 | Advertising, directed at investors. | 100,000 | . . . . . . . . . . . . | an effective tac- |
| 10/15/00 | Advertising, directed at producers. | 5,000 | . . . . . . . . . . . . | tic for on-line |
| 11/15/00 | Web page designs and updated. | 20,000 | . . . . . . . . . . . . | marketers of |
| 11/15/00 | Advertising, directed at investors. | 100,000 | . . . . . . . . . . . . | special interest |
| 11/15/00 | Advertising, directed at producers. | 5,000 | . . . . . . . . . . . . | information. |
| 11/30/00 | Direct mail. | 20,000 | . . . . . . . . . . . . | |
| 12/15/00 | Web page designs and updated. | 20,000 | . . . . . . . . . . . . | |
| 12/15/00 | Advertising, directed at investors. | 100,000 | . . . . . . . . . . . . | |
| 12/15/00 | Advertising, directed at producers. | 5,000 | . . . . . . . . . . . . | |

## VI Expense Summary

Having the first and biggest site on a topic is the key to long-term on-line success. On-line companies will probably wither and die if they can't be the best.

| CATEGORY | TOTAL COST |
|---|---|
| Web Page Updates | $280,000 |
| Publicity | 250,000 |
| Advertising | |
|    Producers | 250,000 |
|    Investors | $2,500,000 |
| Direct Mail | 400,000 |
| Customer Service/Inside Sales | 250,000 |
| Trade Shows | 35,000 |
| Brochures/Mailing | 185,000 |
| Misc. | 50,000 |
| **Total** | $4,150,000 |

Marketing Plan 2000
C-Ya Greeting Cards
Klamath Falls, Oregon

Plan was written in collaboration with Jeff DeLong, C-Ya Greeting Card president.

# Executive Summary

## Company Description

C-Ya Greetings Cards is a greeting card company that sells relationship closure cards, which are cards that people can send to their ex-partner after they break up. Some of C-Ya's key customer group, singles breaking up and couples getting divorced, also use the cards when they leave employers they don't like. A sample greeting card uses the phrase "I Think I Can, I Think I Can, I Think I Can" on one side of the card, and the phrase "Why the Hell Should I" on the other. All the cards then end with the phrase "C-Ya." The company started selling its cards exclusively on an Internet Web site but has now branched out–selling its cards to a wide variety of retail outlets. C-Ya sells over two hundred thousand cards per year with a retail value of $2.99 each.

> C-Ya is a manufacturer that started out on the Internet and subsequently went retail.

## Current Situation

C-Ya's Web site came on-line in September of 1997 and since then has been able to build a brand awareness among its target customer group for its cards and other items such as T-shirts, sweatshirts, and mouse pads. The company has been branching out from its Web base and now sells its cards at hair salons, airport gift shops, and singles bars, and is on the verge of signing contracts with major companies that will greatly expand its distribution.

> The Internet site built brand awareness in the retail market.

While the Internet has been an excellent avenue to introduce the C-Ya greeting card, it is difficult to build a multimillion-dollar business selling $2.99 cards one or two at a time. The company has been able to grow its sales at a faster rate by branching out with new retail outlets that place orders that range from $150 to $1,000. It is now pursuing even larger distribution outlets that can produce in the hundreds of thousands of dollars each year.

## Marketing Strategy

C-Ya's success has been primarily driven by its unique product line that addresses the end of a relationship, a market never addressed by any major greeting card company. The product line drives the company's success and one of the key components of the company strategy is to continue to introduce new cards every year. C-Ya also plans on continuing to build its brand with its Web site and extensive publicity campaign. Its primary sales focus will be expanding its penetration in retail markets and seeking marketing arrangements with major partners that have the potential to rapidly expand sales.

## Marketing Goals

C-Ya's goals for 2000 are to continue to build its brand name as the leading innovative supplier of closure cards and expand its distribution network to expand the number of singles or soon-to-be divorced adults aware of the C-Ya line. C-Ya's specific goal is to ship over five hundred thousand C-Ya cards in 2000.

# Situation Analysis

## Internal Audit

**Company Background.** C-Ya greeting cards were first conceived in 1993 by their founder Jeff DeLong while he was watching *The Oprah Winfrey Show* on the importance of having closure in a relationship. DeLong was going through a divorce at the time and he believed the idea of having a closure card to end a relationship or marriage was a great idea. The company was unable to sell its product successfully until 1997 when it started to sell the product over the Internet.

The Internet proved to be an ideal vehicle for C-Ya for a number of reasons.

1. Web pages for single and divorced people are extremely popular on the Internet and those sites were a perfect fit for interlinks with the C-Ya site.
2. The word closure became popular in 1997 and the C-Ya closure cards came up early in any listing of search engine results. That early listing not only built traffic, but it also was a major factor in the extensive national TV, radio, and print publicity that the company has received.
3. The nature of the Web allowed C-Ya to offer a free C-Ya card that could be downloaded from its site, which provided the company an inexpensive tactic to build traffic to its Web site.

C-Ya provides a product that its target customer wants and that is not readily available from any other source.

C-Ya was successful because there were many Web sites where its target customer group went for information.

C-Ya was able to quickly build its business on the Web to over ten thousand card sales per month. The large number of site visitors that C-Ya attracted also kept C-Ya high on the "top results" list of Internet search engines, which helped build the site's momentum.

Another key factor in the company's success was, and still is, that its product was and still is unique and that the site was reaching a target audience who didn't have any other similar product to buy. Customers showed their cards to friends and those friends became C-Ya customers. This word of mouth also led to retail stores (primarily hair salons at first) calling the company to see if the cards could be purchased on a wholesale basis for resale. The company responded by creating a display for the C-Ya cards and started selling the cards in displays for total prices that ranged from $150 to $500.

> Retail distribution has the advantage of producing a much higher average sale than does the average Internet sale.

The company realized that it wasn't much more work selling a $500 display than it was to sell four cards over the Internet. The company had two choices to continue to grow in the future. It could either add a broader product line to increase its income potential from any one customer, or it could use its brand building success on the Internet to expand its distribution network. The company has added seven other products on the Internet site, but has realized that the company's real growth is expanding distribution. While the company continues to encourage sales to retailers, it doesn't have the resources to set up an effective distribution network, and has therefore decided to pursue major alliances with companies that can distribute its products to a broad market. The emphasis in 2000 is to strike deals with partners that sell direct to consumers in order to continue to build the C-Ya brand, and then in 2001 and 2002 strike alliances with companies that can broaden the company's retail distribution network.

**Product Profile.** C-Ya currently has over 50 card designs available and it offers displays of 125, 250, and 500 cards, with either 25 or 50 card designs in each display. One advantage of C-Ya's Internet site is that it produces instant market research regarding what card designs are most and least popular and that information helps C-Ya ensure that each card it offers to retailers is popular and will sell well. This information also allows C-Ya to put together packs of five of its most popular cards for the major alliance partners it is working with for the year 2000. The packs of five are important as otherwise C-Ya cards at $2.99 are too inexpensive for customers to justify the shipping and handling cost.

> C-Ya packaged its cards together in order to have a price that justified a marketing program by its alliance partners.

**Site Profile.** C-Ya's Web site is designed to take visitors quickly to the cards they want. C-Ya's home page downloads in half the time of most pages, and allows the visitor to quickly view C-Ya's card selection. The site is designed to sell cards, and it moves visitors through the site in a hurry. The site also offers a free card that customers can download, a feature that 3,000 people per day take advantage of. The free card service was started to build site traffic and brand awareness for the C-Ya name. The free downloaded cards will be dropped in 2000 in order to encourage a higher percentage of visitors to purchase a card and to cut the cost of hosting the Web site.

**Interlinks.** Much of C-Ya's initial growth was generated through links with other sites. The company has used rotating banner ads as a method of linking rather than having a special resource section on its site that lists other sites. The banner ad linkage program consists of C-Ya agreeing with another site serving the same target market to include the other site's banner ad in its rotation. This interlink practice has allowed C-Ya to keep its Web site clear of clutter so visitors can concentrate on buying a card. Web sites typical of the ones that C-Ya interlinks with are:

lovestories.com

cupid.net

dateable.com

solosingle.com

divorcecentral.com

getwild.com

singlescoach.com

studentbodies.com

divorcesource.com

singlesmall.com

singlescafe.net

adolescentadulthood.com

dating.about.com

One reason C-Ya has been an attractive interlink partner is that its publicity and high ranking in Internet searches bring an average of over three thousand visitors per day to the site.

**Sales Profile.** The site has produced excellent results, with 2 to 5 percent of the site's visitors making a purchase. Retail stores that have started to sell the C-Ya cards have all contacted the company directly for their initial purchase. Most of the stores are places frequented by young adults, including hair salons, bars, and restaurants. Airport gift shops are another retail group that added the product. All of the retailers like the product because of its unique message and because many of their customers are breaking off a relationship. C-Ya has not had to pursue this business because the retailers have discovered C-Ya greeting cards on their own. The company doesn't have the resources to pursue this market more aggressively. C-Ya has also tried posting pages on various shopping malls, but that sales channel hasn't worked out at all for C-Ya. C-Ya has not been willing to sign on other sites as distribution outlets. The company wanted to maintain its exclusivity as an enticement for a potential major Internet marketing partner.

*Author's note:* The plan as printed in this book does not state specific growth or sales numbers, because the company wanted that information kept proprietary. Instead the plan includes vague statements regarding growth, such as "greater than 20 percent." The actual plan C-Ya uses includes more specific numbers.

**Sales Trends.** C-Ya Greeting Cards was been able to generate an annual increase in sales of over 25 percent per year for both Internet card sales and retail store sales since it started in

Very few on-line businesses will have the feeding system of like-minded sites that C-Ya has.

Retailers want C-Ya's product line because it is so popular with its target customer group.

September of 1997. C-Ya wants to branch away from the Internet over the next two years for several reasons. The first is that today there are over 2.5 billion pages on the Internet. Many of the sites are being heavily advertised through traditional mass media outlets such as TV and print advertising. The media portrays the Internet as a great distribution outlet for smaller companies, but in fact the opposite is true today. Search engine protocols give preference to sites that are visited frequently by a person directly entering the site's Web address on his or her browser. Sites with a large advertising budget draw direct traffic, and jump to the top of the rankings for Internet searches. Smaller companies have a very hard time being pulled up on the Internet when they don't appear in the top 20 search engine placements, and small companies' other distribution outlet, on-line shopping malls, have not performed well for most consumer products aimed at large target markets. C-Ya's ability to survive in the upcoming years as an Internet marketer depends on its ability to develop its brand name, a task that can be more readily accomplished now through retail stores and partnership arrangements.

The second reason that C-Ya is pushing other distribution outlets is simply that it makes more money on large orders. Shipping out an order for two to five cards has more administrative costs as the company has grown larger, and the profit per order has dropped correspondingly.

*The Internet's search engine protocols favor sites that have already established a heavy traffic pattern.*

## Strengths and Weaknesses

### Strengths

1. Company founder Jeff DeLong has been able to continually come up with creative new cards with sayings that connect with his target customer group.
2. C-Ya was on the Internet before the number of Web pages exploded in late 1998 and 1999. This head start has made it impossible for competitors such as Revenge.com or Break-Up.com to develop a significant market presence.
3. Jeff DeLong's willingness to talk to the media has positioned him as the expert on closure cards. He continues to get calls for TV and radio interviews on a regular basis.
4. Holding the leading Web position for a product or as an informational source is proving to be a major competitive advantage. Sites holding this designation are being bought and sold for incredible prices as Web leaders are difficult to dislodge.
5. C-Ya's retail sales also work to reinforce C-Ya's position as a market leader, as well acting as a catalyst for people to visit the Web site.
6. C-Ya has experience in working the Web and keeping its name being listed as a top ranked site by Internet search engines.

*Successful on-line retailers typically have a product that is unique or hard to obtain in the retail market.*

### Weaknesses

1. C-Ya has very little experience setting up a retail distribution network.
2. C-Ya doesn't have the resources to compete with some of the major new greeting card Web sites, such as 123greetings.com, which have initiated a heavy promotional budget in mid-1999. The short- and long-term impact of some of these sites on C-Ya's site is unknown at this time.

## Customer Information

**Customer Profile.** There are 80 million single adults in the United States, 58 percent, or 46.4 million who are under the age of 29. Many of these young singles are Internet savvy and spend a significant amount of time on the Internet, frequently at sites for singles.

These singles appreciate a witty, funny card that delivers the message that a relationship is over. While five hundred thousand cards seems significant, it is only a small percentage of the market of people breaking off a relationship or getting divorced. The cards go a long way toward easing the difficult situation that exists when couples break up.

**Customer Buying Patterns.** Most customers purchase a C-Ya greeting card on impulse when they are breaking up. Breaking off a relationship or getting a divorce is an emotionally draining experience and the people involved in the breakup are more likely to buy a card on an impulse if they see it in a display. This is another major reason the company is branching out into retail stores and why it is looking to find major partners to place C-Ya cards in front of its target customer group as often as possible.

## Market Profile

**Markets Served.** One of the reasons C-Ya had trouble launching its product before it opened its Internet page is that there wasn't a recognized market for relationship closure cards, or for any products that related to the ending of a relationship on less than ideal terms. The number of potential customers was large, possibly as many as 10 to 20 million people per year end a relationship, but there wasn't any organized place where potential customers congregated or bought products. The Internet changed that, with sites for both singles and divorced people to get information, join chat rooms, and participate in forums. C-Ya was a great addition to those sites as it gave people a new outlet for expressing their feelings to a former partner is a relationship.

Outside of the Internet, C-Ya still does not have a recognized market with an established distribution channel. It has built its success selling cards to locations where people who have been disappointed in a relationship might gather. Salons where women often go for a makeover

---

C-Ya is responding to the major new on-line greeting card companies by forming alliances with larger TV and on-line retailers.

---

Evaluating how customers purchase a product helped C-Ya select its distribution network.

---

The Internet has produced a large number of meeting sites and forums for customers that would otherwise be hard to find.

after a breakup have worked out well for C-Ya, as have bars where short-term relationships often start or end. The lack of a definable market is one of the reasons that C-Ya is looking to hook up with alliance partners that can expose the product to a broader market than singles and divorced people who frequent Internet sites targeted at them.

### Past and Current Trends
1. The number of Web users is expanding rapidly.
2. The number of Web pages has expanded so quickly that Internet sites have trouble attracting users to their sites through all the clutter on the Web.
3. The number of single adults is expected to continue to increase.
4. The popularity of singles' sites on the Internet may lead to more retail or TV shopping sites geared toward singles. The singles' market is large with 80 million people, but at the moment it is only served by a few marketers such as Club Med vacation sites and some singles clubs.
5. People are increasingly willing to download greeting cards and then forward them to a friend, relative, or ex-boyfriend or girlfriend.
6. The price for greeting cards, even from industry leaders like Hallmark, is dropping, with many cards now available at 99 cents.

*Author's note:* Larger companies would typically have detailed numbers to define both market trends and customer profiles. In C-Ya's case, it has sold to only a small percentage of the potential market, and the numbers are not that relevant to its potential success. So C-Ya chose not to worry about the exact numbers.

## Opportunities and Threats

### Opportunities
1. C-Ya has just scratched the surface of the market for singles breaking up and divorced people, even at five hundred thousand cards per year.
2. There are few other products targeted at people ending a relationship. C-Ya should be able to market a full line of products over time aimed at people breaking up. C-Ya has just started to offer alternative products.
3. There is also a big market for couples who have a reached a point in their relationship where they have an unresolved issue to work out. One product line to do that is a Ya-But line of cards, for people to let their partners know when communications are breaking down. A sample card could state on one side of the card "Ya But, Ya But, Ya But."

People have a hard time finding small retailers on the Internet because it has become so crowded.

C-Ya has an enormous market opportunity that no other firm is exploiting.

The other side could be "Three Ya-Buts and you're out. Let's talk." The card line could still be sold under the C-Ya product line as it adds a little more urgency to the card.

4. C-Ya has closely held onto its brand and refused to let other companies sell the line, as well as holding the line on retail pricing, staying at $2.99, even though many greeting cards are now sold at 99 cents. C-Ya has protected the brand so that it would be more appealing to a major partner in a marketing agreement.

C-Ya is expanding its product line based on what customers would like to see.

### Threats

1. Some people are predicting that the Web is becoming so crowded that it will stop being effective; some experts even predict the Web will implode from data overload.
2. A large greeting card company will try to compete with C-Ya's relationship closure cards. The main factor preventing that is those companies are used to creating sentimental or humorous cards, and not breakup cards.

**Competitor Audit.** Two competitors have tried to compete with C-Ya. One is revenge.com and the other is breakup.com. Neither company has had much success in knocking C-Ya off of its leadership role, and they are nearly as desirable as an interlink partner or as a media interview as C-Ya. The workings on today's crowed Internet works very much to C-Ya's favor. Once a company establishes a pre-eminent position in search engines, their sites continue to get the most hits, which keeps them at the top of the search engines' "top site" list. The only way to overcome that advantage is an extensive advertising campaign in print, radio, or television to get people to directly enter the site name. That may be a cost-effective tactic for a major market. But it is not effective in smaller niche markets where the potential purchasers (people who are about to break up) are difficult to locate. C-Ya is a perfect size market, substantial, with many sites targeted at the same target customer group, but still too small to justify an extensive advertising program.

The nature of Internet search engines makes it difficult for new companies to compete on most products.

## Positioning

### Positioning Statements

For the target customer group: C-Ya Greeting Cards are far and away the market leader in the relationship closure cards and products.

For the potential distributors or alliance partners: C-Ya Greeting Cards sell fast when placed in locations where single adults visit or congregate. The only factor holding back total sales is that the C-Ya greeting cards do not have a wide enough distribution.

### Positioning Tactics

1. C-Ya will keep expanding its retail distribution. Currently C-Ya is the only relationship greeting card company with retail as well as Internet distribution. C-Ya also wants to have the biggest retail distribution network in case an Internet competitor wants to follow it into the retail market.
2. Continue to add new cards, with 15 to 25 new card designs currently being projected for 2000.
3. Continue to do all requested media interviews
4. Strike deals with two major marketers in 2000 to exponentially expand the market's awareness of C-Ya's greeting cards.

> C-Ya's tactics are all designed to give it exposure and momentum, two factors that hinder potential competitors.

### Other Marketing Tactics

1. Continue its active interlink (also referred to as affiliate) strategy with sites targeted at young single adults and/or divorced adults.
2. Discontinue the free downloaded card to encourage additional card purchases, and to avoid hurting the sales efforts of the major partners.
3. Revise Web site every four to six months to keep it looking fresh to its frequent customers.
4. Continue to promote on the site other products such as apparel and mouse pads.

## Marketing Tactics

**Retail Distribution.** C-Ya will continue to have a wholesale page on its site, and will continue to follow up with both interested inquiries and current customers. Special announcements will be sent to the retailers announcing new cards and also holiday specials.

**New Cards.** C-Ya will continue to add a minimum of four new card designs per quarter. Poor selling cards will be deleted at the same time new cards are added. C-Ya will also experiment with holiday theme cards that people can send to a person who broke off the relationship with them. For instance on Valentine's Day, a card could say on one side "Last year I had a great Valentine's Day" and on the other side "You sure pulled the wool over my eyes" with the customary C-Ya on the bottom. C-Ya has also discovered that many of its customers are using its cards to bid a "fond" farewell to their employer. C-Ya will add several cards next year aimed at people quitting their jobs.

**Publicity.** C-Ya has always received a substantial amount of media coverage due to its unusual product line. This publicity has resulted in many direct hits from Internet users, as well inquiries from retailers. More importantly the continuing publicity on major stations such as CNN and major shows such as *Good Day New York* helps keep C-Ya as the number one name in its market.

**Partnerships.** One pending partnership is with giftpoint.com, a major Internet retailer with a large mass media budget that will offer the cards on its Internet site. This is a key alliance for C-Ya because it exposes its greeting cards to people who aren't at the moment breaking off a relationship. This added exposure to single, married, or divorced adults encourages those adults to return to buy a C-Ya card if the relationship should come to an end. The other partnership is with sitetoshop.com, a site that will be adding a weekly and possibly daily cable TV show to help promote its products. Again this helps C-Ya as it is targeted at more than people breaking up. C-Ya doesn't have the financial resources to reach out to the general population in the way that these two sites do, and their marketing will expose C-Ya Greeting Cards to many more people than it is reaching today.

**Interlink or Affiliate Program.** C-Ya will continue to exchange banner ads with other sites targeted at its market.

**Discontinue the Free Downloaded Cards.** The free downloaded cards were originally offered to build brand awareness and site traffic. Currently about 3,000 cards are downloaded. While not all of those 3,000 downloads will turn into purchases with this change, C-Ya expects that 5 to 10 percent of the downloaders will now purchase a card. The other drawback to downloading cards is that C-Ya pays a fee to the company hosting its site based on usage. With the large number of downloads, C-Ya is paying for over 10 gigabytes of activity per month.

**Web Revisions.** The company will continue to make major revisions to its site every four to six months to mark the arrival of new cards or products to its site.

**Accessory Products.** C-Ya will continue to offer accessory products on its site to produce additional income. The products currently being offered include:

| | |
|---|---|
| T-shirts | Tank Tops |
| Lofteez | Twill Hats |
| Mouse Pads | Sports Shirts |
| Sweatshirts | Coasters |

Alliances allow C-Ya to cost effectively promote its products to people it otherwise would not reach.

Marketers of low-cost products need to try to increase the size of their average sale with auxiliary products.

## Implementation Plan/2000

*Note*: Cost and person responsible have been deleted at the company's request.

| DATE | ACTION | COST | PERSON RESPONSIBLE |
|------|--------|------|--------------------|
| 1/15/00 | Send out announcements for Valentine Cards to Retailers. | . . . . | . . . . . . . . . . . . |
| 1/15/00 | Add/delete sites from affiliate program. | . . . . | . . . . . . . . . . . . |
| 1/30/00 | Discontinue free downloaded card. | . . . . | . . . . . . . . . . . . |
| 2/15/00 | Add/delete sites from affiliate program. | . . . . | . . . . . . . . . . . . |
| 2/15/00 | Add new products or options to wholesale page for retailers. | . . . . | . . . . . . . . . . . . |
| 2/28/00 | Finalize details of first partnership program. | . . . . | . . . . . . . . . . . . |
| 3/15/00 | Add/delete sites from affiliate program. | . . . . | . . . . . . . . . . . . |
| 3/30/00 | Add a minimum of four new cards. | . . . . | . . . . . . . . . . . . |
| 4/15/00 | Add/delete sites from affiliate program. | . . . . | . . . . . . . . . . . . |
| 4/15/00 | Complete Web site revisions. | . . . . | . . . . . . . . . . . . |
| 4/30/00 | Finalize details of second partnership program. | . . . . | . . . . . . . . . . . . |
| 5/15/00 | Add/delete sites from affiliate program. | . . . . | . . . . . . . . . . . . |
| 5/15/00 | Add new products or options to wholesale page for retailers. | . . . . | . . . . . . . . . . . . |
| 6/15/00 | Add/delete sites from affiliate program. | . . . . | . . . . . . . . . . . . |
| 6/30/00 | Add a minimum of four new cards. | . . . . | . . . . . . . . . . . . |
| 7/15/00 | Add/delete sites from affiliate program. | . . . . | . . . . . . . . . . . . |
| 8/15/00 | Add/delete sites from affiliate program. | . . . . | . . . . . . . . . . . . |
| 8/15/00 | Complete Web site revisions. | . . . . | . . . . . . . . . . . . |
| 8/15/00 | Add new products or options to wholesale page for retailers. | . . . . | . . . . . . . . . . . . |
| 9/15/00 | Add/delete sites from affiliate program. | . . . . | . . . . . . . . . . . . |
| 9/30/00 | Add a minimum of four new cards. | . . . . | . . . . . . . . . . . . |
| 10/15/00 | Add/delete sites from affiliate program. | . . . . | . . . . . . . . . . . . |
| 11/15/00 | Add/delete sites from affiliate program. | . . . . | . . . . . . . . . . . . |
| 11/15/00 | Add new products or options to wholesale page for retailers. | . . . . | . . . . . . . . . . . . |
| 11/30/00 | Add a minimum of four new cards. | . . . . | . . . . . . . . . . . . |
| 12/15/00 | Add/delete sites from affiliate program. | . . . . | . . . . . . . . . . . . |
| 12/15/00 | Complete Web site revisions. | . . . . | . . . . . . . . . . . . |

← C-Ya wants to add services and products as it expands its retail distribution.

← C-Ya is spreading its new card introductions throughout the year to keep its momentum strong.

## Final Comments

Internet marketing has introduced a new key element to marketing: building Web site traffic. Although traditional marketing tactics—such as developing a positioning strategy, having a customer focus, and creating a memorable message—still hold true, they don't have anywhere near the importance they have in the non-Internet world. The difference is that the Internet just doesn't create the visual or emotional impact of other media. So the task of an on-line marketer is first, to bring people to it's site, and then to have a reason they should keep coming to the site.

As you read the three on-line marketing plans, you noticed that the companies have more complex strategies than the earlier marketing plans in an effort to bring people to the site. Magnet sites, banner ad trading programs, free products or stock picks, interlinks, and domain name registrations are just a few of the tactics companies use to attract traffic. Companies have to work hard and be innovative if they expect to get traffic. Most successful small on-line companies have programmers or marketers who spend 15 to 30 hours per week working on their site or arranging for banner ad trades in order to build traffic.

Cross promotions and alliances have become a key tactic in the traditional marketing world. They are far more important for Internet marketers because it is impossible for any small company to reach more than just a small percentage of their target customers. C-Ya would not have had a chance on-line if it had not started to partner with all the sites that focused on singles and divorced adults. The difficulty in attracting a large number of customers to a site has made positioning a difficult decision for on-line companies. Typically marketers position themselves to attract a certain type of customer. On the Internet you don't want to lose a visitor if you can help it, and most on-line retailers try to have something for everyone. On-line marketing may turn out to be the one marketing arena where companies are better off not being focused on one group of customers. BHD Corp. is a good example. It has the Short Term Stock Selector for people who want to choose their own stocks, and Mutual Fund Magic for those who want someone else to handle their stock decisions.

> On-line marketers need to have products for every visitor if they want to maximize their revenues.

On-line marketing is still changing rapidly, but one fact has become clear. Web site traffic begets more Web site traffic, and traffic has become the most important element in e-commerce. That's why dot-com companies are advertising so heavily in print and on TV. They want to grab an early lead in traffic because they know that lead may become an insurmountable obstacle to competitors.

There has been a lot written on how on-line companies are all losing money. That's not true. Both BHD Corp. and C-Ya Greeting Cards have made money from their first year. Money can be made if you have a strategy that delivers a product people want and that brings those people to your site. On-line marketing is even the preferred method for markets in which customers are scattered and hard to locate. The important point to remember is that by no means is an Internet Web site like advertising. When you put an ad in a magazine, you know people will see it. You just need to know how to grab the readers' attention and then sell them on your product. On-line you have absolutely no guarantee that anyone will see your Web page. You won't succeed unless you know how to bring people to your site. Unfortunately you can't wait and see what will happen. First come, first served is the rule of the day. If you don't dominate the Web, you will be lost in the Web hinterlands where nobody goes to visit. So I recommend starting by going to Web sites like www.virtualpromote.com to learn every trick of the trade in building traffic, then assign someone to spend 20 to 30 hours per week setting up interlinks, and then launching your program. If you are lucky, you'll get a great on-line program like C-Ya's that not only makes money on the Internet, but that uses its on-line dominance to build a retail distribution network.

Small on-line companies are making money selling products or services on the Internet.

You need to choose a target customer and product that are just right to succeed on the Internet.

## Traffic Stop

If you can answer yes to the following questions, you should be able to launch a profitable on-line business. Be sure to incorporate every one of these elements into your marketing plan. The old adage "Leave no stone unturned" is especially true in on-line marketing.

|  | YES | NO |
|---|---|---|
| 1. Are there many sites on the Web that appeal to your target customer group? | _____ | _____ |
| 2. Is an active banner ad trading program or interlink network established for your target customer? | _____ | _____ |
| 3. Are there distinctive names you can use in your site to attract visitors? For example, C-Ya used the term *closure greeting cards* because closure was a popular term. Oil-N-Gas's name is deliberately chosen because that is how people enter a search term? | _____ | _____ |
| 4. Is your product category still without a dominant Web site? | _____ | _____ |
| 5. Do you have anything valuable to prospects that can be downloaded as a giveaway? | _____ | _____ |
| 6. Are there any associations or other groups that are focused on your customers with whom you could form an alliance? | _____ | _____ |
| 7. Do you have a product or service that people know they want but have trouble finding? | _____ | _____ |

If you haven't checked yes to most of these questions, you will need to market your site through traditional tactics, which can be expensive.

# Marketing Plan Workbook

**CHAPTER 14** THE OPENING **CHAPTER 15** SITUATION ANALYSIS
**CHAPTER 16** STRATEGY, TACTICS, AND IMPLEMENTATION

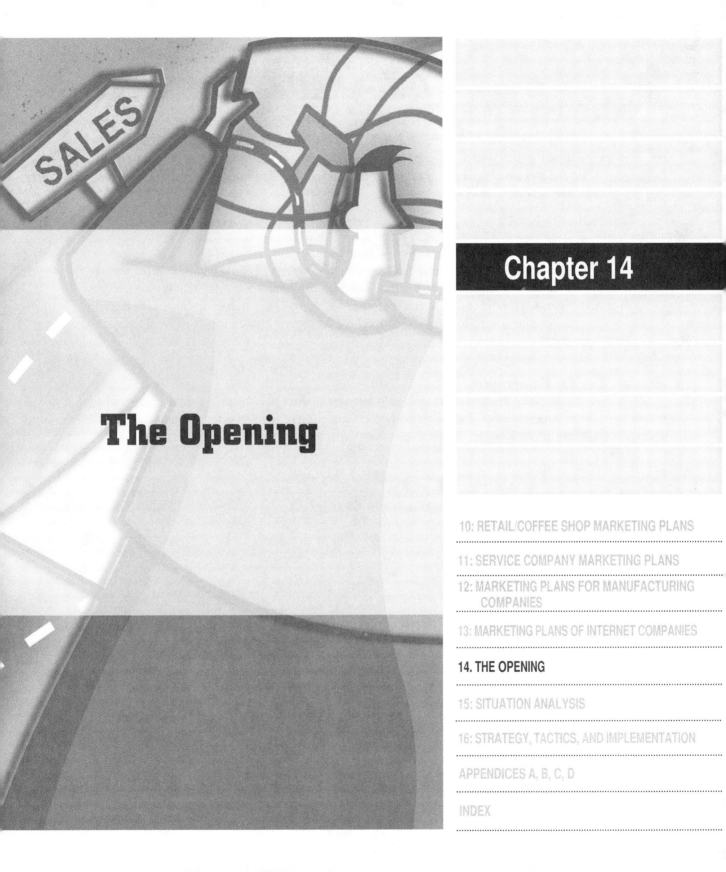

# Chapter 14

## The Opening

10: RETAIL/COFFEE SHOP MARKETING PLANS

11: SERVICE COMPANY MARKETING PLANS

12: MARKETING PLANS FOR MANUFACTURING
COMPANIES

13: MARKETING PLANS OF INTERNET COMPANIES

**14. THE OPENING**

15: SITUATION ANALYSIS

16: STRATEGY, TACTICS, AND IMPLEMENTATION

APPENDICES A, B, C, D

INDEX

The opening of a marketing plan is a short capsule of what you will be trying to do over the next year, ending with the marketing plan's objectives. People should be able to read your opening and know exactly what you are trying to accomplish. The opening is helpful to employees, investors, and customer advisors.

People should be able to read your opening in one to two minutes.

## Executive Summary Section

The summary section of the plan can vary tremendously among marketing plans depending on your situation. What is important is that your executive summary explain what you are doing for the year. You should be able to achieve this in 500 words or less in even the most complicated situation. After you fill in the workbook section, you can go back and add additional information if needed.

### First Paragraph

List your business name, what your business is, where it is located (if appropriate), and your target customer. *Example:* Don Miguel's is a chain of eight Mexican restaurants in Albuquerque, New Mexico that targets young couples between 16 and 35 years old.

Keep your first paragraph simple and direct.

## *MARKETING PLAN*

## Table of Contents

1. Executive Summary
2. Marketing Objectives
3. Situation Analysis
   A. Internal Audit
      1. Company Operations
      2. Product/Service Description and Profile
      3. Sales Trends
      4. Last Year's Commentary
      5. Strengths/Weaknesses
   B. External Evaluation
      1. Customer Information
      2. Market Profile
4. Positioning
   A. Positioning Strategies
      1. New Strategies
      2. Continuing Strategies
   B. Additional Marketing Strategies
      1. New Strategies
      2. Continuing Strategies
   C. Rationale for Strategy
   D. Competitive Positioning
5. Marketing Tactics
   A. Product
   B. Pricing
   C. Distribution
   D. Advertising/Public Relations
   E. Trade Shows
   F. Electronic Media
   G. Events
   H. Alliances/Partnerships
   I. Other Tactics
6. Implementation Plan: (dates, activity, cost summary, person responsible)
7. Expense Summary

The marketing plan describes the situation, your strategy for the situation, and your implementation plan to increase sales.

Every marketing tactic you use, no matter how mundane should be listed in the plan.

Next, you want to add more descriptive details that give readers a little better understanding of your business. Don't describe your business in too much detail; that will come in the internal evaluation section of the plan. *Example:* Don Miguel's restaurants are located in areas of Albuquerque where there are many entertainment options, including movies, bars with entertainment, and sports clubs. The restaurants seat 175 to 225 people and do over 50 percent of their business after 9:00 P.M.

Always start the plan by explaining who you are. Don't assume you will be the only person to read your plan.

Give a brief commentary about the company's sales growth and marketing strategy over the past few years. *Example:* Don Miguel's per-restaurant sales have grown 16 percent per year over the past three years, due primarily to the popularity of their expanded appetizer menus and super-sized margaritas. If your sales have declined or remained stagnant, you may want to list the main reason that sales have not grown. *Example*: Don Miguel's sales have declined 3 percent over the past year because of increased competition from sports clubs and the opening of two popular clubs that feature swing dancing.

I've found that most companies experience substantial changes in their market situation each year.

## Second Paragraph

The second paragraph must capture the major factor in the situation of your business. In some cases you may describe the situation that faces your business such as the appearance of new competitors, the development of new opportunities or threats, or the fact that your competitors have put you in a competitive situation. In other cases the major situation may revolve around the actions you may be taking such as expansion into new markets, expansion of current business, or entry into a new target market. If your business, product, or service is new, your second paragraph should concentrate on the opportunity you are pursuing, listing who the target market is, what need or desire they have that isn't being met, and why your business is well suited to attack this opportunity.

. . . . . . . . . . . . . . . . . . . . . . . . . . . . . . . . . . . . . . . . . . . . . . . . . . . . . . . . . . . . . . . . . . . . . . . . .

. . . . . . . . . . . . . . . . . . . . . . . . . . . . . . . . . . . . . . . . . . . . . . . . . . . . . . . . . . . . . . . . . . . . . . . . .

. . . . . . . . . . . . . . . . . . . . . . . . . . . . . . . . . . . . . . . . . . . . . . . . . . . . . . . . . . . . . . . . . . . . . . . . .

. . . . . . . . . . . . . . . . . . . . . . . . . . . . . . . . . . . . . . . . . . . . . . . . . . . . . . . . . . . . . . . . . . . . . . . . .

. . . . . . . . . . . . . . . . . . . . . . . . . . . . . . . . . . . . . . . . . . . . . . . . . . . . . . . . . . . . . . . . . . . . . . . . .

*Your strategy should be stated as a customer focus. It should be based at least in part on what customers want.*

## Third Paragraph

This paragraph should be a short explanation of your strategy and tactics for the next year. The first sentence should say that your company or product name will address whatever the situation is, using your major marketing strategy. *For example*: If Don Miguel's is being threatened by sports clubs and swing clubs, their plan might concentrate on adding more entertainment value to its restaurants. *Example*: Don Miguel's will respond to the increased competition from sports bars and swing dance clubs by adding more entertainment features to its restaurants. The next part of the paragraph should briefly explain what tactics you will use. *Example*: Don Miguel's will add game nights, live entertainment on the weekends, and mariachis during dinner on Wednesday and Thursday. (Don't list every tactic you plan on implementing, just the major ones.)

. . . . . . . . . . . . . . . . . . . . . . . . . . . . . . . . . . . . . . . . . . . . . . . . . . . . . . . . . . . . . . . . . . . . . . . . .

. . . . . . . . . . . . . . . . . . . . . . . . . . . . . . . . . . . . . . . . . . . . . . . . . . . . . . . . . . . . . . . . . . . . . . . . .

. . . . . . . . . . . . . . . . . . . . . . . . . . . . . . . . . . . . . . . . . . . . . . . . . . . . . . . . . . . . . . . . . . . . . . . . .

. . . . . . . . . . . . . . . . . . . . . . . . . . . . . . . . . . . . . . . . . . . . . . . . . . . . . . . . . . . . . . . . . . . . . . . . .

. . . . . . . . . . . . . . . . . . . . . . . . . . . . . . . . . . . . . . . . . . . . . . . . . . . . . . . . . . . . . . . . . . . . . . . . .

*Be sure that your positioning strategy, if properly executed, will clearly make you a preferred supplier.*

## Last Paragraph

The last paragraph should be very short. It should just list your major positioning goals (no more than two) and your sales objectives. *Example*: In 2000 Don Miguel's will re-establish itself as the premium entertainment restaurant for young couples between 18 and 32 in the Albuquerque area. The company plans on increasing sales 8 percent during the year and improving its critical after–9:00 P.M. business by 15 percent.

. . . . . . . . . . . . . . . . . . . . . . . . . . . . . . . . . . . . . . . . . . . . . . . . . .
. . . . . . . . . . . . . . . . . . . . . . . . . . . . . . . . . . . . . . . . . . . . . . . . . .
. . . . . . . . . . . . . . . . . . . . . . . . . . . . . . . . . . . . . . . . . . . . . . . . . .
. . . . . . . . . . . . . . . . . . . . . . . . . . . . . . . . . . . . . . . . . . . . . . . . . .
. . . . . . . . . . . . . . . . . . . . . . . . . . . . . . . . . . . . . . . . . . . . . . . . . .

**Your goals should be clear, measurable and a stretch to achieve.**

This format will give your executive summary all the information it needs for most readers. You can add details if you feel more information is needed to convey a brief description of your situation and marketing strategy, but don't go overboard. This is a summary section.

## Marketing Objectives and Goals

I like to place this section next in the marketing plan because it contains the key information that management likes to look at. It is also the section that clearly reminds you what you are trying to accomplish for the year. Use the same form first presented in Chapter 6 to prepare the first and third parts of this section on sales and measurable marketing objectives. You first completed the positioning statement for your strategy on the Position Strategy form on pages 78 to 800. You may not have all the information listed on this form. If you don't have it, and can't get it, just leave that information out of your final plan.

### Marketing and Sales Objectives

Sales Dollar Objectives: . . . . . . . . . . . . . . . . . . . . . . . . . . . . . . . . . . . . . . .

Percentage Increase from Prior Year: . . . . . . . . . . . . . . . . . . . . . . . . . . . . . . .

Market Share: . . . . . . . . . . . . . . . . . . . . . . . . . . . . . . . . . . . . . . . . . . . . . . .

Percentage Increase from Prior Year: . . . . . . . . . . . . . . . . . . . . . . . . . . . . . . .

Major Target Customer: . . . . . . . . . . . . . . . . . . . . . . . . . . . . . . . . . . . . . . . .

Market Share: . . . . . . . . . . . . . . . . . . . . . . . . . . . . . . . . . . . . . . . . . . . . . . .

Percentage Increase from Prior Year: . . . . . . . . . . . . . . . . . . . . . . . . . . . . . . .

**Your sales and marketing objectives should be clear and measurable.**

### Positioning Statements

Positioning statement for consumers.

. . . . . . . . . . . . . . . . . . . . . . . . . . . . . . . . . . . . . . . . . . . . . . . . . . .

. . . . . . . . . . . . . . . . . . . . . . . . . . . . . . . . . . . . . . . . . . . . . . . . . . .

. . . . . . . . . . . . . . . . . . . . . . . . . . . . . . . . . . . . . . . . . . . . . . . . . . .

Positioning statement for the distribution network.

. . . . . . . . . . . . . . . . . . . . . . . . . . . . . . . . . . . . . . . . . . . . . . . . . . .

. . . . . . . . . . . . . . . . . . . . . . . . . . . . . . . . . . . . . . . . . . . . . . . . . . .

. . . . . . . . . . . . . . . . . . . . . . . . . . . . . . . . . . . . . . . . . . . . . . . . . . .

Your positioning strategies should provide a significant benefit to your customers.

**Other Measurable Marketing Objectives.** These could include the number of new retailers opened, the number of new accounts, products introduced, new markets penetrated, decrease in cost per sale, increase in the closing rate, the number of salespeople hired, or the percentage of customer complaints.

1. . . . . . . . . . . . . . . . . . . . . . . . . . . . . . . . . . . . . . . . . . . . . . . . .

2. . . . . . . . . . . . . . . . . . . . . . . . . . . . . . . . . . . . . . . . . . . . . . . . .

3. . . . . . . . . . . . . . . . . . . . . . . . . . . . . . . . . . . . . . . . . . . . . . . . .

4. . . . . . . . . . . . . . . . . . . . . . . . . . . . . . . . . . . . . . . . . . . . . . . . .

5. . . . . . . . . . . . . . . . . . . . . . . . . . . . . . . . . . . . . . . . . . . . . . . . .

## Final Comments

Marketers should be able to explain their situation and marketing strategy in just a few paragraphs. If you need more space to explain your strategy, you are not focusing on the key points that will determine your success. Think of a person moving rocks from one side of a river to the other. That person will have the greatest success taking one rock at a time to the other side. He or she won't get any rocks over trying to take them all at once. Marketing is no different. Pick one strategy, and focus on that strategy until you build up enough momentum to impact your business. It might take a year or two, but that's okay as long as you finally make an impact. The BIGGEST mistake I see marketers make is not persevering with a strategy until customers understand it and it starts to make a difference in their business. Positioning your company in your prospects' minds takes time. You can't expect a short marketing program to have much of a long-term impact on potential customers.

Executing a marketing program halfway is a waste of money. Promote a program with the resources it needs to impact the market.

Your plan should have a clear focus on a special characteristic of a target customer group.

## Simplicity Is Power

In an overcrowded marketing world the simplest message is the most easily remembered. I like the executive summary because it is a check on whether you have a simple message and strategy that everyone can easily understand. Wendy's is a good example. It is a fast-food hamburger restaurant. Its target customers are adults and its differential advantage is that it has the best food. Go back and look over your executive summary to see if you can answer yes to these questions.

|  | YES | NO |
|---|---|---|
| 1. Can a new reader understand what your business does? | _____ | _____ |
| 2. Is your target customer clearly identified? | _____ | _____ |
| 3. Have you identified the customer need or desire that your business strategy is based on? | _____ | _____ |
| 4. Does your summary identify the one or two factors in your market situation that are impacting your business? | _____ | _____ |
| 5. Would a new reader understand the logic of your marketing strategy? | _____ | _____ |
| 6. Is it clear that your strategy is one that you can implement? | _____ | _____ |

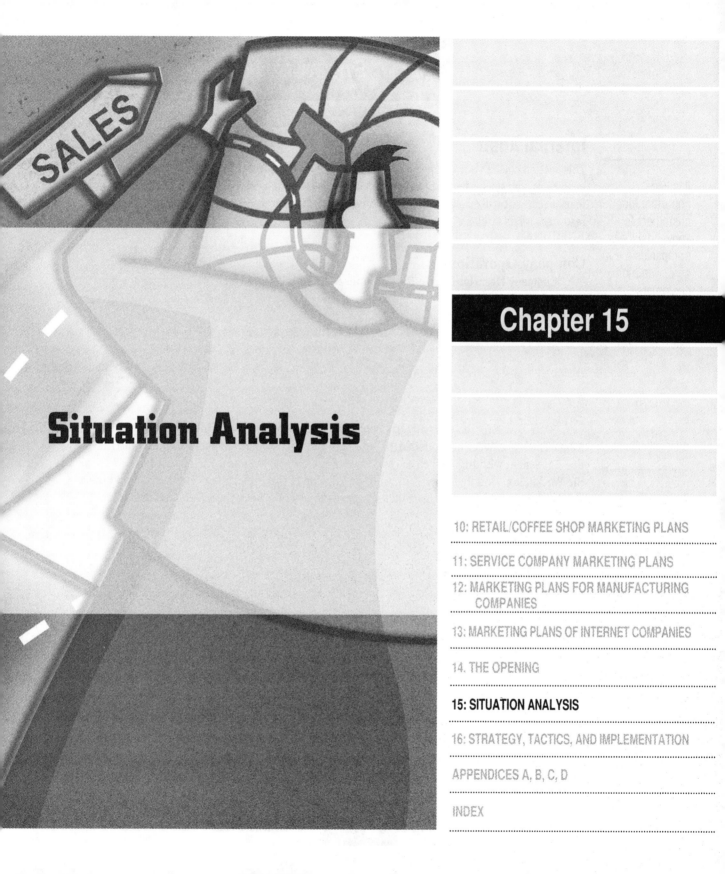

# Situation Analysis

**SALES**

## Chapter 15

10: RETAIL/COFFEE SHOP MARKETING PLANS

11: SERVICE COMPANY MARKETING PLANS

12: MARKETING PLANS FOR MANUFACTURING
COMPANIES

13: MARKETING PLANS OF INTERNET COMPANIES

14. THE OPENING

**15: SITUATION ANALYSIS**

16: STRATEGY, TACTICS, AND IMPLEMENTATION

APPENDICES A, B, C, D

INDEX

# Internal Audit

This section covers your company, what it does, how it operates, what its strengths and weaknesses are, and how it is perceived by customers. This section is longer than the executive summary because it will cover many more items in describing how your company operates and what resources it has available.

## Company Operations

**Company Description and Background.** Start with your business name, what your business is, where it is located (if appropriate), and who your target customer is—just as you did in the executive summary.

. . . . . . . . . . . . . . . . . . . . . . . . . . . . . . . . . . . . . . . . . . . . . . . . . . . . . . . . . . . . . . . . . . . . . . . .

. . . . . . . . . . . . . . . . . . . . . . . . . . . . . . . . . . . . . . . . . . . . . . . . . . . . . . . . . . . . . . . . . . . . . . . .

. . . . . . . . . . . . . . . . . . . . . . . . . . . . . . . . . . . . . . . . . . . . . . . . . . . . . . . . . . . . . . . . . . . . . . . .

State how long the company has been in business and why it was founded. *Example*: John's Hitch and Weld was founded 14 years ago when its owners were able to sign a distribution agreement with Rigid Hitch to carry several premium hitch lines. The market for hitches in the Washington County area was growing rapidly due to the expansion of Highway 95 and the rapid construction of many new middle-class neighborhoods. Also, there were no established competitors.

. . . . . . . . . . . . . . . . . . . . . . . . . . . . . . . . . . . . . . . . . . . . . . . . . . . . . . . . . . . . . . . . . . . . . . . .

. . . . . . . . . . . . . . . . . . . . . . . . . . . . . . . . . . . . . . . . . . . . . . . . . . . . . . . . . . . . . . . . . . . . . . . .

. . . . . . . . . . . . . . . . . . . . . . . . . . . . . . . . . . . . . . . . . . . . . . . . . . . . . . . . . . . . . . . . . . . . . . . .

. . . . . . . . . . . . . . . . . . . . . . . . . . . . . . . . . . . . . . . . . . . . . . . . . . . . . . . . . . . . . . . . . . . . . . . .

. . . . . . . . . . . . . . . . . . . . . . . . . . . . . . . . . . . . . . . . . . . . . . . . . . . . . . . . . . . . . . . . . . . . . . . .

. . . . . . . . . . . . . . . . . . . . . . . . . . . . . . . . . . . . . . . . . . . . . . . . . . . . . . . . . . . . . . . . . . . . . . . .

The next paragraph should discuss changes that have occurred in the business that have brought you to your current situation. These may include changes to your target customer group. *Example*: John's original customers were primarily pickup truck owners who installed hitches to haul boats and utility trailers. When John's opened, 80 percent of its customers were blue-collar workers. Over the past 14 years, five competitors have entered the Washington

It is very important for customers to know how their companies are perceived by customers.

This section should do more than just explain your business. It should also describe the reason you went into business.

County market. In addition, customers are primarily installing hitches on sport utility vehicles or supercab pickup trucks. These vehicles all require special mounting and drop ball mount bars. The average price of John's customers' vehicles has risen from about $8,000 to over $30,000 in the past 14 years. Customers are now more concerned about how the hitch bar is installed on their vehicle. Today, over 50 percent of John's customers are professionals.

If possible, try to respond to market changes by focusing on a customer need or desire.

. . . . . . . . . . . . . . . . . . . . . . . . . . . . . . . . . . . . . . . . . . . . . . . . . . . . . . . .

. . . . . . . . . . . . . . . . . . . . . . . . . . . . . . . . . . . . . . . . . . . . . . . . . . . . . . . .

. . . . . . . . . . . . . . . . . . . . . . . . . . . . . . . . . . . . . . . . . . . . . . . . . . . . . . . .

. . . . . . . . . . . . . . . . . . . . . . . . . . . . . . . . . . . . . . . . . . . . . . . . . . . . . . . .

. . . . . . . . . . . . . . . . . . . . . . . . . . . . . . . . . . . . . . . . . . . . . . . . . . . . . . . .

. . . . . . . . . . . . . . . . . . . . . . . . . . . . . . . . . . . . . . . . . . . . . . . . . . . . . . . .

The next paragraph should describe how the company has responded to the changes over the years. *Example*: John's Hitch and Weld started out as a low-cost operation in an abandoned service station. Over the years John's has responded to changing conditions by moving to an ultra-clean facility, switching to vendors that supply hidden hitch bars, and installing only hitch bars that are specifically designed for each vehicle. John's also posts a large chart in its waiting room that specifies the correct hitch part number for each vehicle and which hitch installation accessories are required for that vehicle. The chart establishes with professionals that John's Hitch and Weld is also professional, and that it is installing the correct hitch for their car.

Make sure your target market is specific and that customers in it buy for somewhat similar reasons.

. . . . . . . . . . . . . . . . . . . . . . . . . . . . . . . . . . . . . . . . . . . . . . . . . . . . . . . .

. . . . . . . . . . . . . . . . . . . . . . . . . . . . . . . . . . . . . . . . . . . . . . . . . . . . . . . .

. . . . . . . . . . . . . . . . . . . . . . . . . . . . . . . . . . . . . . . . . . . . . . . . . . . . . . . .

. . . . . . . . . . . . . . . . . . . . . . . . . . . . . . . . . . . . . . . . . . . . . . . . . . . . . . . .

. . . . . . . . . . . . . . . . . . . . . . . . . . . . . . . . . . . . . . . . . . . . . . . . . . . . . . . .

**Target Market(s)**

. . . . . . . . . . . . . . . . . . . . . . . . . . . . . . . . . . . . . . . . . . . . . . . . . . . . . . . .

. . . . . . . . . . . . . . . . . . . . . . . . . . . . . . . . . . . . . . . . . . . . . . . . . . . . . . . .

. . . . . . . . . . . . . . . . . . . . . . . . . . . . . . . . . . . . . . . . . . . . . . . . . . . . . . . .

### Company's Specialty

John's Hitch and Weld's specialty is that it stocks all the hitches and accessories for SUVs and specializes in installing hidden hitches. Your specialty should tie in somehow to your target markets.

· · · · · · · · · · · · · · · · · · · · · · · · · · · · · · · · · · · · · · · · · · · · · · · · · · · · · · · · · · · · · · · · · · · ·

· · · · · · · · · · · · · · · · · · · · · · · · · · · · · · · · · · · · · · · · · · · · · · · · · · · · · · · · · · · · · · · · · · · ·

· · · · · · · · · · · · · · · · · · · · · · · · · · · · · · · · · · · · · · · · · · · · · · · · · · · · · · · · · · · · · · · · · · · ·

**Mission Statement.** If you have a meaningful mission statement that you use in your business, list it here. If the mission statement has changed over time, explain what the original mission statement was and how it has changed.

A mission statement should be connected in some way to your positioning strategy.

· · · · · · · · · · · · · · · · · · · · · · · · · · · · · · · · · · · · · · · · · · · · · · · · · · · · · · · · · · · · · · · · · · · ·

· · · · · · · · · · · · · · · · · · · · · · · · · · · · · · · · · · · · · · · · · · · · · · · · · · · · · · · · · · · · · · · · · · · ·

· · · · · · · · · · · · · · · · · · · · · · · · · · · · · · · · · · · · · · · · · · · · · · · · · · · · · · · · · · · · · · · · · · · ·

· · · · · · · · · · · · · · · · · · · · · · · · · · · · · · · · · · · · · · · · · · · · · · · · · · · · · · · · · · · · · · · · · · · ·

· · · · · · · · · · · · · · · · · · · · · · · · · · · · · · · · · · · · · · · · · · · · · · · · · · · · · · · · · · · · · · · · · · · ·

· · · · · · · · · · · · · · · · · · · · · · · · · · · · · · · · · · · · · · · · · · · · · · · · · · · · · · · · · · · · · · · · · · · ·

## Product/Service/Description and Profile

The importance of a product or service or section of the store to your business should be roughly in proportion to its importance to the customer.

In this section you want to list your products and services. In the case of a store, list the different sections of the store. For instance, a hardware store has a paint section, a door section, a lock section, and so on. Also list a brief description of the product or service and, if appropriate, who the product is for. For example, a painting store may have a Victorian wallpaper section for a series of Victorian homes in a nearby neighborhood, or a plant care company may combine with a maintenance supplier and waste removal supplier to offer a complete service agreement that's targeted at large office buildings. Then offer a brief comment about the strength or success of the product in the market. *Example*: The Victorian section has made the store the preferred supplier of the nearby Victorian neighborhood; or, the Victorian section has more prestigious wallpaper than the two competitive stores.

# Situation Analysis

Product, Service, or Store Section: . . . . . . . . . . . . . . . . . . . . . . . . . . . . . . . . . . . . . . .

Brief Description: . . . . . . . . . . . . . . . . . . . . . . . . . . . . . . . . . . . . . . . . . . . . . . . . . . . . . .

. . . . . . . . . . . . . . . . . . . . . . . . . . . . . . . . . . . . . . . . . . . . . . . . . . . . . . . . . . . . . . . . . . . .

. . . . . . . . . . . . . . . . . . . . . . . . . . . . . . . . . . . . . . . . . . . . . . . . . . . . . . . . . . . . . . . . . . . .

Target Customer: . . . . . . . . . . . . . . . . . . . . . . . . . . . . . . . . . . . . . . . . . . . . . . . . . . . . . .

Market Status of Product or Service: . . . . . . . . . . . . . . . . . . . . . . . . . . . . . . . . . . . . .

. . . . . . . . . . . . . . . . . . . . . . . . . . . . . . . . . . . . . . . . . . . . . . . . . . . . . . . . . . . . . . . . . . . .

. . . . . . . . . . . . . . . . . . . . . . . . . . . . . . . . . . . . . . . . . . . . . . . . . . . . . . . . . . . . . . . . . . . .

Don't be afraid to drop products that don't satisfy an important customer need. Focus on products that customers want.

Product, Service, or Store Section: . . . . . . . . . . . . . . . . . . . . . . . . . . . . . . . . . . . . . . .

Brief Description: . . . . . . . . . . . . . . . . . . . . . . . . . . . . . . . . . . . . . . . . . . . . . . . . . . . . . .

. . . . . . . . . . . . . . . . . . . . . . . . . . . . . . . . . . . . . . . . . . . . . . . . . . . . . . . . . . . . . . . . . . . .

. . . . . . . . . . . . . . . . . . . . . . . . . . . . . . . . . . . . . . . . . . . . . . . . . . . . . . . . . . . . . . . . . . . .

Target Customer: . . . . . . . . . . . . . . . . . . . . . . . . . . . . . . . . . . . . . . . . . . . . . . . . . . . . . .

Market Status of Product or Service: . . . . . . . . . . . . . . . . . . . . . . . . . . . . . . . . . . . . .

. . . . . . . . . . . . . . . . . . . . . . . . . . . . . . . . . . . . . . . . . . . . . . . . . . . . . . . . . . . . . . . . . . . .

. . . . . . . . . . . . . . . . . . . . . . . . . . . . . . . . . . . . . . . . . . . . . . . . . . . . . . . . . . . . . . . . . . . .

If a product has a weak market position, drop it and concentrate on products where you have an advantage.

Product, Service, or Store Section: . . . . . . . . . . . . . . . . . . . . . . . . . . . . . . . . . . . . . . .

Brief Description: . . . . . . . . . . . . . . . . . . . . . . . . . . . . . . . . . . . . . . . . . . . . . . . . . . . . . .

. . . . . . . . . . . . . . . . . . . . . . . . . . . . . . . . . . . . . . . . . . . . . . . . . . . . . . . . . . . . . . . . . . . .

. . . . . . . . . . . . . . . . . . . . . . . . . . . . . . . . . . . . . . . . . . . . . . . . . . . . . . . . . . . . . . . . . . . .

Target Customer: . . . . . . . . . . . . . . . . . . . . . . . . . . . . . . . . . . . . . . . . . . . . . . . . . . . . . .

Market Status of Product or Service: . . . . . . . . . . . . . . . . . . . . . . . . . . . . . . . . . . . . .

. . . . . . . . . . . . . . . . . . . . . . . . . . . . . . . . . . . . . . . . . . . . . . . . . . . . . . . . . . . . . . . . . . . .

. . . . . . . . . . . . . . . . . . . . . . . . . . . . . . . . . . . . . . . . . . . . . . . . . . . . . . . . . . . . . . . . . . . .

Product, Service, or Store Section: . . . . . . . . . . . . . . . . . . . . . . . . . . . . . . . . . . .

Brief Description: . . . . . . . . . . . . . . . . . . . . . . . . . . . . . . . . . . . . . . . . . . . . . .

. . . . . . . . . . . . . . . . . . . . . . . . . . . . . . . . . . . . . . . . . . . . . . . . . . . . . . . . . . .

. . . . . . . . . . . . . . . . . . . . . . . . . . . . . . . . . . . . . . . . . . . . . . . . . . . . . . . . . . .

Target Customer: . . . . . . . . . . . . . . . . . . . . . . . . . . . . . . . . . . . . . . . . . . . . . . .

Market Status of Product or Service: . . . . . . . . . . . . . . . . . . . . . . . . . . . . . . . . . .

. . . . . . . . . . . . . . . . . . . . . . . . . . . . . . . . . . . . . . . . . . . . . . . . . . . . . . . . . . .

. . . . . . . . . . . . . . . . . . . . . . . . . . . . . . . . . . . . . . . . . . . . . . . . . . . . . . . . . . .

> Marketers are better off with three strong products than seven average ones.

Product, Service, or Store Section: . . . . . . . . . . . . . . . . . . . . . . . . . . . . . . . . . . .

Brief Description: . . . . . . . . . . . . . . . . . . . . . . . . . . . . . . . . . . . . . . . . . . . . . .

. . . . . . . . . . . . . . . . . . . . . . . . . . . . . . . . . . . . . . . . . . . . . . . . . . . . . . . . . . .

. . . . . . . . . . . . . . . . . . . . . . . . . . . . . . . . . . . . . . . . . . . . . . . . . . . . . . . . . . .

Target Customer: . . . . . . . . . . . . . . . . . . . . . . . . . . . . . . . . . . . . . . . . . . . . . . .

Market Status of Product or Service: . . . . . . . . . . . . . . . . . . . . . . . . . . . . . . . . . .

. . . . . . . . . . . . . . . . . . . . . . . . . . . . . . . . . . . . . . . . . . . . . . . . . . . . . . . . . . .

. . . . . . . . . . . . . . . . . . . . . . . . . . . . . . . . . . . . . . . . . . . . . . . . . . . . . . . . . . .

> You need to recharge your marketing strategy if your market share is declining or staying the same. "Old reliable" can quickly become "soon forgotten."

## Sales Trends

| | |
|---|---|
| Sales Three Years Ago:. . . . . . . . . . . . . . . . . . | Percentage Growth:. . . . . . . . . . . |
| Sales Two Years Ago:. . . . . . . . . . . . . . . . . . . | Percentage Growth:. . . . . . . . . . . . |
| Sales Last Year:. . . . . . . . . . . . . . . . . . . . . . | Percentage Growth:. . . . . . . . . . . . |
| Sales Projected This Year: . . . . . . . . . . . . . . | Percentage Growth:. . . . . . . . . . . . |
| Market Share Three Years Ago:. . . . . . . . . . . . | Percentage Growth:. . . . . . . . . . . . |
| Market Share Two Years Ago:. . . . . . . . . . . . . | Percentage Growth:. . . . . . . . . . . . |

Market Share Last Year:.................. Percentage Growth:.................

Market Share Projected This Year: .......... Percentage Growth:.................

You should become more aggressive with your marketing programs if your market share is not increasing.

You may not always have this information, but if you do it should be included in the plan. The sample plans in Section Four omitted this section because either the companies did not want to share this data or it was unavailable.

Comment on why your sales and market share has changed, or remained the same, over the past three years. List any significant events. *Example*: Jeannie's Kids Catalog has managed to hold its market share and sales steady over the past three years even with GapKids and Talbot Kids entering the market. The company has been able to offset losses to these two new catalogs by pulling market share away from the mass merchandisers, by expanding its percentage of exclusive kids designs, and by increasing its mailings to families with two working parents. Jeannie's will continue to add to its exclusive designer selection to counter the new catalogs, and will add a special girls-only section to position itself away from GapKids' mostly boys product orientation.

. . . . . . . . . . . . . . . . . . . . . . . . . . . . . . . . . . . . . . . . . . . . . . . . . . . . . . . . . . . . . . .

. . . . . . . . . . . . . . . . . . . . . . . . . . . . . . . . . . . . . . . . . . . . . . . . . . . . . . . . . . . . . . .

. . . . . . . . . . . . . . . . . . . . . . . . . . . . . . . . . . . . . . . . . . . . . . . . . . . . . . . . . . . . . . .

. . . . . . . . . . . . . . . . . . . . . . . . . . . . . . . . . . . . . . . . . . . . . . . . . . . . . . . . . . . . . . .

. . . . . . . . . . . . . . . . . . . . . . . . . . . . . . . . . . . . . . . . . . . . . . . . . . . . . . . . . . . . . . .

. . . . . . . . . . . . . . . . . . . . . . . . . . . . . . . . . . . . . . . . . . . . . . . . . . . . . . . . . . . . . . .

## Last Year's Commentary

Every company had sales affected by events occurring over the past year. Those events could include competitive activity, economic conditions, success or failure of a new product, changes in the way a product is used, or gains or losses in key distribution outlets. You want to explain the events that impacted you, both positively and negatively, over the past year. Those events typically have a large bearing on your marketing plan for the current year.

Companies can survive one bad year without losing all their market momentum. Two consecutive bad years is often fatal.

. . . . . . . . . . . . . . . . . . . . . . . . . . . . . . . . . . . . . . . . . . . . . . . . . . . . . . . . . . . . . . .

. . . . . . . . . . . . . . . . . . . . . . . . . . . . . . . . . . . . . . . . . . . . . . . . . . . . . . . . . . . . . . .

. . . . . . . . . . . . . . . . . . . . . . . . . . . . . . . . . . . . . . . . . . . . . . . . . . . . . . . . . . . . . . .

. . . . . . . . . . . . . . . . . . . . . . . . . . . . . . . . . . . . . . . . . . . . . . . . . . . . . . . . . . . . . . .

. . . . . . . . . . . . . . . . . . . . . . . . . . . . . . . . . . . . . . . . . . . . . . . . . . . . . . . . . . . . . .

. . . . . . . . . . . . . . . . . . . . . . . . . . . . . . . . . . . . . . . . . . . . . . . . . . . . . . . . . . . . . .

## Strengths and Weaknesses

In Chapter 4 you listed your company's strengths and weaknesses. You will list those again in this section of the plan.

### Company/Product/Service Strengths

1. . . . . . . . . . . . . . . . . . . . . . . . . . . . . . . . . . . . . . . . . . . . . . . . . . . . . . . . . . . . . . . .

2. . . . . . . . . . . . . . . . . . . . . . . . . . . . . . . . . . . . . . . . . . . . . . . . . . . . . . . . . . . . . . . .

3. . . . . . . . . . . . . . . . . . . . . . . . . . . . . . . . . . . . . . . . . . . . . . . . . . . . . . . . . . . . . . . .

4. . . . . . . . . . . . . . . . . . . . . . . . . . . . . . . . . . . . . . . . . . . . . . . . . . . . . . . . . . . . . . . .

5. . . . . . . . . . . . . . . . . . . . . . . . . . . . . . . . . . . . . . . . . . . . . . . . . . . . . . . . . . . . . . . .

6. . . . . . . . . . . . . . . . . . . . . . . . . . . . . . . . . . . . . . . . . . . . . . . . . . . . . . . . . . . . . . . .

### Company/Product/Service Weaknesses

1. . . . . . . . . . . . . . . . . . . . . . . . . . . . . . . . . . . . . . . . . . . . . . . . . . . . . . . . . . . . . . . .

2. . . . . . . . . . . . . . . . . . . . . . . . . . . . . . . . . . . . . . . . . . . . . . . . . . . . . . . . . . . . . . . .

3. . . . . . . . . . . . . . . . . . . . . . . . . . . . . . . . . . . . . . . . . . . . . . . . . . . . . . . . . . . . . . . .

4. . . . . . . . . . . . . . . . . . . . . . . . . . . . . . . . . . . . . . . . . . . . . . . . . . . . . . . . . . . . . . . .

5. . . . . . . . . . . . . . . . . . . . . . . . . . . . . . . . . . . . . . . . . . . . . . . . . . . . . . . . . . . . . . . .

6. . . . . . . . . . . . . . . . . . . . . . . . . . . . . . . . . . . . . . . . . . . . . . . . . . . . . . . . . . . . . . . .

## The External Evaluation

I like to break down the external evaluation into two sections: customer information and market profile. Not everyone does that, but I like to be sure customers have their own section because they are the most important component of your marketing strategy. Everything you do is

Customers remember what happened over the past year. Be ready to respond aggressively if market events have conspired against you.

Make sure that your company's internal operations improve every year.

designed to meet customers' needs and desires. I believe putting customer data into its own section helps ensure that the marketing plan is customer oriented.

Your number one goal in the marketing planning process is to understand your customers.

## Customer Information

**Customer Profile.** In Chapter 2 you completed a Customer Profile form that looked very much like the following one. All you need to do for this section of the plan is to turn your form into a sentence-and-paragraph format. For example, the functional goals and major interest chart for a company selling a new loft wedge for shots 70 to 80 yards from the green might look like this:

PRIORITY (1–5)

| | | |
|---|---|---|
| Customer's Functional Goals: | Have a lower score | 1 |
| | Be able to take a full swing | 3 |
| Customer's Major Interests: | Compete with friends | 2 |
| | Score well in tournaments | 3 |
| | Keep handicap down | 3 |

A sentence-and-paragraph format would appear as follows:

Your target market group needs to be clearly defined.

The target customer group for the new loft club are golfers who either have handicaps of 15 or below, or who play a minimum of eight rounds per month in warm weather. These golfers want to keep their scores as low as possible, and one way to do that is to keep their swing as consistent as possible. The loft wedge eliminates the need for a golfer to take a two-thirds to a half swing on many approach shots. Golfers believe that the less-than-full swing shot is the hardest one in golf, and that it impacts their score. Just as important, taking a two-thirds swing can throw off the golfer's regular swing on his or her next shot.

The target customer group's primary interest is competing with their friends. Good golfers play regularly with the same group of friends or at a club where they play with 15 to 20 other regulars. How they score in comparison to others in their group is of vital interest to regular golfers. The target group also wants to keep their handicap down and score well in tournaments, all desires that the loft club can help deliver.

Start by completing the Customer Profile form I've repeated here. Then turn the information in the form into a sentence-and-paragraph format similar to the example of the loft golf club.

Target Customer Profile:

> Members of a Target Customer Group should buy products for similar reasons.

. . . . . . . . . . . . . . . . . . . . . . . . . . . . . . . . . . . . . . . . . . . . . . . . . . . . . . . . . . . . . . . . . . . . . . . . . . . . . . . . .

. . . . . . . . . . . . . . . . . . . . . . . . . . . . . . . . . . . . . . . . . . . . . . . . . . . . . . . . . . . . . . . . . . . . . . . . . . . . . . . . .

. . . . . . . . . . . . . . . . . . . . . . . . . . . . . . . . . . . . . . . . . . . . . . . . . . . . . . . . . . . . . . . . . . . . . . . . . . . . . . . . .

. . . . . . . . . . . . . . . . . . . . . . . . . . . . . . . . . . . . . . . . . . . . . . . . . . . . . . . . . . . . . . . . . . . . . . . . . . . . . . . . .

*Rank priority by the priority of the item to customers. Rank each item 1 to 5, with 1 being a high value, and 5 a low value

**PRIORITY\* (1–5)**

Customer's Functional Goals:

> I believe over 80 percent of a customer's buying decision is based on his or her primary interest.

Customer's Major Interests:

Use sentence-and-paragraph format to describe the target customer profile:

. . . . . . . . . . . . . . . . . . . . . . . . . . . . . . . . . . . . . . . . . . . . . . . . . . . . . . . . . . . . . . . . . . . . . . . . . . . . . . . . .

. . . . . . . . . . . . . . . . . . . . . . . . . . . . . . . . . . . . . . . . . . . . . . . . . . . . . . . . . . . . . . . . . . . . . . . . . . . . . . . . .

. . . . . . . . . . . . . . . . . . . . . . . . . . . . . . . . . . . . . . . . . . . . . . . . . . . . . . . . . . . . . . . . . . . . . . . . . . . . . . . . .

. . . . . . . . . . . . . . . . . . . . . . . . . . . . . . . . . . . . . . . . . . . . . . . . . . . . . . . . . . . . . . . . . . . . . . . . . . . . . . . . .

. . . . . . . . . . . . . . . . . . . . . . . . . . . . . . . . . . . . . . . . . . . . . . . . . . . . . . . . . . .

. . . . . . . . . . . . . . . . . . . . . . . . . . . . . . . . . . . . . . . . . . . . . . . . . . . . . . . . . . .

Type of Customer Buying Behavior:

|  |  |
|---|---|
| Maximizer | . . . . . . . . . . . . . |
| Judicial | . . . . . . . . . . . . . |
| Low-Cost Buyer | . . . . . . . . . . . . . |
| Minimizer | . . . . . . . . . . . . . |

**PRIORITY\* (1–5)**

Customer's Self Image:

. . . . . . . . . . . . . . . . . .        . . . . . . . . . . . . . . . . . .

. . . . . . . . . . . . . . . . . .        . . . . . . . . . . . . . . . . . .

. . . . . . . . . . . . . . . . . .        . . . . . . . . . . . . . . . . . .

There is nothing a marketer can do to change a customer's buying behavior.

Why is your type of product
 important to the customer

. . . . . . . . . . . . . . . . . .        . . . . . . . . . . . . . . . . . .

. . . . . . . . . . . . . . . . . .        . . . . . . . . . . . . . . . . . .

. . . . . . . . . . . . . . . . . .        . . . . . . . . . . . . . . . . . .

. . . . . . . . . . . . . . . . . .        . . . . . . . . . . . . . . . . . .

. . . . . . . . . . . . . . . . . .        . . . . . . . . . . . . . . . . . .

Use a sentence-and-paragraph format:

. . . . . . . . . . . . . . . . . . . . . . . . . . . . . . . . . . . . . . . . . . . . . . . . . . . . . . . . . . .

. . . . . . . . . . . . . . . . . . . . . . . . . . . . . . . . . . . . . . . . . . . . . . . . . . . . . . . . . . .

. . . . . . . . . . . . . . . . . . . . . . . . . . . . . . . . . . . . . . . . . . . . . . . . . . . . . . . . . . .

A product or service is typically important to a customer for just one or two reasons.

........................................................
........................................................
........................................................

PRIORITY* (1–5)

What features are most

important to customers?

.....................          .....................

.....................          .....................

.....................          .....................

.....................          .....................

As it relates to your product, what mood is your customer typically in when buying your product?

Fun loving          ...............

Practical           ...............

Serious             ...............

PRIORITY* (1–5)

Match the mood of your communications material to the buying mood of your customers.

Why do your customers buy
your brand?                    .....................          .....................
Why don't your customers buy
your brand?                    .....................          .....................

Use a sentence-and-paragraph format:

........................................................
........................................................
........................................................
........................................................

. . . . . . . . . . . . . . . . . . . . . . . . . . . . . . . . . . . . . . . . . . . . . . . . .
. . . . . . . . . . . . . . . . . . . . . . . . . . . . . . . . . . . . . . . . . . . . . . . . .

**Customer Buying Patterns.** In Chapter 3 you filled out a Customer Buying Patterns form, most of which is repeated here. Again, take the information off the form and change it into a sentence-and-paragraph format for the plan.

How does the customer decide to buy?

. . . . . . . . . . . . . . . . . . . . . . . . . . . . . . . . . . . . . . . . . . . . . . . . .
. . . . . . . . . . . . . . . . . . . . . . . . . . . . . . . . . . . . . . . . . . . . . . . . .
. . . . . . . . . . . . . . . . . . . . . . . . . . . . . . . . . . . . . . . . . . . . . . . . .
. . . . . . . . . . . . . . . . . . . . . . . . . . . . . . . . . . . . . . . . . . . . . . . . .
. . . . . . . . . . . . . . . . . . . . . . . . . . . . . . . . . . . . . . . . . . . . . . . . .
. . . . . . . . . . . . . . . . . . . . . . . . . . . . . . . . . . . . . . . . . . . . . . . . .

What are the steps the buyer takes in his or her buying decision?

|  | PRIORITY* (1–5) | IMPORTANCE (1–5) |
|---|---|---|
| Step 1: | | |
| Step 2: | | |
| Step 3: | | |
| Step 4: | | |
| Step 5: | | |
| Step 6: | | |

Use a sentence-and-paragraph format:

. . . . . . . . . . . . . . . . . . . . . . . . . . . . . . . . . . . . . . . . . . . . . . . . .
. . . . . . . . . . . . . . . . . . . . . . . . . . . . . . . . . . . . . . . . . . . . . . . . .
. . . . . . . . . . . . . . . . . . . . . . . . . . . . . . . . . . . . . . . . . . . . . . . . .

Marketers often don't adequately consider how customers buy. That makes this topic an opportunity for most marketers.

You'll want your marketing strategy to focus on one or two key steps in a customer's buying process.

. . . . . . . . . . . . . . . . . . . . . . . . . . . . . . . . . . . . . . . . . . . . . . . . . . . . . . . . . .
. . . . . . . . . . . . . . . . . . . . . . . . . . . . . . . . . . . . . . . . . . . . . . . . . . . . . . . . . .
. . . . . . . . . . . . . . . . . . . . . . . . . . . . . . . . . . . . . . . . . . . . . . . . . . . . . . . . . .

How does your company impact a customer during each stage of the buying cycle?

Step 1: . . . . . . . . . . . . . . . . . . . . . . . . . . . . . . . . . . . . . . . . . . . . . . . . . . . . . .

Step 2: . . . . . . . . . . . . . . . . . . . . . . . . . . . . . . . . . . . . . . . . . . . . . . . . . . . . . .

Step 3: . . . . . . . . . . . . . . . . . . . . . . . . . . . . . . . . . . . . . . . . . . . . . . . . . . . . . .

Step 4: . . . . . . . . . . . . . . . . . . . . . . . . . . . . . . . . . . . . . . . . . . . . . . . . . . . . . .

Step 5: . . . . . . . . . . . . . . . . . . . . . . . . . . . . . . . . . . . . . . . . . . . . . . . . . . . . . .

Step 6: . . . . . . . . . . . . . . . . . . . . . . . . . . . . . . . . . . . . . . . . . . . . . . . . . . . . . .

Use a sentence-and-paragraph format:

Be sure to put your marketing messages where customers look for information.

. . . . . . . . . . . . . . . . . . . . . . . . . . . . . . . . . . . . . . . . . . . . . . . . . . . . . . . . . .
. . . . . . . . . . . . . . . . . . . . . . . . . . . . . . . . . . . . . . . . . . . . . . . . . . . . . . . . . .
. . . . . . . . . . . . . . . . . . . . . . . . . . . . . . . . . . . . . . . . . . . . . . . . . . . . . . . . . .
. . . . . . . . . . . . . . . . . . . . . . . . . . . . . . . . . . . . . . . . . . . . . . . . . . . . . . . . . .
. . . . . . . . . . . . . . . . . . . . . . . . . . . . . . . . . . . . . . . . . . . . . . . . . . . . . . . . . .
. . . . . . . . . . . . . . . . . . . . . . . . . . . . . . . . . . . . . . . . . . . . . . . . . . . . . . . . . .

Where do customers gather information about your product?

| | PRIORITY* (1–5) | IMPORTANCE (1–5) |
|---|---|---|
| 1: . . . . . . . . . . . . . . . . . . . . . . . . . . . . . . | . . . . . | . . . . . |
| 2: . . . . . . . . . . . . . . . . . . . . . . . . . . . . . . | . . . . . | . . . . . |
| 3: . . . . . . . . . . . . . . . . . . . . . . . . . . . . . . | . . . . . | . . . . . |
| 4: . . . . . . . . . . . . . . . . . . . . . . . . . . . . . . | . . . . . | . . . . . |

Where does your company have an advantage in the buying decision?

| | PRIORITY*<br>(1–5) | IMPORTANCE<br>(1–5) |
|---|---|---|
| 1: . . . . . . . . . . . . . . . . . . . . . . . . . . . . . . . . . . . . . . . . | . . . . . . . . . . | . . . . . . . . . . |
| 2: . . . . . . . . . . . . . . . . . . . . . . . . . . . . . . . . . . . . . . . . | . . . . . . . . . . | . . . . . . . . . . |
| 3: . . . . . . . . . . . . . . . . . . . . . . . . . . . . . . . . . . . . . . . . | | . . . . . . . . . . |
| 4: . . . . . . . . . . . . . . . . . . . . . . . . . . . . . . . . . . . . . . . . | | . . . . . . . . . . |

Use a sentence-and-paragraph format:

. . . . . . . . . . . . . . . . . . . . . . . . . . . . . . . . . . . . . . . . . . . . . . . . . . . . . . . . .

. . . . . . . . . . . . . . . . . . . . . . . . . . . . . . . . . . . . . . . . . . . . . . . . . . . . . . . . .

. . . . . . . . . . . . . . . . . . . . . . . . . . . . . . . . . . . . . . . . . . . . . . . . . . . . . . . . .

. . . . . . . . . . . . . . . . . . . . . . . . . . . . . . . . . . . . . . . . . . . . . . . . . . . . . . . . .

. . . . . . . . . . . . . . . . . . . . . . . . . . . . . . . . . . . . . . . . . . . . . . . . . . . . . . . . .

. . . . . . . . . . . . . . . . . . . . . . . . . . . . . . . . . . . . . . . . . . . . . . . . . . . . . . . . .

← Survey customers to see where they get information. Marketers are often surprised at where customers learn about a product or service.

← Marketers gain a sustainable advantage when they dominate a customer information site.

## Market Profile

This section could also be called an industry profile if you compete in a broad market. I've found that most companies compete in a smaller market, and in many cases just a segment of that smaller market. The first step in this section is to list the markets you compete in and then have a chart on the market segments. I like to use this chart if I have it. If you don't compete in a segment, you may not know its actual size. Then, instead of a chart, put the information into a sentence-and-paragraph format that defines your position in the market segment you do compete in. The market segment analysis from Safeplay Systems repeated here is a good example of how companies handle this section when they have a small market share and limited market information.

### Market Analysis

The overall playground market can be broken into several segments: (1) schools, (2) park and recreation playgrounds, (3) residential market, (4) large customer commercial market (i.e., playgrounds at McDonald's), and (5) day care centers. Safeplay Systems has chosen to compete in the day care market because it is the least competitive of the markets, and it is a market where customers value, and will pay for, products that better meet the needs of their users. Safeplay also chose the day care market because there was and still is not as much equipment for infant to five-year-old children, who are most important to day care providers.

*Day Care Market Segments*
According to *Child Care News*, the 100,000 licensed day care centers are divided into these categories:

| | |
|---|---|
| Independents | 26% |
| Church Affiliated | 21% |
| Public/Private Schools | 20% |
| Head Start | 7% |
| Employer Based | 4% |
| Chains | 3% |
| Other | 19% |

Safeplay Systems' main markets are independents, church affiliated, and private schools. These markets have smaller purchases and aren't pursued quite as vigorously by big competitors, and they are interested in buying top-quality equipment with the best features. Safeplay Systems' products are competitively priced, but staying with smaller, quality conscious buyers helps Safeplay avoiding bidding wars from its larger competitors.

List the markets you compete in:

................................................................

................................................................

................................................................

................................................................

................................................................

................................................................

You want to segment markets so you can find one in which your product or service can offer special benefits to the customer.

# SITUATION ANALYSIS

List the different segments of the market.

|  | PERCENTAGE OF MARKET | YOUR PERCENTAGE OF SEGMENT |
|---|---|---|
| 1. . . . . . . . . . . . . . . . . . . . . . . . . . . . . . . . . . . . . . . . . . . . . . . . . . . . . . |  |  |
| 2. . . . . . . . . . . . . . . . . . . . . . . . . . . . . . . . . . . . . . . . . . . . . . . . . . . . . . |  |  |
| 3. . . . . . . . . . . . . . . . . . . . . . . . . . . . . . . . . . . . . . . . . . . . . . . . . . . . . . |  |  |
| 4. . . . . . . . . . . . . . . . . . . . . . . . . . . . . . . . . . . . . . . . . . . . . . . . . . . . . . |  |  |

If you are going to use a sentence-and-paragraph format rather than a chart, list your comments here.

. . . . . . . . . . . . . . . . . . . . . . . . . . . . . . . . . . . . . . . . . . . . . . . . . . . . . . . . . . . . . . . . . . . . . . . . . . . .

. . . . . . . . . . . . . . . . . . . . . . . . . . . . . . . . . . . . . . . . . . . . . . . . . . . . . . . . . . . . . . . . . . . . . . . . . . . .

. . . . . . . . . . . . . . . . . . . . . . . . . . . . . . . . . . . . . . . . . . . . . . . . . . . . . . . . . . . . . . . . . . . . . . . . . . . .

. . . . . . . . . . . . . . . . . . . . . . . . . . . . . . . . . . . . . . . . . . . . . . . . . . . . . . . . . . . . . . . . . . . . . . . . . . . .

. . . . . . . . . . . . . . . . . . . . . . . . . . . . . . . . . . . . . . . . . . . . . . . . . . . . . . . . . . . . . . . . . . . . . . . . . . . .

. . . . . . . . . . . . . . . . . . . . . . . . . . . . . . . . . . . . . . . . . . . . . . . . . . . . . . . . . . . . . . . . . . . . . . . . . . . .

**Past and Current Trends.** For each segment, you want to list any trends that have been occurring in the market. These trends can include the emergence of superstores in a product category, the merger of two major competitors, several suppliers forming an alliance agreement to supply a complete package, new processing techniques, a movement toward automation, the tendency for companies to outsource some of their human resources, or any other trend in your market that has a potential impact on your business. You can consolidate the markets if similar trends affect each market. If the trends are different, you should comment on each market segment separately.

Use a sentence-and-paragraph format.

. . . . . . . . . . . . . . . . . . . . . . . . . . . . . . . . . . . . . . . . . . . . . . . . . . . . . . . . . . . . . . . . . . . . . . . . . . . .

. . . . . . . . . . . . . . . . . . . . . . . . . . . . . . . . . . . . . . . . . . . . . . . . . . . . . . . . . . . . . . . . . . . . . . . . . . . .

. . . . . . . . . . . . . . . . . . . . . . . . . . . . . . . . . . . . . . . . . . . . . . . . . . . . . . . . . . . . . . . . . . . . . . . . . . . .

In the ideal market segment, you have something special to offer, and you are protected from excessive competition.

When listing market segments, I prefer to use a chart format because it is easier to understand.

. . . . . . . . . . . . . . . . . . . . . . . . . . . . . . . . . . . . . . . . . . . . . . . . . . . . . . . . . . . . . . . . . . . . .

. . . . . . . . . . . . . . . . . . . . . . . . . . . . . . . . . . . . . . . . . . . . . . . . . . . . . . . . . . . . . . . . . . . . .

. . . . . . . . . . . . . . . . . . . . . . . . . . . . . . . . . . . . . . . . . . . . . . . . . . . . . . . . . . . . . . . . . . . . .

Small companies often grow rapidly when they are the first competitor to respond to a new trend.

**Opportunities and Threats.** These should be any major developments that either offer you large opportunities or present a distinct threat to your business. This section isn't in many of the marketing plans listed in this book, because those businesses don't have a significant opportunity or threat over the next year. I prefer to list the opportunities and threats with a number format, and a brief description of each tactic, but you may also talk about opportunities and threats in a paragraph format.

### Opportunities

1. . . . . . . . . . . . . . . . . . . . . . . . . . . . . . . . . . . . . . . . . . . . . . . . . . . . . . . . . . . . . . . .

. . . . . . . . . . . . . . . . . . . . . . . . . . . . . . . . . . . . . . . . . . . . . . . . . . . . . . . . . . . . . . .

. . . . . . . . . . . . . . . . . . . . . . . . . . . . . . . . . . . . . . . . . . . . . . . . . . . . . . . . . . . . . . .

2. . . . . . . . . . . . . . . . . . . . . . . . . . . . . . . . . . . . . . . . . . . . . . . . . . . . . . . . . . . . . . .

Evaluate each opportunity or threat carefully. You don't want to be left behind when the market shifts.

. . . . . . . . . . . . . . . . . . . . . . . . . . . . . . . . . . . . . . . . . . . . . . . . . . . . . . . . . . . . . . .

. . . . . . . . . . . . . . . . . . . . . . . . . . . . . . . . . . . . . . . . . . . . . . . . . . . . . . . . . . . . . . .

### Threats

1. . . . . . . . . . . . . . . . . . . . . . . . . . . . . . . . . . . . . . . . . . . . . . . . . . . . . . . . . . . . . . .

. . . . . . . . . . . . . . . . . . . . . . . . . . . . . . . . . . . . . . . . . . . . . . . . . . . . . . . . . . . . . . .

. . . . . . . . . . . . . . . . . . . . . . . . . . . . . . . . . . . . . . . . . . . . . . . . . . . . . . . . . . . . . . .

2. . . . . . . . . . . . . . . . . . . . . . . . . . . . . . . . . . . . . . . . . . . . . . . . . . . . . . . . . . . . . . .

. . . . . . . . . . . . . . . . . . . . . . . . . . . . . . . . . . . . . . . . . . . . . . . . . . . . . . . . . . . . . . .

. . . . . . . . . . . . . . . . . . . . . . . . . . . . . . . . . . . . . . . . . . . . . . . . . . . . . . . . . . . . . . .

**Competitor Audit.** You can use a chart to show your competitors, or you can format the information into a sentence-and-paragraph format.

A. . . . . . . . . . . . . . . . . . . . . . . . . . . . . . . . . . . . . . . . . . . . . . . . . . . . . . . . . . . . . . . . . . . . . . . . . . .

Dollar Sales Level: . . . . . . . . . . . . . . . . . . . . .     Market Share: . . . . . . . . . . . . . . . . . . . . .

Major Advantage: . . . . . . . . . . . . . . . . . . . . . . . . . . . . . . . . . . . . . . . . . . . . . . . . . . . . . .

Positioning Strategy: . . . . . . . . . . . . . . . . . . . . . . . . . . . . . . . . . . . . . . . . . . . . . . . . . . . .

Comments: . . . . . . . . . . . . . . . . . . . . . . . . . . . . . . . . . . . . . . . . . . . . . . . . . . . . . . . . . . . .

. . . . . . . . . . . . . . . . . . . . . . . . . . . . . . . . . . . . . . . . . . . . . . . . . . . . . . . . . . . . . . . . . . . . . . . . .

. . . . . . . . . . . . . . . . . . . . . . . . . . . . . . . . . . . . . . . . . . . . . . . . . . . . . . . . . . . . . . . . . . . . . . . . .

. . . . . . . . . . . . . . . . . . . . . . . . . . . . . . . . . . . . . . . . . . . . . . . . . . . . . . . . . . . . . . . . . . . . . . . . .

You'll get battered and bruised if you try to take on a large competitor head to head. Look for market niches they ignore.

B. . . . . . . . . . . . . . . . . . . . . . . . . . . . . . . . . . . . . . . . . . . . . . . . . . . . . . . . . . . . . . . . . . . . . . . . . . .

Dollar Sales Level: . . . . . . . . . . . . . . . . . . . . .     Market Share: . . . . . . . . . . . . . . . . . . . . .

Major Advantage: . . . . . . . . . . . . . . . . . . . . . . . . . . . . . . . . . . . . . . . . . . . . . . . . . . . . . .

Positioning Strategy: . . . . . . . . . . . . . . . . . . . . . . . . . . . . . . . . . . . . . . . . . . . . . . . . . . . .

Comments: . . . . . . . . . . . . . . . . . . . . . . . . . . . . . . . . . . . . . . . . . . . . . . . . . . . . . . . . . . . .

. . . . . . . . . . . . . . . . . . . . . . . . . . . . . . . . . . . . . . . . . . . . . . . . . . . . . . . . . . . . . . . . . . . . . . . . .

. . . . . . . . . . . . . . . . . . . . . . . . . . . . . . . . . . . . . . . . . . . . . . . . . . . . . . . . . . . . . . . . . . . . . . . . .

. . . . . . . . . . . . . . . . . . . . . . . . . . . . . . . . . . . . . . . . . . . . . . . . . . . . . . . . . . . . . . . . . . . . . . . . .

Include in comments when a positioning strategy is unique or especially effective.

C. . . . . . . . . . . . . . . . . . . . . . . . . . . . . . . . . . . . . . . . . . . . . . . . . . . . . . . . . . . . . . . . . . . . . . . . . . .

Dollar Sales Level: . . . . . . . . . . . . . . . . . . . . .     Market Share: . . . . . . . . . . . . . . . . . . . . .

Major Advantage: . . . . . . . . . . . . . . . . . . . . . . . . . . . . . . . . . . . . . . . . . . . . . . . . . . . . . .

Positioning Strategy: . . . . . . . . . . . . . . . . . . . . . . . . . . . . . . . . . . . . . . . . . . . . . . . . . . . .

Comments: . . . . . . . . . . . . . . . . . . . . . . . . . . . . . . . . . . . . . . . . . . . . . . . . . . . . . . . . . . . .

. . . . . . . . . . . . . . . . . . . . . . . . . . . . . . . . . . . . . . . . . . . . . . . . . . . . . . . . . . . . . . . . . . . . . . . . .

Your positioning statement needs to be different from your competitors. Otherwise your customers will be confused.

. . . . . . . . . . . . . . . . . . . . . . . . . . . . . . . . . . . . . . . . . . . . . .

. . . . . . . . . . . . . . . . . . . . . . . . . . . . . . . . . . . . . . . . . . . . . .

D. . . . . . . . . . . . . . . . . . . . . . . . . . . . . . . . . . . . . . . . . . . . . . .

Dollar Sales Level: . . . . . . . . . . . . . . . . . . . .    Market Share: . . . . . . . . . . . . . . . . . . . . .

Major Advantage: . . . . . . . . . . . . . . . . . . . . . . . . . . . . . . . . . . . . . . . . . . . . . . . .

Positioning Strategy: . . . . . . . . . . . . . . . . . . . . . . . . . . . . . . . . . . . . . . . . . . .

Comments: . . . . . . . . . . . . . . . . . . . . . . . . . . . . . . . . . . . . . . . . . . . . . . . . . . .

. . . . . . . . . . . . . . . . . . . . . . . . . . . . . . . . . . . . . . . . . . . . . . . . . . . . . . . .

. . . . . . . . . . . . . . . . . . . . . . . . . . . . . . . . . . . . . . . . . . . . . . . . . . . . . . . .

. . . . . . . . . . . . . . . . . . . . . . . . . . . . . . . . . . . . . . . . . . . . . . . . . . . . . . . .

**Competitor Chart.** You might also want to include a competitor chart if you have just a few competitors in a small market where customers can choose from all of the competitors.

Markers like to use charts because they highlight which competitors have the strongest market position.

Rank competitors based on the following features with 1 being the top rank:

| COMPETITOR | PRICE | PRICE/VALUE | FEATURES | SALES DISTRIBUTION | QUALITY | SERVICE |
|---|---|---|---|---|---|---|
| . . . . . . . . . . . | . . . . . | . . . . . . | . . . . . | . . . . . . . . . | . . . . | . . . . |
| . . . . . . . . . . . | . . . . . | . . . . . . | . . . . . | . . . . . . . . . | . . . . | . . . . |
| . . . . . . . . . . . | . . . . . | . . . . . . | . . . . . | . . . . . . . . . | . . . . | . . . . |
| . . . . . . . . . . . | . . . . . | . . . . . . | . . . . . | . . . . . . . . . | . . . . | . . . . |
| . . . . . . . . . . . | . . . . . | . . . . . . | . . . . . | . . . . . . . . . | . . . . | . . . . |
| . . . . . . . . . . . | . . . . . | . . . . . . | . . . . . | . . . . . . . . . | . . . . | . . . . |
| . . . . . . . . . . . | . . . . . | . . . . . . | . . . . . | . . . . . . . . . | . . . . | . . . . |

**Competitor Commentary.** You might want to include a section of commentary if you have different things happening among your competitors, such as a bigger competitor that is failing in the market, or a couple of new competitors that are moving up fast with innovative product lines. This section should also show how you are differentiated from your competitors.

........................................................................................

........................................................................................

........................................................................................

........................................................................................

........................................................................................

........................................................................................

........................................................................................

Several effective marketing strategies should be obvious if you've thoroughly analyzed your current situation.

## Final Comments

I feel strongly that marketing is a process and not an intuitive skill. Marketers don't find the solutions to their problems by instinct. They find the answers by evaluating the situation and learning what their customers want. If you've done your evaluation correctly, your marketing strategy should be obvious. A more experienced marketer's only advantage is that he or she has been exposed to more situations and has seen the results of dozens, if not hundreds, of marketing programs. But the key to a successful program is to find one special customer characteristic that allows you to set your company apart in an important way. Marketers who spend the time to really understand their customer and their market typically find that characteristic.

If a marketing strategy isn't screaming out at you after you finish your situation analysis, you need to go back and try a little harder. Don't start off with a program that doesn't give your company a competitive advantage. If you do, you'll probably find that your marketing efforts won't produce the types of results you want.

Keep looking for that one special customer characteristic that will lead to your success.

Today your marketing situation will change dramatically every year or two.

## Do You Really Have the Answers?

I've found that many small business marketers tend to slide over their situation analysis and move right into positioning tactics. That's the exact reverse of what they should do. If you analyze your situation carefully, your strategy should be clear. You should answer yes to these questions before moving forward to the strategy section of the plan.

|  | YES | NO |
|---|---|---|
| 1. Have your identified a market segment where your competitive advantage will make you a preferred supplier? | _____ | _____ |
| 2. Do your customers say, "Wow that's great!" when they hear what your competitive advantage is? | _____ | _____ |
| 3. Are your products and services based on customer needs rather than on your company's capabilities? | _____ | _____ |
| 4. Do you know how to impact customers at key points in their buying process? | _____ | _____ |
| 5. Is your company on the cutting edge with new developments in the market? | _____ | _____ |
| 6. Do you know why customers think you are better than the competition? | _____ | _____ |
| 7. Have you discovered a customer characteristic that will allow you an exclusive advantage in the market? | _____ | _____ |

If you can answer yes to these questions, you will be able to create a dynamite marketing strategy. If you can't answer yes to at least five of the questions, the success of your plan will depend on luck. That's not a position you want to be in.

# Strategy, Tactics, and Implementation

## Chapter 16

10: RETAIL/COFFEE SHOP MARKETING PLANS

11: SERVICE COMPANY MARKETING PLANS

12: MARKETING PLANS FOR MANUFACTURING COMPANIES

13: MARKETING PLANS OF INTERNET COMPANIES

14: THE OPENING

15: SITUATION ANALYSIS

16: STRATEGY, TACTICS, AND IMPLEMENTATION

APPENDICES A, B, C, D

INDEX

## Positioning and Marketing Strategies

A positioning strategy creates a desired image that you want to establish in the minds of your customers or your distribution network. A marketing strategy implements a program that will either support the positioning strategy, or will act in some way to increase sales or cut marketing costs.

Consider Flowertown, a florist that wants to increase its sales to wedding parties. It has decided that it wants to position itself as *the* wedding florist. Parts of its positioning strategy are:

1. Assigning a florist/designer to each wedding party
2. Creating a TLC Wedding Package which includes three consultations with the florist/designer and having the florist/designer present three hours before the wedding to ensure that every last detail with the flowers is correct
3. Setting up a wedding center with photos and other materials in the store to help brides select floral arrangements
4. Presenting classes in the spring at the store and in local community center on the use of flowers to create a memorable wedding experience
5. Adding other products to the wedding center, such as wedding registers to encourage more visits from brides

All of these steps are part of the florist's positioning strategy. Flowertown will also implement other marketing tactics to promote and sell its business move effectively. Some of those strategies include:

1. Maximizing sales at key holidays such as Valentine's Day, Mother's Day, and Secretary's Day
2. Maximizing sales to repeat customers in the area such as churches, funeral homes, and flowers by phone
3. Encouraging impulse sales by walk-in traffic
4. Adding gift items appropriate to each holiday to encourage impulse purchases

These strategies help the florist sell more products, but they aren't at the core of Flowertown's positioning strategy. Still, they are an important part of the florist's success. Next, the tactics need to be divided into tactics that support the company's positioning strategy, and those geared to supporting other marketing strategies.

---

*Always decide on your positioning tactics first. Typically, they have the most impact on your business.*

*For every tactic you are proposing, ask yourself, "Will this have a significant impact on my business?" If the answer is no, why use it?*

Positioning Tactics:

1. Form an alliance with a wedding photographer and bakery to print a brochure on the perfect wedding that can be passed out at each business.
2. Attend the four annual spring bridal fairs that occur in the area.
3. Continue to offer the Lover's Special for Valentines Day, a $120 special bouquet sold for $70. The bouquet has been very popular with men considering proposing marriage.
4. Prepare brochures on the TLC Wedding Package.
5. Set aside a 10-by-10-foot area of the store to use as the wedding center.

Other Tactics:

1. Continue to offer the option of having flowers on Secretary's Day delivered by a Victorian maid.
2. Continue as a member of the Flowers by Phone program.
3. Maintain a 3-inch ad in the Yellow Pages.
4. Add a new line of upscale baskets for bouquets over $50.
5. Offer a 30 percent discount to churches for their Sunday flowers.
6. Encourage impulse purchases with special value-priced prepared bouquets on days other than special holidays.

Be sure to list new *and* previously used tactics in your plan. The plan should contain everything you will do in the next year.

Not every marketer separates positioning and marketing tactics as clearly as this example. But I think it helps marketers focus on just what they are trying to accomplish in the upcoming year. Keeping the two types of strategies separate helps ensure the company will effectively execute both parts of their overall marketing strategy.

*Note*: When filling out this section, refer to the Positioning Strategy form in Chapter 6.

## Positioning Strategies

New Strategies

1. . . . . . . . . . . . . . . . . . . . . . . . . . . . . . . . . . . . . . . . . . . . . . . . . . . . . . . . . . . . . . . .

. . . . . . . . . . . . . . . . . . . . . . . . . . . . . . . . . . . . . . . . . . . . . . . . . . . . . . . . . . . . . . .

. . . . . . . . . . . . . . . . . . . . . . . . . . . . . . . . . . . . . . . . . . . . . . . . . . . . . . . . . . . . . . .

2. . . . . . . . . . . . . . . . . . . . . . . . . . . . . . . . . . . . . . . . . . . . . . . . . . . . . . . . . . . . . . . .

. . . . . . . . . . . . . . . . . . . . . . . . . . . . . . . . . . . . . . . . . . . . . . . . . . . . . . . . . . . . . . .

. . . . . . . . . . . . . . . . . . . . . . . . . . . . . . . . . . . . . . . . . . . . . . . . . . . . . . . . . . . . . . .

New positioning strategies should have a clear connection to your situation analysis.

Continuing Strategies

1. .........................................................................................

2. .........................................................................................

*Note*: I separate the continuing strategies from the new ones so that it is clear to readers of the plan what elements of the strategy are being implemented for the first time.

## Additional Marketing Strategies

New Strategies

1. .........................................................................................

2. .........................................................................................

Continuing Strategies

1. .........................................................................................

2. .........................................................................................

New strategies will take effort to implement properly. Try to have a balance of old and new strategies.

People who read your plan should understand exactly why you have decided on a certain strategy.

## Rationale for Strategy

You want to give a short three or four paragraph rationale for your new positioning strategies and any other significant marketing strategies. For example, Flowertown's rationale would be as follows:

*Positioning Strategy Rationale*

The biggest percentage of flower sales in the local communities is weddings. The decision of which flowers to use is usually made by the bride and her mother. Both target groups want the wedding day to be a perfect event, and they tend to dwell on every detail of the wedding. To reassure the brides and their mothers that the wedding floral arrangements will be perfect, we are implementing our TLC Package. It offers each wedding party a point of contact, provides three meetings when the bride and her mother can look at many different options, and sends the florist/designer to the wedding site to ensure that the flowers are perfect for the wedding.

> Flowertown's strategy is based on offering its customers confidence that their wedding day will be perfect.

*Marketing Strategy Rationale.* Customers normally don't think that much about buying flowers. Instead they tend to go to a florist they can locate quickly or one they have used before. To make the store memorable, Flowertown will continue its tactics of delivering flowers with Victorian maids on Secretary's Day. The store will continue its Yellow Page ads and its membership in Flowers by Phone to generate its share of purchases from customers who buy occasionally for funerals or other special events. Flowertown will also continue its regular program of promotional window displays to encourage walk-by traffic to stop in and make a purchase.

> Flowertown's marketing strategy is based on how its customers buy.

You can comment on the strategies that you feel are significant. Also remember to include tactics for your distribution network if they are relevant to your business.

*Positioning Strategy Rationale*

. . . . . . . . . . . . . . . . . . . . . . . . . . . . . . . . . . . . . . . . . . . . . . . . . . . . . . . . . . . . . . . .

. . . . . . . . . . . . . . . . . . . . . . . . . . . . . . . . . . . . . . . . . . . . . . . . . . . . . . . . . . . . . . . .

. . . . . . . . . . . . . . . . . . . . . . . . . . . . . . . . . . . . . . . . . . . . . . . . . . . . . . . . . . . . . . . .

. . . . . . . . . . . . . . . . . . . . . . . . . . . . . . . . . . . . . . . . . . . . . . . . . . . . . . . . . . . . . . . .

. . . . . . . . . . . . . . . . . . . . . . . . . . . . . . . . . . . . . . . . . . . . . . . . . . . . . . . . . . . . . . . .

> Standard marketing tactics are typically centered on how customers buy, or on where they go to look for information.

*Marketing Strategy Rationale*

........................................................................

........................................................................

........................................................................

........................................................................

........................................................................

Your positioning statement should be powerful enough for customers to take a moment to check you out.

## Competitive Positioning

In Chapter 6, you filled out the following positioning statements.

**Your basic positioning statement for end users** should read as follows:

.............. (your company name) provides ............. (your product or service) to ....
.......... (your target market). .............. (your company name) offers .............
(your competitive advantage) to the ............. (target customer group) to meet or satisfy
the ............. (target customer group's major want or desire that your company meets).

Be sure to consider your distribution channel as a customer group.

**Your basic positioning statement for the distribution network** should read as follows:

.............. (your company name) provides ............. (your product or service) to ....
.......... (your target part of the distribution network). .............. (your company name)
offers ............. (your competitive advantage) to the ............. (target customer
group) to meet or satisfy the ............. (target customer group's major want or desire that
your company meets).

## Marketing Tactics for ............(List the Year)

In this part you want to list every marketing tactic you will use over the next year. (Refer back to
Chapters 7, 8, and 9 for the specific tactics you selected earlier.)

You should give a brief explanation, no more than three or four sentences of how you will be implementing each tactic. List every tactic that must implemented so it can be included in the implementation timetable (coming up at the end of the plan). For example, Flowertown might have the following explanation of its promotional program.

*Promotional Programs.* Flowertown will continue to offer its special cut-flower bouquets on Fridays at $4.95 and $6.95, and its twelve roses for $25.95 special on Fridays that aren't holidays during the year. It will also expand its selection of comedy gift items from Garnett Hill, and its sweetheart gift selections from Sweet Mary's, which will be offered on promotional specials throughout the year.

Be sure to include several tactics targeted at your distribution network, if you rely on one to get your product to customers.

Tactic 1. . . . . . . . . . . . . . . . . . . . . . . . . . . . . . . . . . . . . . . . . . . . . . . . . . . . . . . . . . . . . . . . .

Comments: . . . . . . . . . . . . . . . . . . . . . . . . . . . . . . . . . . . . . . . . . . . . . . . . . . . . . . . . . . .

. . . . . . . . . . . . . . . . . . . . . . . . . . . . . . . . . . . . . . . . . . . . . . . . . . . . . . . . . . . . . . . . . . . . . . . . . . . .

. . . . . . . . . . . . . . . . . . . . . . . . . . . . . . . . . . . . . . . . . . . . . . . . . . . . . . . . . . . . . . . . . . . . . . . . . . . .

. . . . . . . . . . . . . . . . . . . . . . . . . . . . . . . . . . . . . . . . . . . . . . . . . . . . . . . . . . . . . . . . . . . . . . . . . . . .

Evaluate all your tactics to see if they are cost effective. Many strategies such as big catalogs are no longer as cost effective as they once were.

Tactic 2. . . . . . . . . . . . . . . . . . . . . . . . . . . . . . . . . . . . . . . . . . . . . . . . . . . . . . . . . . . . . . . . .

Comments: . . . . . . . . . . . . . . . . . . . . . . . . . . . . . . . . . . . . . . . . . . . . . . . . . . . . . . . . . . .

. . . . . . . . . . . . . . . . . . . . . . . . . . . . . . . . . . . . . . . . . . . . . . . . . . . . . . . . . . . . . . . . . . . . . . . . . . . .

. . . . . . . . . . . . . . . . . . . . . . . . . . . . . . . . . . . . . . . . . . . . . . . . . . . . . . . . . . . . . . . . . . . . . . . . . . . .

. . . . . . . . . . . . . . . . . . . . . . . . . . . . . . . . . . . . . . . . . . . . . . . . . . . . . . . . . . . . . . . . . . . . . . . . . . . .

. . . . . . . . . . . . . . . . . . . . . . . . . . . . . . . . . . . . . . . . . . . . . . . . . . . . . . . . . . . . . . . . . . . . . . . . . . . .

Be sure you implement tactics that ensure that your product or service is exposed to customers. A great positioning strategy doesn't help if customers don't see it.

Tactic 3. . . . . . . . . . . . . . . . . . . . . . . . . . . . . . . . . . . . . . . . . . . . . . . . . . . . . . . . . . . . . . . . .

Comments: . . . . . . . . . . . . . . . . . . . . . . . . . . . . . . . . . . . . . . . . . . . . . . . . . . . . . . . . . . .

. . . . . . . . . . . . . . . . . . . . . . . . . . . . . . . . . . . . . . . . . . . . . . . . . . . . . . . . . . . . . . . . . . . . . . . . . . . .

. . . . . . . . . . . . . . . . . . . . . . . . . . . . . . . . . . . . . . . . . . . . . . . . . . . . . . . . . . . . . . . . . . . . . . . . . . . .

. . . . . . . . . . . . . . . . . . . . . . . . . . . . . . . . . . . . . . . . . . . . . . . . . . . . . . . . . . . . . . . . . . . . . . . . . . . .

. . . . . . . . . . . . . . . . . . . . . . . . . . . . . . . . . . . . . . . . . . . . . . . . . . . . . . . . . . . . . . . . . . . . . . . . . . . .

Tactic 4. . . . . . . . . . . . . . . . . . . . . . . . . . . . . . . . . . . . . . . . . . . . . . . . . . . . . . . . .

Comments: . . . . . . . . . . . . . . . . . . . . . . . . . . . . . . . . . . . . . . . . . . . . . . . . . . . .

. . . . . . . . . . . . . . . . . . . . . . . . . . . . . . . . . . . . . . . . . . . . . . . . . . . . . . . . . . . . . .

. . . . . . . . . . . . . . . . . . . . . . . . . . . . . . . . . . . . . . . . . . . . . . . . . . . . . . . . . . . . . .

. . . . . . . . . . . . . . . . . . . . . . . . . . . . . . . . . . . . . . . . . . . . . . . . . . . . . . . . . . . . . .

. . . . . . . . . . . . . . . . . . . . . . . . . . . . . . . . . . . . . . . . . . . . . . . . . . . . . . . . . . . . . .

Be sure at least some of your promotional programs go out into the customer's world.

Tactic 5. . . . . . . . . . . . . . . . . . . . . . . . . . . . . . . . . . . . . . . . . . . . . . . . . . . . . . . . .

Comments: . . . . . . . . . . . . . . . . . . . . . . . . . . . . . . . . . . . . . . . . . . . . . . . . . . . .

. . . . . . . . . . . . . . . . . . . . . . . . . . . . . . . . . . . . . . . . . . . . . . . . . . . . . . . . . . . . . .

. . . . . . . . . . . . . . . . . . . . . . . . . . . . . . . . . . . . . . . . . . . . . . . . . . . . . . . . . . . . . .

. . . . . . . . . . . . . . . . . . . . . . . . . . . . . . . . . . . . . . . . . . . . . . . . . . . . . . . . . . . . . .

. . . . . . . . . . . . . . . . . . . . . . . . . . . . . . . . . . . . . . . . . . . . . . . . . . . . . . . . . . . . . .

You don't need to have a large number of tactics; you just need them to be effective.

Tactic 6. . . . . . . . . . . . . . . . . . . . . . . . . . . . . . . . . . . . . . . . . . . . . . . . . . . . . . . . .

Comments: . . . . . . . . . . . . . . . . . . . . . . . . . . . . . . . . . . . . . . . . . . . . . . . . . . . .

. . . . . . . . . . . . . . . . . . . . . . . . . . . . . . . . . . . . . . . . . . . . . . . . . . . . . . . . . . . . . .

. . . . . . . . . . . . . . . . . . . . . . . . . . . . . . . . . . . . . . . . . . . . . . . . . . . . . . . . . . . . . .

. . . . . . . . . . . . . . . . . . . . . . . . . . . . . . . . . . . . . . . . . . . . . . . . . . . . . . . . . . . . . .

. . . . . . . . . . . . . . . . . . . . . . . . . . . . . . . . . . . . . . . . . . . . . . . . . . . . . . . . . . . . . .

Tactic 7. . . . . . . . . . . . . . . . . . . . . . . . . . . . . . . . . . . . . . . . . . . . . . . . . . . . . . . . .

Comments: . . . . . . . . . . . . . . . . . . . . . . . . . . . . . . . . . . . . . . . . . . . . . . . . . . . .

. . . . . . . . . . . . . . . . . . . . . . . . . . . . . . . . . . . . . . . . . . . . . . . . . . . . . . . . . . . . . .

. . . . . . . . . . . . . . . . . . . . . . . . . . . . . . . . . . . . . . . . . . . . . . . . . . . . . . . . . . . . . .

..................................................  ←

Evaluate some of
your minor tac-
tics. Would you
be better off

Tactic 8. ..........................................................  dropping those
tactics and
Comments: ..........................................  investing the
money in one
.........................................................  of your major
tactics?
.........................................................

.........................................................

.........................................................


Tactic 9. ..........................................................

Comments: ..........................................

.........................................................

.........................................................  ←

.........................................................  Your tactics
should include at
.........................................................  least one new
tactic, such as

Tactic 10. ..........................................................  an alliance, cross
promotion, or on-
Comments: ..........................................  line marketing
program.
.........................................................

.........................................................

.........................................................

.........................................................

Tactic 11. . . . . . . . . . . . . . . . . . . . . . . . . . . . . . . . . . . . . . . . . . . . . . . . . . . . . . . . . . . . . . . . . . . . . . . . . . . . . . . . . . . . . . .

Comments: . . . . . . . . . . . . . . . . . . . . . . . . . . . . . . . . . . . . . . . . . . . . . . . . . . . . . . . . . . . . . . . . . . . . . . . . . . . . . . . .

. . . . . . . . . . . . . . . . . . . . . . . . . . . . . . . . . . . . . . . . . . . . . . . . . . . . . . . . . . . . . . . . . . . . . . . . . . . . . . . . . . . . . . . . . . . . .

. . . . . . . . . . . . . . . . . . . . . . . . . . . . . . . . . . . . . . . . . . . . . . . . . . . . . . . . . . . . . . . . . . . . . . . . . . . . . . . . . . . . . . . . . . . . .

. . . . . . . . . . . . . . . . . . . . . . . . . . . . . . . . . . . . . . . . . . . . . . . . . . . . . . . . . . . . . . . . . . . . . . . . . . . . . . . . . . . . . . . . . . . . .

. . . . . . . . . . . . . . . . . . . . . . . . . . . . . . . . . . . . . . . . . . . . . . . . . . . . . . . . . . . . . . . . . . . . . . . . . . . . . . . . . . . . . . . . . . . . .

The implementation plan acts as your yearly calendar. Set it up in your office so you can check to be sure you complete every action step.

Tactic 12. . . . . . . . . . . . . . . . . . . . . . . . . . . . . . . . . . . . . . . . . . . . . . . . . . . . . . . . . . . . . . . . . . . . . . . . . . . . . . . . . . . . . . .

Comments: . . . . . . . . . . . . . . . . . . . . . . . . . . . . . . . . . . . . . . . . . . . . . . . . . . . . . . . . . . . . . . . . . . . . . . . . . . . . . . . .

. . . . . . . . . . . . . . . . . . . . . . . . . . . . . . . . . . . . . . . . . . . . . . . . . . . . . . . . . . . . . . . . . . . . . . . . . . . . . . . . . . . . . . . . . . . . .

. . . . . . . . . . . . . . . . . . . . . . . . . . . . . . . . . . . . . . . . . . . . . . . . . . . . . . . . . . . . . . . . . . . . . . . . . . . . . . . . . . . . . . . . . . . . .

. . . . . . . . . . . . . . . . . . . . . . . . . . . . . . . . . . . . . . . . . . . . . . . . . . . . . . . . . . . . . . . . . . . . . . . . . . . . . . . . . . . . . . . . . . . . .

. . . . . . . . . . . . . . . . . . . . . . . . . . . . . . . . . . . . . . . . . . . . . . . . . . . . . . . . . . . . . . . . . . . . . . . . . . . . . . . . . . . . . . . . . . . . .

Make sure you have the resources to effectively implement each tactic. If not, drop it.

Tactic 13. . . . . . . . . . . . . . . . . . . . . . . . . . . . . . . . . . . . . . . . . . . . . . . . . . . . . . . . . . . . . . . . . . . . . . . . . . . . . . . . . . . . . . .

Comments: . . . . . . . . . . . . . . . . . . . . . . . . . . . . . . . . . . . . . . . . . . . . . . . . . . . . . . . . . . . . . . . . . . . . . . . . . . . . . . . .

. . . . . . . . . . . . . . . . . . . . . . . . . . . . . . . . . . . . . . . . . . . . . . . . . . . . . . . . . . . . . . . . . . . . . . . . . . . . . . . . . . . . . . . . . . . . .

. . . . . . . . . . . . . . . . . . . . . . . . . . . . . . . . . . . . . . . . . . . . . . . . . . . . . . . . . . . . . . . . . . . . . . . . . . . . . . . . . . . . . . . . . . . . .

. . . . . . . . . . . . . . . . . . . . . . . . . . . . . . . . . . . . . . . . . . . . . . . . . . . . . . . . . . . . . . . . . . . . . . . . . . . . . . . . . . . . . . . . . . . . .

. . . . . . . . . . . . . . . . . . . . . . . . . . . . . . . . . . . . . . . . . . . . . . . . . . . . . . . . . . . . . . . . . . . . . . . . . . . . . . . . . . . . . . . . . . . . .

Tactic 14. . . . . . . . . . . . . . . . . . . . . . . . . . . . . . . . . . . . . . . . . . . . . . . . . . . . . . . . . . . . . . . . . . . . . . . . . . . . . . . . . . . . . . .

Comments: . . . . . . . . . . . . . . . . . . . . . . . . . . . . . . . . . . . . . . . . . . . . . . . . . . . . . . . . . . . . . . . . . . . . . . . . . . . . . . . .

. . . . . . . . . . . . . . . . . . . . . . . . . . . . . . . . . . . . . . . . . . . . . . . . . . . . . . . . . . . . . . . . . . . . . . . . . . . . . . . . . . . . . . . . . . . . .

. . . . . . . . . . . . . . . . . . . . . . . . . . . . . . . . . . . . . . . . . . . . . . . . . . . . . . . . . . . . . . . . . . . . . . . . . . . . . . . . . . . . . . . . . . . . .

. . . . . . . . . . . . . . . . . . . . . . . . . . . . . . . . . . . . . . . . . . . . . . . . . . . . . . . .

. . . . . . . . . . . . . . . . . . . . . . . . . . . . . . . . . . . . . . . . . . . . . . . . . . . . . . . .

Tactic 15. . . . . . . . . . . . . . . . . . . . . . . . . . . . . . . . . . . . . . . . . . . . . . . . . . . . . . .

Comments: . . . . . . . . . . . . . . . . . . . . . . . . . . . . . . . . . . . . . . . . . . . . . . . . . . . . . .

. . . . . . . . . . . . . . . . . . . . . . . . . . . . . . . . . . . . . . . . . . . . . . . . . . . . . . . . . . .

. . . . . . . . . . . . . . . . . . . . . . . . . . . . . . . . . . . . . . . . . . . . . . . . . . . . . . . . . . .

. . . . . . . . . . . . . . . . . . . . . . . . . . . . . . . . . . . . . . . . . . . . . . . . . . . . . . . . . . .

Every action step for every tactic needs to be on the plan. Otherwise you are likely to forget to finish a step in time.

## Implementation Plan and Budget

### Implementation Plan

In effect, the implementation plan is a calendar for you to follow throughout the year. Every month it tells you what action items need to be done, who is supposed to do them, and how much they will cost. In Chapters 10, 11, and 12, you put together an implementation plan for each tactic you plan on using during the year. Your job now is to put all the steps for each tactic into one final implementation plan. This is a time-consuming task if you have more than 10 tactics you'll be implementing, but it will pay off over the next year. I've found that most companies without an implementation plan are lucky to execute even half of their planned tactics because they simply fail to get some of the preliminary steps done on time.

Break out each action step for every tactic from Appendices B,C, and D.

| DATE | ACTION | COST | PERSON RESPONSIBLE |
|------|--------|------|--------------------|
| | | | |
| | | | |
| | | | |
| | | | |
| | | | |
| | | | |

| DATE | ACTION | COST | PERSON RESPONSIBLE |
|------|--------|------|--------------------|
| | | | |
| | | | |
| | | | |
| | | | |
| | | | |
| | | | |
| | | | |
| | | | |
| | | | |
| | | | |
| | | | |
| | | | |
| | | | |
| | | | |
| | | | |
| | | | |
| | | | |
| | | | |
| | | | |
| | | | |
| | | | |
| | | | |
| | | | |
| | | | |

Avoid having too many action steps occur too closely together,

Only one person should be responsible for each action. If two or more people are involved, list the person with ultimate responsibility first.

# Strategy, Tactics, and Implementation

| DATE | ACTION | COST | PERSON RESPONSIBLE |
|------|--------|------|--------------------|
|      |        |      |                    |

Be sure that the costs for each month can be covered by your sales level.

Be sure to spread out the responsibility for a program to the people who will make it happen.

| DATE | ACTION | COST | PERSON RESPONSIBLE |
|------|--------|------|--------------------|
| | | | |

Make sure each action step could be understood by a new employee.

Post your implementation plan on your office wall to ensure you keep on schedule.

## Expense Summary

How you separate action items out for your budget depends on your company. Most larger companies break out the budget into rather detailed categories, but smaller companies typically just break the marketing budget down to five to 12 simple categories—much like the companies in Section Four broke down their budgets. Some companies also include marketing and sales personnel salary in the marketing budget. I've included those categories here for readers who are writing plans for companies that include salaries. You don't need to rigidly follow this budget format. Revise it so it fits your company's budgeting process.

Companies use many different formats in their budgeting process.

### Budget

| ITEM | TOTAL $ |
|---|---|
| Marketing department salaries | . . . . . . . . . . . . . . . . . . . . |
| Marketing department travel | . . . . . . . . . . . . . . . . . . . . |
| Sales—administrative and management salaries | . . . . . . . . . . . . . . . . . . . . |
| Sales—field sales-force salaries | . . . . . . . . . . . . . . . . . . . . |
| Sales—management travel | . . . . . . . . . . . . . . . . . . . . |
| Sales—field sales-force travel | . . . . . . . . . . . . . . . . . . . . |
| Printing, brochures, manuals, sales materials | . . . . . . . . . . . . . . . . . . . . |
| Trade shows—booth costs | . . . . . . . . . . . . . . . . . . . . |
| Trade shows—space rental, transportation, and travel | . . . . . . . . . . . . . . . . . . . . |
| Advertising | . . . . . . . . . . . . . . . . . . . . |
| Publicity costs | . . . . . . . . . . . . . . . . . . . . |
| Direct-mail costs | . . . . . . . . . . . . . . . . . . . . |
| Internet site development and adjustment costs | . . . . . . . . . . . . . . . . . . . . |
| Internet hosting fees | . . . . . . . . . . . . . . . . . . . . |
| Special event costs | . . . . . . . . . . . . . . . . . . . . |
| Cost of promotions, giveaways, etc. | . . . . . . . . . . . . . . . . . . . . |
| Seminar or presentation costs | . . . . . . . . . . . . . . . . . . . . |
| Newsletters, publication, and mailing costs | . . . . . . . . . . . . . . . . . . . . |
| Technical service costs, including personnel | . . . . . . . . . . . . . . . . . . . . |
| Customer service costs, including personnel | . . . . . . . . . . . . . . . . . . . . |
| Customer service, other costs | . . . . . . . . . . . . . . . . . . . . |
| Other costs | . . . . . . . . . . . . . . . . . . . . |
| **Total** | . . . . . . . . . . . . . . . . . . . . |

You can set your budget categories either by type of activity (such as printing) or by tactic.

List your budget in enough detail that you can see where your money is being spent.

## Final Comments

A marketing plan has many jobs to do and it has to be balanced to get every job done. The major tasks of a marketing program are as follows:

1. To position your company so customers will perceive your competitive advantage
2. To contact customers, or to be in places where customers will find you
3. To provide customers with the information, installation, or service support they need to make a purchase
4. To have a distribution plan that gives customers an easy way to buy your product
5. To develop communication materials that are easy to use and understand

You can't simply decide to split your tactics up evenly among the tasks. Instead, you have to decide which of the five marketing tasks is the most difficult for your company, and then concentrate some of your tactics on that task. For example, an office building sales company doesn't have trouble locating prospects. It has trouble selling them. So the company would want to concentrate on positioning tactics and sales efforts. Another company that specializes in high-end installations of backyard koi ponds may have an easy time making the sale once it finds an interested prospect. Its problem is finding true prospects. It might concentrate its tactics on trade shows or other events where it has a chance of finding customers.

A major task of a marketing plan is to allocate resources to tactics that will produce the most result.

## Do You Have the Right Game Plan?

Rate the five categories from 1 to 5, with 1 being the aspect of marketing that is most difficult for your company and 5 being the aspect that is easiest for your company.

_____ 1. Position your company so customers will perceive your competitive advantage.

_____ 2. Contact customers, or be in places where customers will find you.

_____ 3. Provide customers the information, installation, or service support they need to make a purchase.

_____ 4. Have a distribution plan that gives customers an easy way to buy your product.

_____ 5. Develop communication materials that are easy to use and understand.

Now rate the five categories by where you place your marketing emphasis. Rank them from 1 to 5, with 1 as the marketing aspect you most emphasize and 5 as the aspect you least emphasize.

_____ 1. Position your company so customers will perceive your competitive advantage.

_____ 2. Contact customers, or be in places where customers will find you.

_____ 3. Provide customers the information, installation, or service support they need to make a purchase.

_____ 4. Have a distribution plan that gives customers an easy way to buy your product.

_____ 5. Develop communication materials that are easy to use and understand.

A balanced plan places most of the marketing emphasis on the marketing tasks that are most difficult to complete successfully. Go back and rework your strategy and tactics if you aren't emphasizing the right areas.

Be prepared to go back and forth several times before you settle on a final plan.

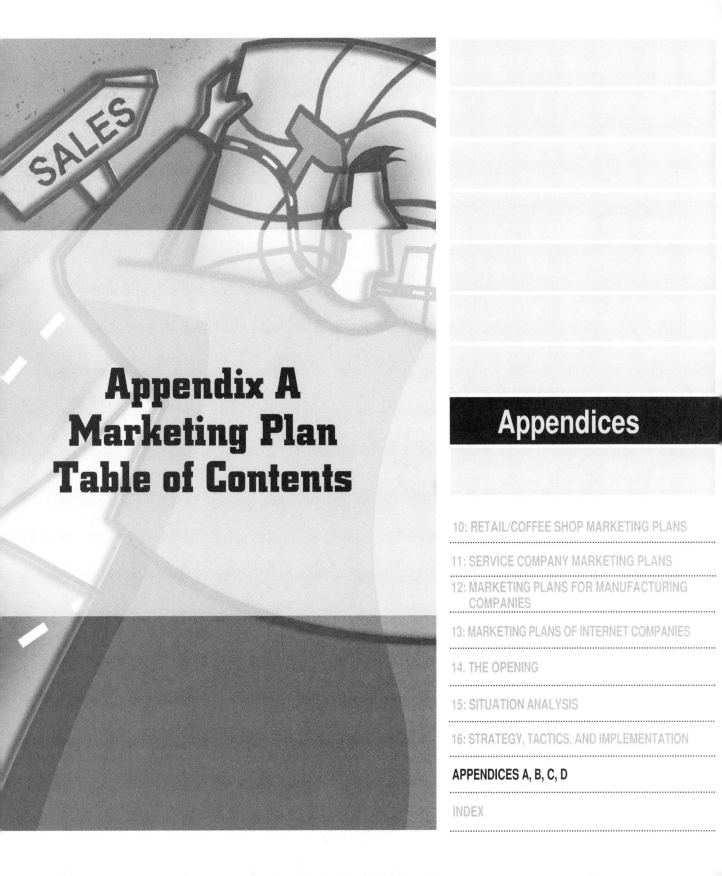

# Appendix A
# Marketing Plan
# Table of Contents

## Appendices

10: RETAIL/COFFEE SHOP MARKETING PLANS

11: SERVICE COMPANY MARKETING PLANS

12: MARKETING PLANS FOR MANUFACTURING
COMPANIES

13: MARKETING PLANS OF INTERNET COMPANIES

14. THE OPENING

15: SITUATION ANALYSIS

16: STRATEGY, TACTICS, AND IMPLEMENTATION

**APPENDICES A, B, C, D**

INDEX

**Marketing Plan**
**Table of Contents**

The situation analysis should be a quarter to a half of the content of a marketing plan.

1. Executive Summary
2. Marketing Objectives
3. Situation Analysis
    A. Internal Audit
        1. Company Description
        2. Product/Service Description and Profile
        3. Sales Trends
        4. Last Year's Commentary
        5. Strengths/Weaknesses
    B. External Evaluation
        1. Customer Information
        2. Market Profile
4. Positioning
    A. Positioning Strategies
        1. New Strategies
        2. Continuing Strategies
    B. Additional Marketing Strategies
        1. New Strategies
        2. Continuing Strategies
    C. Rationale for Strategy
    D. Competitive Positioning

Every plan should include product, pricing, distribution and promotion tactics.

5. Marketing Tactics
    A. Product
    B. Pricing
    C. Distribution
    D. Advertising/PR
    E. Trade Shows
    F. Electronic Media
    G. Events
    H. Alliances/Partnerships
    I. Other Tactics
6. Implementation Plan: (dates, activity, cost summary, person responsible)
7. Expense Summary

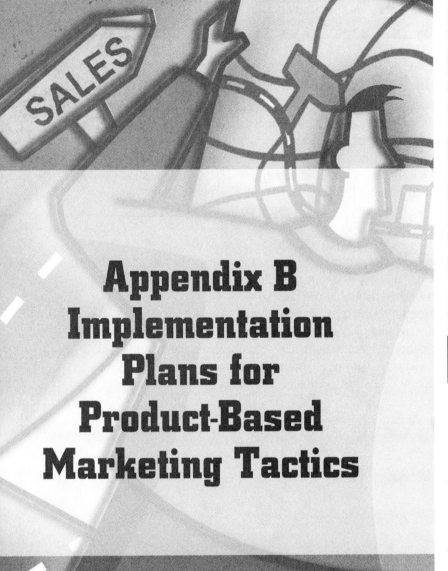

# Appendix B
# Implementation
# Plans for
# Product-Based
# Marketing Tactics

## Appendices

10: RETAIL/COFFEE SHOP MARKETING PLANS

11: SERVICE COMPANY MARKETING PLANS

12: MARKETING PLANS FOR MANUFACTURING COMPANIES

13: MARKETING PLANS OF INTERNET COMPANIES

14. THE OPENING

15: SITUATION ANALYSIS

16: STRATEGY, TACTICS, AND IMPLEMENTATION

**APPENDICES A, B, C, D**

INDEX

## Implementation Plan for Product-Based Marketing Tactics

Products and services have a short product life cycle today. You need to introduce new products or services at least every other year.

The next three appendices contain workbook sections. You will complete an implementation timetable for each tactic you'll use in the next year. Each appendix starts with an example of an implementation timetable for a tactic. Then there are eight pages of forms for you to fill out. You don't have to fill out eight tactics, just list the tactics you will actually be using. The reason for a timetable is to keep track of the key dates for implementing a tactic. At the end of the marketing plan is an implementation calendar for all the tactics you plan to use during the year. You'll want to keep this calendar hardy, so you'll know you are on schedule to meet all your deadlines.

The implementation calendar also helps you space your tactics evenly throughout the year. Most companies can only execute a limited number of tactics at one time. They aren't capable of executing dozens of tactics simultaneously. Without an implementation calendar, you'll find that it is quite easy to schedule too many activities in one month.

I've separated the implementation of tactics into three appendices because I believe it is important to have a balanced marketing program. You need to have tactics to generate momentum in all three categories: product, communications, and sales distribution and promotions. Without a balanced program, you may improve operations in one category, while your position in another category rapidly declines. Be sure to include tactics in each major category.

## SAMPLE IMPLEMENTATION PLAN

*Note*: This plan is for a clothing store that targets girls and young women from 13 to 26 years old, who like an eclectic look.

Displays are all important for a retail store.

Tactic: Change the window and store displays

Purpose of Tactic: To better reflect the store's unconventional merchandise

Person Responsible: Julie Sanborn

Final Implementation Date: July 1, 2000

| DATE | ACTION | COST | PERSON RESPONSIBLE |
|------|--------|------|--------------------|
| 1/15/00 | Check with suppliers to see what display material they have available. | | Julie S. |
| 2/15/00 | Make trip to Chicago to review displays at similar stores to get new ideas. | $ 750 | Julie S. |
| 3/15/00 | Complete scan of industry magazines for display ideas. | | Julie S. |
| 3/30/00 | Prepare pictures of display options that appear to work best. | | Julie S. |
| 4/15/00 | Conduct informal surveys of customers to determine which display option they prefer. | | Julie S. |
| 4/30/00 | Decide on final display configuration. | | Julie S. |
| 5/15/00 | Order all new display equipment. | 2,400 | Julie S. |
| 6/30/00 | Finalize display installation in both windows and store. | 500 | Julie S. |
| | | Total $3,650 | |

Tactic: .....................................................................................

Purpose of Tactic: .........................................................................

Person Responsible: .......................................................................

Final Implementation Date: ..............................................................

| DATE | ACTION | COST | PERSON RESPONSIBLE |
|------|--------|------|--------------------|
| | | | |
| | | | |
| | | | |
| | | | |
| | | | |
| | | | |
| | | | |
| | | | |
| | | | |
| | | | |
| | | | |
| | | | |
| | | | |
| | | | |
| | | | |
| | | | |
| | | | |

**Total    $**

## IMPLEMENTATION PLANS FOR PRODUCT-BASED MARKETING TACTICS

Tactic: .......................................................................................................

Purpose of Tactic: ...........................................................................

Person Responsible: .........................................................................

Final Implementation Date: ...............................................................

| DATE | ACTION | COST | PERSON RESPONSIBLE |
|------|--------|------|--------------------|
| | | | |
| | | | |
| | | | |
| | | | |
| | | | |
| | | | |
| | | | |
| | | | |
| | | | |
| | | | |
| | | | |
| | | | |
| | | | |
| | | | |
| | | | |
| | | | |
| | | | |
| | | | |

Total     $

Tactic: .....................................................................................................................

Purpose of Tactic: ..................................................................................................

Person Responsible: ...............................................................................................

Final Implementation Date: ...................................................................................

| DATE | ACTION | COST | PERSON RESPONSIBLE |
|------|--------|------|--------------------|
| | | | |
| | | | |
| | | | |
| | | | |
| | | | |
| | | | |
| | | | |
| | | | |
| | | | |
| | | | |
| | | | |
| | | | |
| | | | |
| | | | |
| | | | |
| | | | |
| | | | |

**Total $**

# IMPLEMENTATION PLANS FOR PRODUCT-BASED MARKETING TACTICS

Tactic: .............................................................................................

Purpose of Tactic: ...............................................................................

Person Responsible: .............................................................................

Final Implementation Date: ...................................................................

| DATE | ACTION | COST | PERSON RESPONSIBLE |
|------|--------|------|--------------------|
| | | | |
| | | | |
| | | | |
| | | | |
| | | | |
| | | | |
| | | | |
| | | | |
| | | | |
| | | | |
| | | | |
| | | | |
| | | | |
| | | | |
| | | | |
| | | | |
| | | | |
| | | | |

**Total    $**

Tactic: ...........................................................................................................................................

Purpose of Tactic: ...........................................................................................................

Person Responsible: .......................................................................................................

Final Implementation Date: ............................................................................................

| DATE | ACTION | COST | PERSON RESPONSIBLE |
|------|--------|------|--------------------|
| | | | |
| | | | |
| | | | |
| | | | |
| | | | |
| | | | |
| | | | |
| | | | |
| | | | |
| | | | |
| | | | |
| | | | |
| | | | |
| | | | |
| | | | |
| | | | |
| | | | |

Total $

# IMPLEMENTATION PLANS FOR PRODUCT-BASED MARKETING TACTICS

Tactic:

Purpose of Tactic:

Person Responsible:

Final Implementation Date:

| DATE | ACTION | COST | PERSON RESPONSIBLE |
|------|--------|------|--------------------|
|  |  |  |  |
|  |  |  |  |
|  |  |  |  |
|  |  |  |  |
|  |  |  |  |
|  |  |  |  |
|  |  |  |  |
|  |  |  |  |
|  |  |  |  |
|  |  |  |  |
|  |  |  |  |
|  |  |  |  |
|  |  |  |  |
|  |  |  |  |
|  |  |  |  |
|  |  |  |  |
|  |  |  |  |

**Total $**

Tactic: .............................................................................................................

Purpose of Tactic: ..........................................................................................

Person Responsible: ........................................................................................

Final Implementation Date: ............................................................................

| DATE | ACTION | COST | PERSON RESPONSIBLE |
|------|--------|------|--------------------|
| | | | |
| | | | |
| | | | |
| | | | |
| | | | |
| | | | |
| | | | |
| | | | |
| | | | |
| | | | |
| | | | |
| | | | |
| | | | |
| | | | |
| | | | |
| | | | |
| | | | |

Total    $

# IMPLEMENTATION PLANS FOR PRODUCT-BASED MARKETING TACTICS

Tactic: ................................................................................................

Purpose of Tactic: ................................................................................

Person Responsible: ...............................................................................

Final Implementation Date: .....................................................................

| DATE | ACTION | COST | PERSON RESPONSIBLE |
|------|--------|------|--------------------|
| | | | |
| | | | |
| | | | |
| | | | |
| | | | |
| | | | |
| | | | |
| | | | |
| | | | |
| | | | |
| | | | |
| | | | |
| | | | |
| | | | |
| | | | |
| | | | |
| | | | |
| | | | |

**Total  $**

Tactic: ..................................................................................................................

Purpose of Tactic: ................................................................................................

Person Responsible: ..............................................................................................

Final Implementation Date: ...................................................................................

| DATE | ACTION | COST | PERSON RESPONSIBLE |
| --- | --- | --- | --- |
| | | | |
| | | | |
| | | | |
| | | | |
| | | | |
| | | | |
| | | | |
| | | | |
| | | | |
| | | | |
| | | | |
| | | | |
| | | | |
| | | | |
| | | | |
| | | | |
| | | | |
| | | | |
| | Total | $ | |

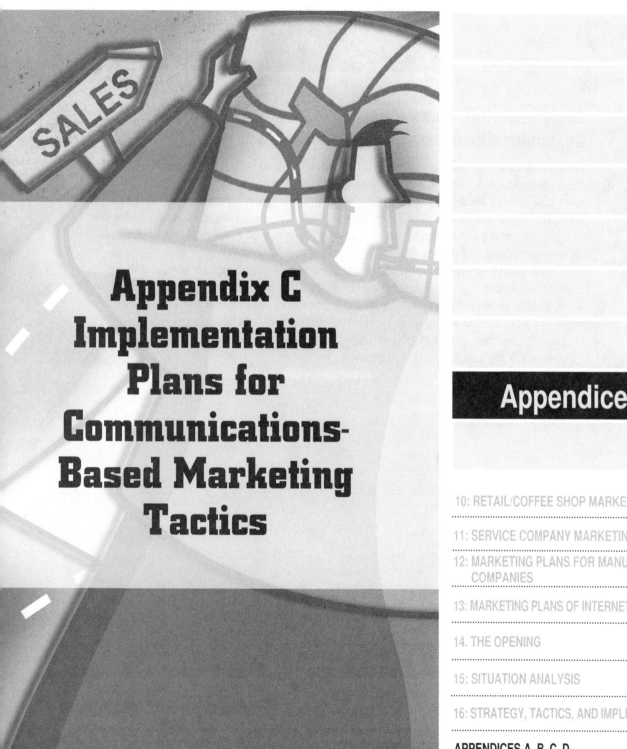

# Appendix C
# Implementation Plans for Communications-Based Marketing Tactics

## Appendices

10: RETAIL/COFFEE SHOP MARKETING PLANS

11: SERVICE COMPANY MARKETING PLANS

12: MARKETING PLANS FOR MANUFACTURING COMPANIES

13: MARKETING PLANS OF INTERNET COMPANIES

14. THE OPENING

15: SITUATION ANALYSIS

16: STRATEGY, TACTICS, AND IMPLEMENTATION

**APPENDICES A, B, C, D**

INDEX

## Implementation Plans for
## Communications-Based Marketing Tactics

Many small companies will hire a graphic artist, advertising agency, or other specialist to help them implement most communications-based programs. I recommend that you do that. A marketer may excel at deciding what customers want, and what point a brochure, ad, or flyer should make. But that doesn't mean they will be able to create the visual images and eye-catching layouts that customers will remember. In most cases marketers aren't really capable of the same creative artistic job as a professional.

Many small business owners try to design their own brochure or want to have complete creative control over all of their marketing materials. Although they certainly need to have input, small business owners need to realize that customers live in a visual world, and that the visual impact of any marketing material to a large part determines how effective the piece will be. Don't be reluctant to hire graphic artists or other creative specialists to give your pieces the "professional look" that the market demands.

Marketers succeed when they send one specific message When you say too much, customers lose sight of your main message.

## SAMPLE IMPLEMENTATION PLAN

*Note*: This plan is for a consultant who offers workshops and seminars for customer service representatives to become customer advocates in order to resolve their problems.

Tactic: Release an informational article highlighting a success story at a national bank

Purpose of Tactic: To make financial institutions aware of another option for improved service

Person Responsible: Jack Swanson

Final Implementation Date: August 15, 2000

| DATE | ACTION | COST | PERSON RESPONSIBLE |
|------|--------|------|--------------------|
| 1/31/00 | Convince the bank to agree to have a story written about their success with customer service advocate training. | | Sheila G. |
| 2/10/00 | Hire a freelance writer to write the story. | $1,200 | Jack S. |
| 2/28/00 | Hire a photographer to get pictures to go along with the story. | 500 | Sheila G. |
| 3/15/00 | Complete initial contacts with editors of trade magazines to explain the story's concept, and why other banks will be interested in reading the story. | | Jack S. |
| 4/30/00 | Complete story along with photos. | | Jack S. |
| 5/15/00 | Send story with photos to editors who expressed interest in featuring the story. | 200 | Sheila G. |
| 5/30/00 | Print story in a magazine format for distribution to prospects and customers. | 1,200 | Sheila G. |
| 6/30/00 | Finalize arrangement with magazine that will carry story. | | Jack S. |
| | | Total $3,100 | |

Don't be afraid to hire outside sources if they can do a better job than you.

# STREETWISE MARKETING PLAN

Tactic: ......................................................................................................................

Purpose of Tactic: ...........................................................................................

Person Responsible: .........................................................................................

Final Implementation Date: ...............................................................................

| DATE | ACTION | COST | PERSON RESPONSIBLE |
|------|--------|------|--------------------|
| ........................................................................................................ | | | |
| ........................................................................................................ | | | |
| ........................................................................................................ | | | |
| ........................................................................................................ | | | |
| ........................................................................................................ | | | |
| ........................................................................................................ | | | |
| ........................................................................................................ | | | |
| ........................................................................................................ | | | |
| ........................................................................................................ | | | |
| ........................................................................................................ | | | |
| ........................................................................................................ | | | |
| ........................................................................................................ | | | |
| ........................................................................................................ | | | |
| ........................................................................................................ | | | |
| ........................................................................................................ | | | |
| ........................................................................................................ | | | |
| ........................................................................................................ | | | |

Total   $

## IMPLEMENTATION PLANS FOR COMMUNICATIONS-BASED MARKETING TACTICS

Tactic: ...................................................................................................

Purpose of Tactic: .......................................................................................

Person Responsible: .....................................................................................

Final Implementation Date: ...............................................................................

| DATE | ACTION | COST | PERSON RESPONSIBLE |
|------|--------|------|--------------------|
| | | | |
| | | | |
| | | | |
| | | | |
| | | | |
| | | | |
| | | | |
| | | | |
| | | | |
| | | | |
| | | | |
| | | | |
| | | | |
| | | | |
| | | | |
| | | | |
| | | | |
| | | | |

Total   $

# STREETWISE MARKETING PLAN

Tactic: ..........................................................................................................................

Purpose of Tactic: ..........................................................................................

Person Responsible: ........................................................................................

Final Implementation Date: ..........................................................................

| DATE | ACTION | COST | PERSON RESPONSIBLE |
|------|--------|------|--------------------|
| | | | |
| | | | |
| | | | |
| | | | |
| | | | |
| | | | |
| | | | |
| | | | |
| | | | |
| | | | |
| | | | |
| | | | |
| | | | |
| | | | |
| | | | |
| | | | |
| | | | |
| | | | |
| | | | |

Total    $

# IMPLEMENTATION PLANS FOR COMMUNICATIONS-BASED MARKETING TACTICS

Tactic:

Purpose of Tactic:

Person Responsible:

Final Implementation Date:

| DATE | ACTION | COST | PERSON RESPONSIBLE |
|------|--------|------|--------------------|
| | | | |
| | | | |
| | | | |
| | | | |
| | | | |
| | | | |
| | | | |
| | | | |
| | | | |
| | | | |
| | | | |
| | | | |
| | | | |
| | | | |
| | | | |
| | | | |
| | | | |
| | | | |

**Total    $**

Tactic: ..................................................................................................

Purpose of Tactic: ....................................................................................

Person Responsible: ................................................................................

Final Implementation Date: ......................................................................

| DATE | ACTION | COST | PERSON RESPONSIBLE |
|------|--------|------|---------------------|
| . . . . . . . . . . . . . . . . . . . . . . . . . . . . . . . . . . . . . . . . . . . . . . . . . . . . . . . . . . . . . . . |
| . . . . . . . . . . . . . . . . . . . . . . . . . . . . . . . . . . . . . . . . . . . . . . . . . . . . . . . . . . . . . . . |
| . . . . . . . . . . . . . . . . . . . . . . . . . . . . . . . . . . . . . . . . . . . . . . . . . . . . . . . . . . . . . . . |
| . . . . . . . . . . . . . . . . . . . . . . . . . . . . . . . . . . . . . . . . . . . . . . . . . . . . . . . . . . . . . . . |
| . . . . . . . . . . . . . . . . . . . . . . . . . . . . . . . . . . . . . . . . . . . . . . . . . . . . . . . . . . . . . . . |
| . . . . . . . . . . . . . . . . . . . . . . . . . . . . . . . . . . . . . . . . . . . . . . . . . . . . . . . . . . . . . . . |

**Total  $**

# IMPLEMENTATION PLANS FOR COMMUNICATIONS-BASED MARKETING TACTICS

Tactic: .................................................................................................

Purpose of Tactic: ....................................................................................

Person Responsible: ..................................................................................

Final Implementation Date: ...........................................................................

| DATE | ACTION | COST | PERSON RESPONSIBLE |
|------|--------|------|--------------------|
| | | | |
| | | | |
| | | | |
| | | | |
| | | | |
| | | | |
| | | | |
| | | | |
| | | | |
| | | | |
| | | | |
| | | | |
| | | | |
| | | | |
| | | | |
| | | | |
| | | | |
| | | | |
| | | | |

Total    $

Tactic: ...............................................................................................................................................

Purpose of Tactic: ................................................................................................................

Person Responsible: .............................................................................................................

Final Implementation Date: ..................................................................................................

| DATE | ACTION | COST | PERSON RESPONSIBLE |
|------|--------|------|--------------------|
| | | | |
| | | | |
| | | | |
| | | | |
| | | | |
| | | | |
| | | | |
| | | | |
| | | | |
| | | | |
| | | | |
| | | | |
| | | | |
| | | | |
| | | | |
| | | | |
| | | | |
| | | | |

**Total** $

# IMPLEMENTATION PLANS FOR COMMUNICATIONS-BASED MARKETING TACTICS

Tactic: ..............................................................................................................

Purpose of Tactic: ..........................................................................................

Person Responsible: ........................................................................................

Final Implementation Date: .............................................................................

| DATE | ACTION | COST | PERSON RESPONSIBLE |
|------|--------|------|--------------------|
| .......................................................................................................................... |
| .......................................................................................................................... |
| .......................................................................................................................... |
| .......................................................................................................................... |
| .......................................................................................................................... |
| .......................................................................................................................... |
| .......................................................................................................................... |
| .......................................................................................................................... |
| .......................................................................................................................... |
| .......................................................................................................................... |
| .......................................................................................................................... |
| .......................................................................................................................... |
| .......................................................................................................................... |
| .......................................................................................................................... |
| .......................................................................................................................... |
| .......................................................................................................................... |
| .......................................................................................................................... |

Total     $

Tactic: ........................................................................................................

Purpose of Tactic: ....................................................................................

Person Responsible: ..................................................................................

Final Implementation Date: ......................................................................

| DATE | ACTION | COST | PERSON RESPONSIBLE |
|------|--------|------|--------------------|
| . . . . . . . . . . . . . . . . . . . . . . . . . . . . . . . . . . . . . . . . . . . . . . . . . . . . . . . . . |
| . . . . . . . . . . . . . . . . . . . . . . . . . . . . . . . . . . . . . . . . . . . . . . . . . . . . . . . . . |
| . . . . . . . . . . . . . . . . . . . . . . . . . . . . . . . . . . . . . . . . . . . . . . . . . . . . . . . . . |
| . . . . . . . . . . . . . . . . . . . . . . . . . . . . . . . . . . . . . . . . . . . . . . . . . . . . . . . . . |
| . . . . . . . . . . . . . . . . . . . . . . . . . . . . . . . . . . . . . . . . . . . . . . . . . . . . . . . . . |
| . . . . . . . . . . . . . . . . . . . . . . . . . . . . . . . . . . . . . . . . . . . . . . . . . . . . . . . . . |
| . . . . . . . . . . . . . . . . . . . . . . . . . . . . . . . . . . . . . . . . . . . . . . . . . . . . . . . . . |

**Total   $**

# Appendix D
# Implementation
# Plans for Marketing
# Tactics for Sales,
# Promotions, and
# Distribution

## Appendices

10: RETAIL/COFFEE SHOP MARKETING PLANS

11: SERVICE COMPANY MARKETING PLANS

12: MARKETING PLANS FOR MANUFACTURING COMPANIES

13: MARKETING PLANS OF INTERNET COMPANIES

14. THE OPENING

15: SITUATION ANALYSIS

16: STRATEGY, TACTICS, AND IMPLEMENTATION

**APPENDICES A, B, C, D**

INDEX

## Implementation Plans for Marketing Tactics for Sales, Promotions, and Distribution

A big mistake marketers make is to underestimate the effort needed to effectively implement promotional and distribution programs.

Sales, promotions, and distribution tactics are typically the most effective marketing tactics because they generally result in immediate sales. They are also the most time-consuming to execute. You must be careful not to schedule too many tactics in this category or you'll end up executing all of them poorly. If you look back at the examples in the last two appendices—changing a store's display and running a publicity program with an information article—you'll notice that most of the work is done within the company or with just one or two people. When you run an event, you may need to coordinate two alliance partners and dozens of other organizations, from hotels to caterers to a temporary help agency. Each group you work with may require several meetings and many phone calls.

Sales and distribution tactics also take more time to implement than you might expect. You need to contact at least a few salespeople and distributors to get their feedback before implementing the program. Then you have to introduce the program to the parties involved. That might require regional meetings or trips to major customers. Sales and distribution tactics can impact many people within your company. Over the past thirty years, I've found that it can be an enormous mistake to put together a distribution tactic and then announce it. You need to get out and sell the program to everyone involved, and show everyone why it's a great program. Their excitement will feed off your energy. In other words, salespeople and distributors won't get excited about a new program unless you're excited about it. Be sure to include a proper introduction for your program in the implementation plan.

## SAMPLE IMPLEMENTATION PLAN

Workshops at national conventions are an extremely effective promotional tactic.

*Note*: This plan is for a distributor of toys, mats, books, and other items for day care facilities.

Tactic: Sponsor workshop at national convention on innovative indoor activity centers

Purpose of Tactic: To increase awareness of company's catalog and improve credibility

Person Responsible: Bruce Miller

Final Implementation Date: Nov. 15, 2000

| DATE | ACTION | COST | PERSON RESPONSIBLE |
|---|---|---|---|
| 1/5/00 | Have workshop scheduled at the national convention for commercial day care facilities. Reserve room for 200 at convention center. | $3,000 | Judy W. |
| 1/30/00 | Contact manufacturers' suppliers to see what presentation they can do for the workshop. | | Bruce M. |
| 1/30/00 | Contact leading experts on play and childhood development to see if they have a presentation for the workshop. | 2,000 | Judy W. |
| 2/15/00 | Decide which experts to have present. Prepare contracts for them. | | Bruce M. |
| 2/28/00 | Prepare preliminary schedule of speakers and presenters for workshop. | | Bruce M. |
| 3/30/00 | Send out to presenters information on the date the presentation material is needed for workshop publication. | | Sue L. |
| 4/30/00 | Prepare flyer for presentation that can be used by presenters to pass out to their customers and prospects. | 1,500 | Bruce M. |
| 5/15/00 | Send out appeal to manufacturers to cover their share of workshop cost. Ask each manufacturer for $2,500 contribution. Donating companies will have a table for their materials. | | Sue L. |
| 5/30/00 | Check with all presenters to check on their progress. | | Judy W. |
| 6/15/00 | Visit convention site during electronics show, check room to determine services available from convention facilities. | 1,400 | Judy W. |
| 7/15/00 | Get a list from presenters of any equipment needs for workshop. | | Sue L. |

Promotional programs frequently have dozens of details marketers have to watch closely.

| 8/15/00 | Get commitments from manufacturers about their contribution toward workshop costs. | | Bruce M. |
| 8/30/00 | Send out letter to manufacturers requesting giveaway items for workshop. | | Judy W. |
| 9/10/00 | Double-check that presentations will be ready. | | Sue L. |
| 9/15/00 | Have all materials in to print booklet for participants. | | Sue L. |
| 10/1/00 | Check presenters who want to buy additional booklet copies. | | Sue L. |
| 10/1/00 | Decide what materials company will distribute. | | Bruce M. |
| 10/15/00 | Have booklet printed. | 2,500 | Judy W. |
| 10/15/00 | Create manifest of all items needed to come in for workshop. List date items need to be shipped, who is shipping it, and how it will be used. | | Sue L. |
| 10/15/00 | Do a setup of room—where materials will be, where each presenter will make presentation, and where handouts and company tables will be set up. | | Bruce M. |
| 11/1/00 | Check shipment status on all items on manifest. | | Sue L. |
| 11/5/00 | Visit convention site, review room, prepare action list for arrival. | | Judy W. |
| 11/15/00 | Arrive two days early to make sure everything is in place and to set up a contact person and contact location for presenter requests. | | Judy W. |
| 11/17/00 | Run the workshop. | | Bruce M. |
| 11/30/00 | Send out list of attendees to manufacturers. | | Sue L. |
| 12/15/00 | Send follow-up mailing to attendees promoting company's catalog. | | Sue L. |

**Total** $10,400

Tactic:

Purpose of Tactic:

Person Responsible:

Final Implementation Date:

| DATE | ACTION | COST | PERSON RESPONSIBLE |
|------|--------|------|--------------------|
| | | | |
| | | | |
| | | | |
| | | | |
| | | | |
| | | | |
| | | | |
| | | | |
| | | | |
| | | | |
| | | | |
| | | | |
| | | | |
| | | | |
| | | | |
| | | | |
| | | | |
| | | | |

Total    $

Tactic:

Purpose of Tactic:

Person Responsible:

Final Implementation Date:

| DATE | ACTION | COST | PERSON RESPONSIBLE |
|------|--------|------|--------------------|
| | | | |
| | | | |
| | | | |
| | | | |
| | | | |
| | | | |
| | | | |
| | | | |
| | | | |
| | | | |
| | | | |
| | | | |
| | | | |
| | | | |
| | | | |
| | | | |
| | | | |
| | | | |

**Total  $**

# IMPLEMENTATION PLANS FOR MARKETING TACTICS FOR SALES, PROMOTIONS, AND DISTRIBUTION

Tactic: ..........................................................................................................

Purpose of Tactic: ..............................................................................

Person Responsible: ............................................................................

Final Implementation Date: ..................................................................

| DATE | ACTION | COST | PERSON RESPONSIBLE |
|------|--------|------|--------------------|
| | | | |
| | | | |
| | | | |
| | | | |
| | | | |
| | | | |
| | | | |
| | | | |
| | | | |
| | | | |
| | | | |
| | | | |
| | | | |
| | | | |
| | | | |
| | | | |
| | | | |
| | | Total | $ |

Tactic: .......................................................................................................................

Purpose of Tactic: ........................................................................................................

Person Responsible: ......................................................................................................

Final Implementation Date: ...........................................................................................

| DATE | ACTION | COST | PERSON RESPONSIBLE |
|------|--------|------|--------------------|
| | | | |
| | | | |
| | | | |
| | | | |
| | | | |
| | | | |
| | | | |
| | | | |
| | | | |
| | | | |
| | | | |
| | | | |
| | | | |
| | | | |
| | | | |
| | | | |
| | | | |

**Total    $**

# IMPLEMENTATION PLANS FOR MARKETING TACTICS FOR SALES, PROMOTIONS, AND DISTRIBUTION

Tactic: ....................................................................................................

Purpose of Tactic: ......................................................................................

Person Responsible: ....................................................................................

Final Implementation Date: ..........................................................................

| DATE | ACTION | COST | PERSON RESPONSIBLE |
|------|--------|------|--------------------|
| | | | |
| | | | |
| | | | |
| | | | |
| | | | |
| | | | |
| | | | |
| | | | |
| | | | |
| | | | |
| | | | |
| | | | |
| | | | |
| | | | |
| | | | |
| | | | |

**Total** **$**

Tactic:

Purpose of Tactic:

Person Responsible:

Final Implementation Date:

| DATE | ACTION | COST | PERSON RESPONSIBLE |
|------|--------|------|--------------------|
| | | | |
| | | | |
| | | | |
| | | | |
| | | | |
| | | | |
| | | | |
| | | | |
| | | | |
| | | | |
| | | | |
| | | | |
| | | | |
| | | | |
| | | | |
| | | | |
| | | | |
| | | | |

**Total  $**

# Implementation Plans for Marketing Tactics for Sales, Promotions, and Distribution

Tactic: .............................................................................................................

Purpose of Tactic: .............................................................................................

Person Responsible: ...........................................................................................

Final Implementation Date: ..................................................................................

| DATE | ACTION | COST | PERSON RESPONSIBLE |
|------|--------|------|--------------------|
| | | | |
| | | | |
| | | | |
| | | | |
| | | | |
| | | | |
| | | | |
| | | | |
| | | | |
| | | | |
| | | | |
| | | | |
| | | | |
| | | | |
| | | | |
| | | | |
| | | | |
| | | | |

**Total $**

Tactic: .......................................................................................................................................

Purpose of Tactic: ......................................................................................................................

Person Responsible: ....................................................................................................................

Final Implementation Date: ...........................................................................................................

| DATE | ACTION | COST | PERSON RESPONSIBLE |
|------|--------|------|--------------------|
| | | | |
| | | | |
| | | | |
| | | | |
| | | | |
| | | | |
| | | | |
| | | | |
| | | | |
| | | | |
| | | | |
| | | | |
| | | | |
| | | | |
| | | | |
| | | | |
| | | | |

Total    $

# INDEX

## A

Advertising, 112–115
  co-op, 137
  Internet banner, 139
Advisory councils, 132
Alliances, 128–129, 132–133
Analysis. *See* External audit, of business;
  Internal audit, of business
Apple Computer, 68

## B

Banner ads, 139. *See also* BHD Corp.
BHD Corp., sample marketing plan,
  220–233, 259
Bidding policies, 104, 131
*Blair Witch Project, The*, 18, 24
Boise Cascade, 81, 82–83
Brand preferences, of customers, 22–23
Brochures, 116–117
Budget samples
  Internet company, 246
  manufacturing company, 215
  retail shops, 153, 166
  service companies, 178, 187
Bundling pricing, 101
Burger King, 66
Burley Rink Supplies, 34
Business, analysis of. *See* External audit,
  of business; Internal audit, of
  business
Buyers, types of, 20–21
Buying patterns, of customers, 31–33,
  38–39
  changes in, 3
  competitive advantage and, 35–36
  information gathering about, 34–35
  marketing's impact on, 33–34
  marketing plan form, 28–30
  tactics to influence, 36–38

## C

Captive pricing, 101
Catalogs, 117
Changes, 2–5
  in competitors, 51
  importance of, in marketing, 55
  responding to, 74
  *see also* Trends
Checklists
  about budget, 189
  about communication tactics, 123
  about customers, 12, 25, 93
  about executive summary, 270
  about expenses, 39
  about implementation plan, 309
  about internal audit, 55
  about marketing changes/
    innovations, 107, 142, 218
  about market share, 74
  about marketing plan, 168
  about on-line business, 260
  about situation analysis, 252
Chrysler, 70
Claire's Boutiques, 49
Classified advertising, 113
Clean Shower, 38
Coffee shop, sample marketing plan,
  154–167
Communication-based marketing tactics,
  112
  advertising, 112–115
  brochures/flyers, 116–117
  direct mail, 120–122
  marketing messages, 115–116
  marketing plan form, 110–111
  publicity, 118–120
  sample plans, 326–336
  trade shows, 117–118
Competitive advantage
  of competitors, 35, 36–37, 64

  positioning strategy and, 64–66, 86
  preserving own, 35–36, 37
  sample analysis, 194–195, 205–207
Competitive rankings, 66–69
Competitors. *See* Competitive advantage
Contests, 137–138
Coppertone, 37
Credibility building, 132–133
Cross promotions, 138
Customers
  buying patterns of, 31–33, 38–39
    changes in, 3
    competitive advantage and, 35–36
    gathering information about,
      31–33, 34–35
    marketing's impact on, 33–34
    marketing plan form, 28–30
    tactics to influence, 36–38
  changes in, 4
  commitments of, 131
  profile of, 18–19, 24–25
    buying types, 20–21
    functional goals of, 19
    interests of, 20
    marketing plan form, 16–17
    mood of, 24
    in plan workbook, 279–285
    product and, 22–23
    samples, 148–149, 173–174,
      225–228, 236–237
    self-image, 21
Customer service, 103–105
C-Ya Greeting cards, sample marketing
  plan, 247–257, 259

## D

Database marketing, 121, 129
Dell Computer, 71, 72
DeLong, Jeff, 247, 248, 251
Demonstrations, 102–103

Description, of business, 48
Direct mail, 120–122
Directory advertising, 113
Direct-response television, 114–115
Displays, in-store, 101–103, 135
Distribution
    competitive ranking of, 67–68
    implementations plans for, 338–348
    network for, 68, 86, 87–89
    positioning strategy for, 89–90
    tactics for, 128–129, 133–135

**E**

Embark, 139
Emhart Fastening Technologies, 8–9
Employees, 48, 50
Endorsements, 132
Enticements, 102
Events, special, 136
Exclusivity, 134
Executive summary
    in plan workbook, 264–268
    samples
        Internet companies, 220–221,
            234–235, 247–248
        manufacturing companies,
            192–193, 204–205
        retail shops, 146, 154–155
        service company, 179
Expertise, of management, 54
External audit, of business, 62, 72–73
    competitive rankings, 66–69
    competitor advantages, 64
    marketing plan form for, 58–61
    opportunities in market, 70–71
    in plan workbook, 278–291
    positioning strategies, 64–65
    samples, 159–160, 207–210
    segments of market, 63–64
    target markets, 63
    threats to company, 71–72
    trends in market, 62, 69–70

**F**

Features, of product
    adding new, 98–99, 100
    competitive ranking of, 67
    importance of, to customer, 23, 25
Feedback, from customer, 22–24
Fender Guitar Company, 47, 48
Financial Ad Trader. *See* BHD Corp.
Financial capability, of business, 53–54
Flyers, 116–117
Forms
    communication-based marketing,
        110–111
    customer buying patterns, 28–30
    customer profile, 16–17
    external audit, 58–61
    internal audit, 44–46
    product-based marketing, 96
FUBU (For Us By Us), 70

**G**

General Motors, 71
Goals
    customer's functional, 19
    of marketing plan, 5, 268–269
    positioning strategy and, 82–86
    for sales levels, 6–7
    sample marketing, 221
GoRu Toys, 112
Guinness, 31
G-Vox Interactive Music, 47–49

**H**

H&R Trains, 62, 102, 136
    sample marketing plan, 146–153, 167
Hessler, Robert, 222
History, of business, 48–49
Humor, 24

**I**

Image pricing, 100–101
Implementation plan

in plan workbook, 303–307
samples
    communication-based, 326–336
    Internet companies, 233, 244–245,
        257
    manufacturing companies, 203, 215
    product-based, 314–324
    retail shops, 152, 164–166
    service companies, 177, 186
    tactics, 338–348
Importance, how to rank on forms, 13
Informational publicity stories, 119
Internal audit, of business, 47–48, 54
    description, 48
    expertise of management, 54
    financial capabilities, 53
    history, 48–49
    marketing plan form for, 44–46
    in plan workbook, 272–278
    sales growth, 51
    samples, 155–158, 179–181,
        222–230, 248–254
    secondary markets, 49–50
    specialties, 50–51
    strengths/weaknesses, 51–53
    target markets, 49
Internet, marketing on, 138–140
Internet companies, sample marketing
    plans, 220–259

**J**

Joint presentations, 119
Judicial buyer, 21

**K**

Key account strategy, 130
Kitchen Koncepts, 9–10
Kraft, Dan, 222, 223

**L**

Larami, 4
Leasing options, 131

Low-cost buyer, 21
Loyalty programs, 137

## M

Macy's, 70
Magazine advertising, 113
Mailing lists. *See* Direct mail
Management
  expertise of, 54
  sales visits by, 130–131
Manufacturing companies, sample
  marketing plans, 192–217
Market(s)
  access to new, 88, 90
  profile of, 285–291
  secondary, 49–50
  trends of, 62, 69–70
  *see also* Target markets
Marketing plan
  goals of, 5
  importance of, 6–11
  sales growth and, 2–11
  samples
    Internet companies, 220–259
    manufacturing companies, 192–217
    retail shops, 146–167
    service companies, 170–188
Marketing plan workbook
  opening, 264–271, 312
  situation analysis
    external audit, 278–291
    internal audit, 272–278
  strategy, tactics, implementation,
    294–309
Marketing strategy
  communications-based, 110–123
    sample plan, 326–336
  critical steps in developing, 71
  objectives
    measurable, 80, 81, 91
    positioning strategy, 64–66,
      78–79, 81–91, 239–240

product-based, 96–107
  sample plan, 314–324
tactics for, 126–129, 140–142
  credibility building, 132–133
  distribution, 128–129, 133–135
  Internet, 138–140
  in plan workbook, 298–303
  promotions, 136–138
  sales, 129–131
  sample plans, 338–348
  samples, 149–151, 161–163,
    183–185, 200–201, 212–214,
    231–232, 240–243, 255–256
MARS (Music and Recording
  Superstores), 64
Maximizer buyer, 21
McDonald's, 66
McGraw-Hill, 48, 51
Might Grounds Coffee Shop, sample
  marketing plan, 154–167
Mills, Wayne, 179–180
Minimizer buyer, 21
Mitchell, Hayden, 222
Momentum, 37–38
Moods, of customer, 24
Motwani, Lajoo, 222, 223
Mutual Fund Magic. *See* BHD Corp.

## N

Names(s)
  marketing value of good, 116
  trading of prospects', 120–121
Networking, 129–130
Newsletters, 119–120
Newspaper advertising, 113–114
Non-negotiated pricing, 101

## O

Oil-N-Gas, Inc., sample marketing plan,
  234–246
Opportunities, in market, 70–71

## P

Packaging, 99–100, 101–103
Paper Warehouse, 64–65
Parker Brothers, 136
Payment terms, 105, 131
Pay-one-price pricing, 101
Perceptions, importance of, 53, 54
Perkins Restaurant, 65
Phone calls, to customer, 22, 23, 24
Positioning statements, 71, 91
  samples, 230–231
Positioning strategies, 64–66
  marketing plan form, 78–79
  to meet marketing objectives, 81–91
  in plan workbook, 294–298
  samples, 149, 160–161, 174–175,
    182–183, 211–212, 254–255
Press releases, 118
Prices/pricing, 100–101
  competitive ranking of, 66–67
  special, 136
Price/value relationship, competitive
  ranking of, 68
Priority, how to rank on forms, 13
Product(s)
  author's use of word, *xiii–xiv*
  company's orientation toward, 72–73
  features of, 23, 25, 67, 98–99, 100
  importance of, to customer, 22–23
Product-based marketing, 97–98
  customer service, 103–105
  marketing plan form, 96
  packaging/store display, 101–103
  pricing, 100–101
  product/store/service, 98–100
  sample plan, 314–324
Profile, of customer, 18–19, 24–25
  buying types, 20–21
  functional goals of, 19
  interests of, 20
  marketing plan form, 16–17
  mood of, 24

in plan workbook, 279–285
product and, 22–23
samples, 148–149, 173–174,
    225–228, 236–237
self-image, 21
Profitability, 87–88, 90
Promotions, 122
    implementations plans for, 338–348
    tactics for, 126–127, 136–138
Prospect names, trading of, 120–121
Publicity, 118–120, 133
Public perceptions, changes in, 3–4

**Q**

Quality, competitive ranking of, 68–69

**R**

Radio advertising, 114
*Radio-TV Interview Report*, 118
Reactive marketing, 2, 71–72
Research projects, 133
Resnick Associates, 119
    sample marketing plan, 170–178, 188

**S**

Safeplay Systems, Inc., 49, 50, 88
    sample marketing plan, 192–203,
        216–217
Sales
    goals for, 6–7
    growth in, 51
    implementation plans for, 338–348
    level of, 87, 89
    tactics for, 126–127, 129–131
Sampling, 137
Schulco, sample marketing plan,
    204–217
Secondary markets, 49–50
Self-image, of customer, 21
Seminars, 136–137
Service
    competitive ranking of, 67

customer, 103–105
    hassle-free, 88–89, 90
Service company, sample marketing
    plans, 170–188
7UP, 53
Short Term Stock Selector. *See* BHD
    Corp.
Situation analysis. *See* External audit, of
    business; Internal audit, of business
Slice, 53
Slogans, 115
Small companies, 49, 63, 218
Snapple, 53
Southwest Painting, 128–129
    sample marketing plan, 179–188
Specialty, of business, 50–51, 130
Starbucks, 37–38
Strategy. *See* Marketing strategy
Street Glow, 97–98
Strengths, of business, 51–52
    examples, 158, 172, 180, 196–197,
        225, 238, 251
    list of, 52–53
Surveys, 118–119

**T**

Tag lines, 115
Target customers. *See* Customers
Target markets
    external audit of, 63
    goals and desires of, 82–86
    internal audit of, 49
    segments of, 63–64
    *see also* Markets
Technology, changes in, 3
Television advertising, 114
Threats, to business, 71–72
Tier pricing, 101
Trademarks, 115–116
Trade shows, 117–118
Trends, 62, 69–70. *See also* Changes
Trial pricing, 100

**U**

University studies, 120

**V**

Value-added pricing, 101
Value/price relationship, competitive
    ranking of, 68
Visual images, 102

**W**

Warranty cards, 22
Weaknesses, of business, 51–52, 54
    examples, 158, 172, 181, 196–197,
        225, 239, 252
    list of, 52–53
Weiss, Nathaniel, 47
Wendy's, 66
Workbook. *See* Marketing plan
    workbook

**Y**

Yellow Pages advertising, 112–113

# ADAMS *STREETWISE*® BOOKS FOR GROWING YOUR BUSINESS

## Visit the rest of the *Streetwise*® series at *www.adamsmedia.com*

**Complete Business Plan**
$19.95 ($29.95 CAN)
ISBN 1-55850-845-7

**24 Hour MBA**
$19.95 ($29.95 CAN)
ISBN 1-58062-256-9

**Customer-Focused Selling**
$19.95 ($29.95 CAN)
ISBN 1-55850-725-6

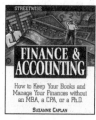

**Finance & Accounting**
$17.95 ($27.95 CAN)
ISBN 1-58062-196-1

**Hiring Top Performers**
$17.95 ($27.95 CAN)
ISBN 1-58062-684-5

**Small Business Start-Up**
$17.95 ($27.95 CAN)
ISBN 1-55850-581-4

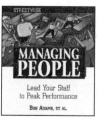

**Managing People**
$19.95 ($29.95 CAN)
ISBN 1-55850-726-4

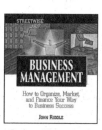

**Business Management**
$19.95 ($29.95 CAN)
ISBN 1-58062-540-1

**Business Letters w/CD-ROM**
$24.95 ($37.95 CAN)
ISBN 1-58062-133-3

**Motivating & Rewarding Employees**
$19.95 ($29.95 CAN)
ISBN 1-58062-130-9

**Relationship Marketing on the Internet**
$17.95 ($27.95 CAN)
ISBN 1-58062-255-0

**Time Management**
$17.95 ($27.95 CAN)
ISBN 1-58062-131-7

**Do-It-Yourself Advertising**
$19.95 ($29.95 CAN)
ISBN 1-55850-727-2

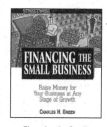

**Financing the Small Business**
$19.95 ($29.95 CAN)
ISBN 1-58062-765-X

**Independent Consulting**
$19.95 ($29.95 CAN)
ISBN 1-55850-728-0

## Available wherever books are sold.

If you cannot find these titles at your favorite retail outlet, you may order them directly from the publisher. BY PHONE: Call 1-800-872-5627. We accept Visa, MasterCard, American Express, and Discover. $4.95 will be added to your total order for shipping and handling. BY MAIL: Write out the full titles of the books you'd like to order and send payment, including $4.95 for shipping and handling, to: Adams Media Corporation, 57 Littlefield Street, Avon, MA 02322. 30-day money-back guarantee.

# FIND MORE ON THIS TOPIC BY VISITING
# BusinessTown.com
## The Web's big site for growing businesses!

☑ **Separate channels on all aspects of starting and running a business**

☑ **Lots of info of how to do business online**

☑ **1,000+ pages of savvy business advice**

☑ **Complete web guide to thousands of useful business sites**

☑ **Free e-mail newsletter**

☑ **Question and answer forums, and more!**

**Accounting**
Basic, Credit & Collections, Projections, Purchasing/Cost Contro

**Advertising**
Magazine, Newspaper, Radio, Television, Yellow Pages

**Business Opportunities**
Ideas for New Businesses, Business for Sale, Franchises

**Business Plans**
Creating Plans & Business Strategie

**Finance**
Getting Money, Money Problem Solutions

**Letters & Forms**
Looking Professional, Sample Letter & Forms

**Getting Started**
Incorporating, Choosing a Legal Structure

**Hiring & Firing**
Finding the Right People, Legal Issu

**Home Business**
Home Business Ideas, Getting Start

**Internet**
Getting Online, Put Your Catalog on the Web

**Legal Issues**
Contracts, Copyrights, Patents, Trademarks

**Managing a Small Busines**
Growth, Boosting Profits, Mistakes Avoid, Competing with the Giants

**Managing People**
Communications, Compensation, Motivation, Reviews, Problem Employees

**Marketing**
Direct Mail, Marketing Plans, Strate Publicity, Trade Shows

**Office Setup**
Leasing, Equipment, Supplies

**Presentations**
Know Your Audience, Good Impres

**Sales**
Face to Face, Independent Reps, Telemarketing

**Selling a Business**
Finding Buyers, Setting a Price, Le Issues

**Taxes**
Employee, Income, Sales, Property, U

**Time Management**
Can You Really Manage Time?

**Travel & Maps**
Making Business Travel Fun